The Consequences of
Cotton in
Antebellum America

ALSO BY WILLIAM J. PHALEN

*American Evangelical Protestantism and
European Immigrants, 1800–1924* (McFarland, 2011)

The Consequences of Cotton in Antebellum America

WILLIAM J. PHALEN

McFarland & Company, Inc., Publishers
Jefferson, North Carolina

LIBRARY OF CONGRESS CATALOGUING-IN-PUBLICATION DATA

Phalen, William J., 1942–
    The consequences of cotton in antebellum America / William J. Phalen.
        p.   cm.
    Includes bibliographical references and index.

    ISBN 978-0-7864-7700-5 (softcover : acid free paper) ∞
    ISBN 978-1-4766-1490-8 (ebook)

    1. Cotton trade—United States—History—19th century. 2. Industrialization—United States—History—19th century. 3. United States—Economic conditions. 4. United States—Social conditions. 5. United States—History—1783–1865. I. Title.
HD9075.P43 2014
338.1'7351097509034—dc23
                                    2014003448

BRITISH LIBRARY CATALOGUING DATA ARE AVAILABLE

© 2014 William J. Phalen. All rights reserved

No part of this book may be reproduced or transmitted in any form or by any means, electronic or mechanical, including photocopying or recording, or by any information storage and retrieval system, without permission in writing from the publisher.

On the cover: Picking cotton on the Alexander plantation © Ben Shahn (Library of Congress)

Manufactured in the United States of America

McFarland & Company, Inc., Publishers
  Box 611, Jefferson, North Carolina 28640
    www.mcfarlandpub.com

For my mother and father

Table of Contents

Preface   1
Introduction   3

1. Mechanization   11
2. Transportation   30
3. The Founding Fathers   46
4. Slavery   62
5. The Impact of Tariffs   78
6. The Effect on the Economy   95
7. Mills in the North   117
8. Mills in the South   137
9. The International Situation   152

Conclusion   171
Chapter Notes   177
Bibliography   191
Index   201

Preface

In this volume I have sought to discuss the impact of cotton on the United States before the Civil War, examining those things that were touched in an important way by cotton's existence through a broad lens, rather than statistics. While other products have affected different regions of the nation at different times, cotton, of all the products of our soil and industry, fashioned the thinking and way of life of the whole nation. Even though cotton was produced in only one part of the country, and despite marked disparities among the country's various parts, this one product affected the United States as no other has. Anne O'Hare McCormick, writing in the *New York Times Magazine* in 1931, said of it: "For cotton is more than a crop or an industry; it is a dynastic system, with a set of laws and standards always under assault and peculiarly resistant to change. It is a map-maker, trouble-maker, history maker.... It was cotton that made the South into a section.... On cotton ... the South built up a social and political economy essentially different from that prevailing in the rest of the country."

The Old South was dominant for only about twenty years before the Civil War, but in that short span of time, because of cotton, it created giant industries in the North, a shipping system up and down the Atlantic Coast and to Europe, new machines and new applications for older ones. Cotton was also the foundation of the Industrial Revolution and thus transformed the economic world. Its significance was not lost upon the political economist Karl Marx, who wrote in 1846 that "without cotton you have no modern industry." Cotton brought wealth, power, and prosperity to both America and Europe. Affordable textile garments woven from American cotton improved the quality of life for people throughout the world. But this material progress came with a human cost, for cotton production played the leading role in a racial tragedy of epic proportions.

The fabric of the cotton culture is highly complex, as it contains elaborately intermingled elements of politics, finance, business and social organization, manufacturing, shipping, and the international relations of the United States. A complete study of the impact of cotton on life in the United States before the Civil War would require not one volume but many volumes. Such an inquiry is beyond the aim of this book. Here I have attempted merely to tell something of an agricultural product that fashioned the life of the nation and profoundly affected the destiny of the American people.

Introduction

When a southern journalist remarked in the 1920s that "Cotton is Religion, Politics, Law, Economics, and Art,"[1] he was of course talking about the commodity that had served as an engine of growth for not only a major portion of the country, but also as a preeminent export product for the entire nation. If he had been an economic historian, he might have also been thinking about a system of production and an approach to economic decision-making that had been established in the South long before cotton became king. In other words, before cotton was predominant in the South, commodities like tobacco, rice, and indigo served as the "Religion, Politics, Law, Economics and Art" of the region.

In examining the importance of cotton, a useful place to start is applying the staple thesis to the history of the antebellum United States—that the export sector played the leading role in economic growth and that the specific character of the exports of each region shaped the economic development of that region. In the case of cotton during this period of time, the product did of course shape the character of the South, but it also did much to shape the character of the other regions of the nation, as well as reinforcing the economic well-being of foreign countries.

After the Revolutionary War, when older engines of economic growth in the South—tobacco, rice, and indigo—declined, they were replaced by a new staple commodity to which established systems of production could be applied. This new product, cotton, initially took advantage of the development of new technology in England to manufacture cotton cloth, and the existence of slave-owning plantations in the upper South that had been established during the eighteenth century. As Joyce Chaplin makes clear in her analysis of the transition to cotton in the lower South, "Early cotton cultivators used cotton to preserve a world already shaped by commercial agriculture and slavery."[2] The inventions made by Arkwright, Cartwright, and others in England allowed the South to continue its economic development when the crops it formerly depended on were no longer viable. The growing markets for a range of cotton products in Europe and America influenced the drive for technological improvements in the eighteenth century, contributing to the English industrial revolution. This and the advent of a practical cotton gin invented by Eli Whitney to clean the short staple cotton facilitated the creation and expansion of factories which produced huge quantities of spun and woven cotton textiles.

In addition to Whitney, between 1760 and 1820, there were concerted efforts to create new technology and to update existing machinery for the production of cotton textiles. Samuel Slater's introduction of spinning machinery was only one spectacular illustration of this. Francis Cabot Lowell's investigation of the British textile industry, and his subsequent construction of a power loom, represented the real beginning of large-scale, efficient cotton textile pro-

Interior of a cotton mill showing machinery producing cotton thread (Library of Congress, Prints & Photographs Division, LC-DIG-prokc–20019).

duction in the United States. This start in the textile industry clearly indicated the willingness and ability of American entrepreneurs and mechanics to take over foreign inventions as their use became practicable. One student of New England textile machinery, speaking of the Lowell mills, declared that "the Industrial Revolution in its infancy produced surprisingly few basic skills not already familiar to American mechanics."[3] The same author also concluded:

> The manufacture of cloth was America's greatest industry. For a considerable part of the 1813–1853 period the manufacture of textile machinery appears to have been America's greatest heavy goods industry, occupying the primary position in point of size and value of product among all industries which fabricated metal. Size, however is not the most critical measure of importance. From the textile mills and the textile machine shops came the men who supplied most of the tools for the American Industrial Revolution. From these mills and shops sprang directly the machine tool and locomotive industries together with a host of less basic metal fabricating trades. The part played by the textile machinery industry in fostering American metal working skills in the early nineteenth century was a crucial one.[4]

Cotton production was a highly profitable endeavor for the planters engaged in it, as they took advantage of the southern soil, climate, and a legal system of slavery to meet the extraordinary growth of world demand for raw cotton. The expansion of the cotton textile industry happened first in England and then in the northeastern United States. According to the calculations of Stanley Engerman, per capita income of the free population of the South in 1840 stood at $105, compared to $130 for the Northeast, a region that was experiencing an economic transformation, and $66 for the Old Northwest, then undergoing settlement. During the next two decades, to 1860, the rate of growth of per capita income in the South at 42.9 percent was higher than that of either the Northeast at 40.8 percent, or the Middle West at 34.4 percent.[5]

While the basic pattern of the relationship of the South with the outside world changed little from the days of the exporting of tobacco and rice, the business side of product exporting did. In the past, London and Glasgow had directed the colonial trade in tobacco, rice, and indigo. Now the cotton trade was run domestically from New York. New York ships carried cargoes of manufactured goods to southern ports and shipments of cotton to the Northeast and to Europe. Banking was also centered in New York. The whole commercial mechanism was well-oiled, with credit extended by New York banks that financed the transfer of slaves and the purchase of land, and provided working capital during the period of clearing the land, preparing the soil and raising a cotton crop. Locally, cotton factors in major port cities like New Orleans,

Charleston, Mobile, and Savannah who were connected to lending institutions and businesses in the North arranged for the storage, shipment, and sale of the cotton they received from the planters. They also supplied credit to the planters and purchased consumer goods for them.

While this concentration on one main product in the South inhibited the growth of an urban network of manufacturers, retail trade, and financial institutions in the region, these entities were growing in the North, the Northwest, and the West, partially to supply the South with non-plantation products.

A tragic consequence of cotton's rise to prominence was the effect on the supply of labor for the plantation system—the slaves. They were the major capital investment in the system and, as noted by Conrad and Meyer, economically they were an essential intermediate good. The rise in the price of slaves over the period from 1802 to 1860 from $600 to $1,800 (for a prime field hand) represented a rational increased capitalization of slaves. The crop value per slave rose from $14.68 in 1802 to $101.09 in 1860; and when the price of a slave is divided into crop value per slave it showed no tendency to decline, but was on the average higher in 1860 than at the turn of the nineteenth century.

Slaves were not the only group to suffer for the sake of "King Cotton." In 1823, Robert Crittenden, acting governor of the Arkansas Territory, wrote to John C. Calhoun, secretary of war, about the Qupaw Indian land claim:

> Obviously such Indian wretches should not own rich cotton lands that ought to belong to deserving whites.... This would not do: rich cotton lands on navigable streams in the hands of heathen Indians; lands that ought to be owned by God-fearin', church-going, white men.

The Creeks and Choctaws abandoned 17 million acres in Mississippi and Alabama and moved west across the Mississippi River. As the Indians moved out, the white men moved in. These latter moved so rapidly that by 1837 uncleared Alabama lands were bringing $35 an acre and clearing costs were an additional $15 an acre. The southern Alabama cotton crop increased from 11,000 bales in 1820 to 195,000 bales in 1836.[6]

The early development of a capital market in the Northeast around foreign trade due to cotton production as compared with the relatively primitive state of capital markets in other regions of the nation was an important influence on manufacturing. The growth of the New England textile industry was implemented by the shift of capital from shipping into textiles.[7] While the location of sites with abundant water power dictated specific manufacturing locations within New England, the predilection of Boston capitalists for textile manufacturing within the region was a major factor. The abundance of financial intermediaries in Boston and the Northeast provided the large amounts of loan capital essential to rapid expansion of the textile firms.[8]

Banking, insurance, port facilities, warehousing, the development of a distribution system for exports and the early growth of roads and turnpikes connecting the hinterlands with the major ports were all investments aiding the development of manufacturing, mainly cotton textiles. The vast array of consumer goods manufactured to meet the needs of the northeastern urban dweller, the southern slave and planter, and the western farmer made the complex of industries which grew up around cotton the most important in pre–Civil War America.

Cotton also played a part in a new type of employee. The town of Lowell, a showpiece of early New England industrialism and founded by Nathan Appleton. a successful merchant turned industrialist, was run like a large family. The workers themselves were mainly women (the "mill girls"), whose moral welfare would be safeguarded by the wise paternalists who owned and managed the mills. Indeed "the model that influenced the founders of Lowell most of all was the pre-industrial New England village, with its traditional patterns of deference made more rigid by a corporate table of organization." This paternalistic scheme gradually disintegrated as the employers shifted to Irish immigrant labor. Its frankly experimental character and the tentativeness with which even the most committed politicians viewed the growth of the factory system are apparent in a remark of Henry Clay. "Lowell," Clay predicted (as late as 1843), "will tell whether the Manufacturing system is compatible with social virtues."[9]

While the foreign demand for cotton provided capital to bolster domestic credit institutions, it also acted in other ways to encourage American growth. Most important of all the consequences of that demand—most important because of its own potent ability to generate subsequent events—was the rise and spread of specialized economic activity. It is worth repeating and bearing in mind a fundamental precept of Adam Smith: the degree of specialization depends upon the width of the market (the quality of demand). An individual's productivity, that is his output per unit of labor input, will be low in comparison with that of a specialist doing one thing alone and depending upon exchange with other specialists for the goods he needs but does not himself produce. The greater the degree of specialization, the greater will be the volume of trade.

These things are true not only for individuals but also for the economic sectors and regions that make up an economy. Specialized agriculture is more productive than diversified agriculture. If a region tends to concentrate its resources on a particular kind of production and depends upon other specialized regions for what it needs but does not itself produce in sufficient quantities, not only its own productivity but also that of the whole economy will tend to rise. Precisely this kind of specialized regional activity tended to develop in the United States during the antebellum decades, and so too did both sectoral and occupational specialization.

The demand for cotton during the antebellum period does not alone suffice to explain these occurrences; yet it was a necessary condition for them. The foreign demand for cotton enabled the South—the Southwest in particular—to concentrate its resources to a significant degree on the production of that staple, using the earnings from that sale to pay the East for manufactured goods and financial and shipping services and the West for food supplies and livestock. The internal market for the goods and services of each of the regions, in sum, widened in part because of the foreign market for cotton. Both the growth of specialized commercial agriculture in the West and the development of industry in the East thus partly depended upon the demand for cotton.

Those involved also depended on improved forms of internal transport to knit the separate regions into an interdependent, and therefore national, economy. Transportation improvements in turn owed much to the movement of cotton from the South to the North and the West. Additionally, it was the ensuing rivalry of Atlantic Coast cities for the trade of the Southwest that induced state governments to build roads, canals, bridges, and railroads, or to charter and aid numerous quasi-public business corporations for that purpose. The growth of New York City's port owed as much to the enterprising foresight of her private businessmen who established both Atlantic and coastal packet lines to serve the needs of the cotton trade as it did to the state government that built the Erie Canal.

The relative importance of the cotton crop to the antebellum United States becomes manifest when compared to other leading agricultural products of the nation and other principal articles of our domestic and foreign commerce. The growth of the American population, the extension of the United States' territory, and the additions to our agricultural labor in both our native and emigrant populations have given the country today increased resources and ability for greater agricultural production. However, the greater proportions of most of these agricultural products and manufactured items, except cotton, are consumed in the United States. The fact that the export of many of this country's most important products did not increase in proportion to the nation's increase in population, resources, and ability, and that raw cotton is the single exception is evidence of that product's value and its prominent position in bringing wealth and prosperity to the United States. Additionally, before the Civil War, the total amount of imports into the country did not equal the value of our exports of cotton, giving the nation a favorable balance of payments. Finally, the value of the cotton used in domestic manufacture in 1849 amounted to $27,540,000. If not for American cotton, it would have had to be imported.

This book deals with those areas of the American way of life that were impacted by the development of cotton from a plant growing wild in the American South to a finished product that would change the nation in both beneficial and malevolent ways. When the rocky ground in New England would no longer support all who wished to farm there, cotton mills were part of the means of making a living that supplanted agriculture. The reader will see how these mills did that and also the difference and similarities between the cotton mills in the North and those in the South. Cotton was also at the forefront of the development of the American economy and played an important part in the evolution of the nation's tariff system. Additionally, this work will show how cotton influenced American shipping and played a role in the country's international relations.

The crop had an impact on the Founding Fathers and their efforts to use its importance to benefit the new nation. It also became an item to be acted upon as American inventors both improved foreign means of cotton production and created new machines to enhance its value.

Cotton unfortunately had a harmful side. This was the subjugation of millions of human beings to bring about all of the advantages of the product for the United States.

1

Mechanization

The manufacture of raw cotton is not a young industry. In the United States, as in England, it was the earliest of the textile industries to be reorganized for power-driven machinery and for the modern factory system. The change came about partially because of the quality of the raw material used and its abundant supply, but it was also because of the ease with which the product could be processed by machines. The same causes which made the textile industry the first one to be affected by the English industrial revolution facilitated its early growth in the United States. Since this was the case, it became the ideal product to be taken up and successfully processed by Americans and especially by New Englanders.[1]

The development of technology in America is a totally improbable chapter in world history. Starting on the edge of an unknown continent, the new Americans within ten generations not only filled the continent and subdued it, but also reached out to change the rest of the world. Innovators being urged on by ideologies of mechanization and expansion, tools grew in size and complexity until, in the eyes of the world, the most visible and compelling feature of the American nation was its technology.

The historiography of early American technology may be broken down into roughly three narratives. The first, the least popular, is the argument that American inventors lifted their ideas part and parcel from Europe in general and Great Britain in particular. For example, Eli Whitney's claim of cotton gin paternity has been effectively disputed by the historian Robert Woodbury, who called attention to the machines of Bentham and Brunel in England and Le Blanc in France.[2] Second is the "economic school" of technological history, which believed that American inventors, given an incentive, would come up with something new. The facts that labor scarcity and the hope of financial reward provided sufficient traditionally closed the case. It came down to a neat triangle of shrewd capitalist, bold entrepreneur and ambitious mechanic

(Samuel Colt's Exposition of interchangeable parts manufacturing astonished the British in 1851). The third school might be called "behavioral." John Sawyer presents a list of social and cultural attributes which accounted for the distinctiveness of American technology:

> [There were] differences in the nature and diffusion of education in America; the absence of rigidities and restraints of class and craft; the freedom from hereditary definitions of the tasks or hardened ways of going about them; the high focus on personal advancement and drives to higher material welfare; and the mobility, flexibility, adaptability of Americans and their boundless belief in progress. These and closely related patterns are linked directly to economic behavior and economic results—to initiative, originality, systematic effort and boldness; the "eager resort to machinery" and productive use of small capital, at a time when small capital was decisive; the ceaseless search and ready adoption of the new and more efficient; the intensive responsiveness to shifting opportunities and expanding horizons; the "go-aheadism" that visitors from all categories so often placed at the root of the "immense drive" of American manufacturing.[3]

But what drove Americans to create technology, and what was behind the drive to "create?" First it was individualism. This trait, so described, was a prominent feature of the early American industrial milieu. Striking evidence of it was found in the prevailing attitude toward "craftsmanship." Craftsmanship, of course was the hallmark of the ancient guild system, and it was passed along to the trade unions, which in Europe replaced that system. There was apparently very little of it to be found in America. British observers constantly called attention to the want of "perfect skill" and to the crudity and flimsiness of American construction.[4] Often as not, machinery which in Britain was made of heavy metal and finished to gleaming perfection was in America made of wood, was "much simplified," and was, according to the standards of the day, rough-hewn at best. Yet such jerry-building had its advantages. It cost less, required less time, and the items in question could be discarded more easily for an improved model. Moreover, the American de-emphasis on "craftsmanship" led to a corresponding emphasis on function and efficiency.

Important as it was, the craft tradition—and its relative absence in America—was but one aspect of individualism. Another was the impact of mobility. Because the traditional crafts were not dominant in America, workers from all walks of life found themselves side by side. In Colt's factory, for example, "one had been a butcher, another a tailor, another a gentleman's servant."[5] Nor were they to stay long at a particular occupation: "The citizen of the United States seems really to pride himself in not remaining over long at any particular occupation, and being able to turn his hand to some dozen different pursuits in the course of his life."[6] Eli Whitney Blake got his start in his uncle Eli's arms factory. He then developed an improved lock, a new system of geared power transmission, and the Blake stone crusher, which made possible the American concrete industry. At the age of 92, he was studying aerodynamics and still going strong.

American mechanics were also constantly talking to one another, exchanging ideas, cross-fertilizing from one industry to another: "The successful application of mechanical means to one manufacture has been, as a matter of course, simulative of their application to another, however different...."[7] To an extent unimaginable in Europe, Americans traded successfully in information and inspiration. Thus the clockmakers Eli Terry and Chauncey Jones learned from the arms makers at the Colt factory. Elisha King Root, the man who perfected Colt's machinery, got his start with the Collins brothers and adapted the principles of their ax manufactory to the production of handguns. The clearest case of intellectual spin-off was seen at the Lowell factory, where the perfection of textile machinery demonstrably led to machine tool production, to the development of locomotives, to the Worcester wire industry, and, through Joseph Chickering, to the wire piano. Some of this proliferation represented piracy of a sort, but most of it did not. This attitude of intellectual free trade was America's secret weapon in the battle for intellectual supremacy.[8]

The second feature of the American drive to "create" was egalitarianism. It was probably no accident that the period of American technological takeoff and the Age of the Common Man were one. Nowhere was the contrast between America and Great Britain more apparent than in the manner and significance of basic education. The British commissioners who were so struck by the absence in America of an apprenticeship system were equally struck by the pervasiveness of public education. American mechanics, they noted, were "educated up to a far higher standard than those of a much superior social grade ... in the Old World." The result, as they saw it, was a particular "vivacity" in "inquiring into the first principles" of things, a "theoretical knowledge of the process," which stood in marked contrast to the European mechanics.[9]

Another difference between the systems was that American innovation was not happening at the top, but rather at the bottom, at the level of the ordinary workman. This fact is borne out because we know so few of the inventors of specific devices. Partly because their ambitions were high, partly because their jobs were secure, but partly too because they lived in an unfettered society, the American mechanics made a different kind of response to the problems they faced. They literally "bombarded" their employers with innovative suggestions, some of them outlandish, some of them brilliant.

Then, too, in Jacksonian America the common man was becoming, in addition to a political phenomenon, a symbol of the Machine Age, the ideal person to embrace mechanism and make it respond. As such he was culturally encouraged to express his creativity as few creative people have been. In less than two generations these halcyon days would vanish, and the common man would be counted a Machine Age casualty. But in those few decades when labor was dear and machinery new, it was doubly fortunate for the workingman that a new phase of American folk myth coincided with that stage of Western technological development in which "tinkering" on a broad front could produce astonishing results—as it never could before or would again.[10] Ambition was another factor in the success of the American mechanic. "You may be sure," de Tocqueville wrote, "that the more democratic, enlightened, and free a nation is ... the more will discoveries immediately applicable to productive industry confer on their authors gain, fame, and even power."[11]

What is uniquely American about these successes? For one thing, there is its ubiquity. We are not dealing with limited areas or isolated instances, but rather with a pattern that by 1850 had become recognized and well established. The example of "ingenious men who have solved economic and mechanical problems to their own profit and elevation" was, in the words of one Briton, "constantly before" the American mechanic, engendering a "restless activity of mind and body," an "anxiety to improve his own department": "It may be said that there is not a working boy of average ability in the New England states, at least, who has not an idea of some mechanical invention or improvement in manufactures by which, in good time, he hopes to better his position, or rise to fortune and social distinction."[12]

But even more distinctive is the fact that in America personal ambition came first—literally taking precedence over order and stability. Samuel Slater, in whose incredible memory the Arkwright machine was smuggled into the United States, came in for a surprise when the mill hands he had hired and trained suddenly revolted, devised their own machinery, and set up a number of rival manufacturing companies.

Unlike his European contemporaries, the American mechanic did not think of himself as a permanent wage earner. His work as a laborer was seen as a tour of duty, a preparation for the greater things to come, which came with such frequency that he had an example of success constantly before him. Whatever else the spirit of equality gave him, it generated, as de Tocqueville noted, "an all pervading and restless activity, a super abundant force, an energy which is inseparable from it." Such activity, force and energy, he added, could "produce wonders."[13]

The last condition that benefited the American workman was the open-ended society that he lived in as opposed to the one in Europe. There society existed in a closed and finished universe in which it was futile to advocate change. Traditional values were eclipsed by the more utilitarian values of industriousness and creativity. America was, as Harvard professor Levi Frisbie said in 1818, "full of youthful freshness. We are free from any of those institutions by which other nations are enthralled."[14] He doubtless agreed with Noah Webster that "Europe has grown old in folly, corruption, and tyranny—in that country laws are perverted, manners are licentious, literature is declining, and human nature is debased."[15] But it was probably Samuel Colt who put the American case most succinctly. "There is nothing," he said, "that cannot be produced by machinery."[16]

In 1885, Henry James looked back upon the antebellum United States and saw a land that had "no sovereign, no court, no personal loyalty, no aristocracy, no church, no clergy, no army, no diplomatic service, no country gentlemen, no palaces, no castles, nor manors, nor old country houses, nor parsonages, nor thatched cottages, nor ivied ruins; no cathedrals, nor abbeys, nor little Norman churches; no great universities nor public schools...; no literature, no novels, no museums, no pictures, no political society." In short, it was a land with no past. Though part of the indictment was obviously wrong, the America of Andrew Jackson had undeniably divested itself of an Old World past which, as James suggested, still lived on in Europe.

In examining the benefits that were created by the production of cotton in the United States, we find first there was an additional profit, not from manufacturing itself, but from disseminating manufacturing information. As an example, consider the agreement between the Boston Manufacturing Company and the Dover Cotton Factory, dated October 12, 1821. By the terms of the agreement, the Dover Cotton Factory was granted the free right to use all patented machinery and patented improvements on machinery then held by the Boston Manufacturing Company. Moreover, the Dover Cotton Factory, through its agent, was given free access "to examine the buildings, works, tools, implements, machinery, modes of operation, processes, improvements, and modifications as well relating to the making and using machinery, as to the general manufacture of cotton goods xxx." For these privileges the Dover Cotton Factory agreed to pay six thousand dollars with the further agreement that they would "not communicate to others, or for the interest of others, such information as they may receive under this agreement, but will adopt such measures as the said Boston Manufacturing Company shall communicate for the purpose of preventing publicity to such things as the said parties shall require not to be made public."

A new means of profit was not the only motive behind the policy of extending the use of the power loom to other manufacturers. The merchants who turned from commerce to manufacturing were vitally interested in business, but they were also patriotic citizens keenly interested in the progress of the new nation. Studies of the lives of the New England cotton manufacturers show the mixed motives of private enterprise and public service which characterized their political opinions. And something of a like nature appears in their attitudes towards the expansion of domestic industries. This can be seen in Francis Cabot Lowell's uncompromising attitude towards a bargain; yet it is a fact that he cherished a patriotic vision of making the new nation economically independent of the mother country. That this motive was shared by his associates in the Boston Manufacturing Company appears in a article written years later by one of the partners, Nathan Appleton. In the article Appleton said that in the beginning he did not share Lowell's optimism regarding the financial possibilities of the venture (selling manufacturing secrets), but for the benefit of the country, he was quite willing to lose the full amount of his share in the company in order that so important an experiment be tried.[17]

The nineteenth century industrialization process in the United States was quite unbalanced geographically. The major manufacturing industries were highly concentrated in New England and to a lesser degree the Middle Atlantic States, while the South lagged far behind. Why New England? Before the industrial revolution, the region displayed both a low productivity in the cultivation of the soil relative to the rest of the nation and a high productivity in trade, because of its abundance of harbors, and in fishing. These maritime industries, in turn, provided linkages to shipbuilding, forest products, spinning and weaving (flax for sails), iron manufacture (for nails and tools), and finance (for merchant capital). By the early nineteenth century, the region had been accumulating a stock of native mechanical ability and entrepreneurial talents for dealing with risky capital ventures that was to prove invaluable in the coming industrial development.[18] Along with the two main industries in New England, the cotton textile industry and the firearms industry, the region also had by 1820 the beginnings of an excellent general education system, high skills levels, a growing economy, prosperous people, and social networks that made possible communication of information and supported cooperative ventures.

Even given the above, during the initial decades of the nineteenth century American manufacturing was characterized predominately by an emphasis on consumer rather than capital goods, by handicraft rather than machine techniques, by household and workshop rather than factory organization and by rural dispersion rather than concentration in major urban centers. Even in the textile industries, where factories were the most important production units by the 1830s,[19] activity was largely confined to rural waterfall sites and mill towns in these rural areas. The factory and industrial capitalism had not yet become the cornerstones of metropolitan growth. Added to this was the fact that industrial growth was hampered by Britain's restrictive policies before the Revolution and afterwards by import-restricting legislation and protective tariffs (the Embargo and Non-Intercourse acts functioned as protective measures between 1808 and 1815).

In 1810, Albert Gallatin argued that "the want of sufficient capital" was one of the "most prominent of those causes" impeding the growth of manufacturing in the United States.[20] Adequate capital supplies frequently existed, but the problem most often confronting the factory or workshop owner was that of obtaining a portion of those excess funds. Since it was in the larger cities that the potential investor encountered the widest spectrum of financial outlets and opportunities, the development of large-scale, capital-intensive urban industries was particularly hampered under the prevailing conditions of investment capital scarcity.

Although merchants became somewhat more sympathetic toward industrial investments during the 1820s, for a number of decades the majority still preferred to speculate in land purchases[21] or to enlarge their spheres of trade rather than back manufacturing projects. (Mercantile conservatism regarding industrial developments had been briefly interrupted by the War of 1812, when American ports were cut off from British manufacturers. But even this turn of events tended to favor the textile mills of Massachusetts and Paterson rather than the manufacturing of the larger cities. Also, when the war ended, poor harvests in Europe increased the value of American agricultural commodities considerably.)[22]

Until the enormous migrations of the late 1840s, the problems of capital availability were intensified by the costliness and elasticity of labor supplies. Economic historians have repeatedly demonstrated that the abundance of cheap and fertile land led to a high output per man in early nineteenth century American agriculture, and that these productivity conditions exerted a negative effect on industrial wage levels and the quantity of labor available for manufacturing purposes. Although American urban industrial salaries were high by the standards of English and other European competitors, "even a temporary cessation of work caused employees to scatter widely in search of other employment, and even to leave permanently the occupations in which they previously had been engaged." As opposed to, "The temporary suspension of a factory in Great Britain did not mean the dispersion of all available labor for operating it. A plant could resume operations at any time with a full compliment of qualified workmen."[23]

The shortage of labor was particularly acute in Boston, where "there were no appreciable numbers of men ready and willing to work at wages low enough to foster the establishment of profitable new enterprises," and "a constant deficiency of labor had seriously hampered the growth of industry until the forties." Between 1837 and 1845 few Boston industries underwent sizeable growth, "and many actually declined. The prospective manufacturer desiring a site for a new establishment, or a capitalist with an abundance of money seeking an outlet found little encouragement. And even those already established who wished to expand were inhibited by the inflexible labor supply."[24] Boston boot and shoe entrepreneurs found that it was more profitable to maintain workshops outside of the city, where labor was more plentiful. Similarly, 75 percent of the city's hat dealers were manufacturing their products in neighboring towns. These conditions persisted in Boston and the other major Atlantic ports despite the flow of migrants through these cities. The bulk of the newcomers were either attracted away from the urban labor market by the lure of agricultural prosperity or did not possess the skills requisite to participate in most of the city's handicraft and workshop industries.[25]

The most persuasive point in any discussion regarding the state of technology in antebellum America was that waterpower, then the most important source of energy used to drive factory machinery, constituted an immobile raw material—it simply could not be moved to the larger cities. The mechanized cotton textile industry could flourish in Waltham, Paterson, or the Schuykill suburbs of Roxborough, Spring Garden, and Kensington, but not in Boston, New York, or Philadelphia proper. Similarly, factories utilizing waterpower functioned profitably beside the Patapsco Falls, and at the foot of at least nine other falls within a thirty-mile radius of Baltimore; but no large scale water driven machinery operated within the its corporate limits.[26]

Cost was the greatest constraint on the adoption of steam power in the larger cities. By 1839 at Easton, Pennsylvania, a point accessible to coal, the relative annual cost per horsepower for water and steam was $23 and $105 respectively.[27] Of course Boston, New York, New Orleans, and Baltimore did not possess immediate accessibility to coal. Thus the expense of steam power in those cities was compounded by transport outlays for either coal or wood. The volume of coal consumed, as well as the cost of moving it, was such that even the steam engines of Philadelphia were still quite dependent on wood in the 1830s—despite the relative ease with which Lehigh Valley anthracites could be procured by an all-water route. Because face-to-face contacts were so vital within the context of an essentially primitive communications system, merchant capital was rarely risked in nonlocal industrial projects.

As textile factories were anchored to immobile water power sources, it may be conjectured that large-scale integrated cotton spinning and weaving would have initially emerged as a major industry in the cities if an alternative economical energy source had existed. Although steam power was used widely in manufacturing by 1840, most of its use was concentrated in a few industries and it provided the main power supply for almost none. Since the direct costs of steam power were higher than the costs for waterpower, industries used steam only when its benefits were large. In other words, in the years before it became important as a supplier of land transportation, the steam engine functioned as a substitute for such transportation, allowing power to be brought to the raw materials when it was expensive to bring the materials to the waterpower sites.

The great inventors during this period were disproportionately concentrated in the Northeast, and especially in southern New England and New York, where low-cost transportation networks had facilitated a rapid expansion of commerce early in the antebellum period. This geographic distribution was characteristic of where they filed their patents as well as where they were born.

The situation in the South, especially as applied to mechanization in the textile industry, was completely different. The following excerpts from a letter written on August 11, 1858 by J.M. Wesson, president of the Mississippi Manufacturing Company, to Col. John F.H. Claiborne, a Mississippi elected official and writer, shed some light on the position of the South, not only on textiles but also on manufacturing[28]:

> Mississippi alone possesses all the elements of national wealth and greatness. It is true she has no waterpower, but in this fast age we prefer Steam to Water, as it is more reliable. And where wood is as cheap as it is in the pine hills of Mississippi, it is less expensive than water—unless we should be permitted to draw upon our imagination for a small river that should neither overflow nor "dry up" just suited to our "liking." We say draw upon our imagination, because such a thing does not exist in reality. For in most of the Manufactoring districts North, the waterpower is created by expensive canals that is the source of much expense and trouble.
>
> The citizens, generally, of Mississippi did not appreciate Manufacturing until very recently. It is true that politicians *resolved* many very pretty things upon the subject, but like the scribes and Pharisees, they would not so much as move a finger for its support. We, therefore, had to battle against all the prejudices against Broken Banks, Rail Roads & Manufacturing Co. We believe our Citizens are now waking up to their interests, both in Agriculture and Manufacturing, and their minds should be properly diverted and instructed. And the Agricultural journals of the country are the proper mediums through which it should be done.
>
> What would be our condition now if we were alone dependent upon Old England for all the articles we buy of New England? What would be our interest as a nation in that case? The Answer is clear, and with our present knowledge of its advantages to us we would not hesitate. We know she would monopolize our cotton trade and know no rule of charging us for her manufacturers but our ability to pay. Then if making New England a competitor with Old England for our trade has placed us in so much better condition than we would have been in the hands of Old England alone, work it by the rule of three and the answer will be

our condition when we do our own business. This idea may appear extravagant to some, and it may not be strictly true in Cotton and Cotton goods, but in almost every article it would: in wool hats and Negro shoes, in hoes and axes, in ploughs & wagons. And yet did you ever see a weeding hoe that was made in Miss., *or did you ever see a blanket that was manufactured south of the Potomac*?

The South stands in the same relation to New England now that we as a nation did to Old England fifty years ago. If it was good policy to adopt and support a general system of manufacturing, the same policy is equally good now when applied to the South. And should the next Congress find it necessary to make any material change in the Tarriff, which we think is plainly indicated both by the wants of the Treasury and the receipts of the Customs House, we hope to see Southern members [converted?] to the protective policy.[29]

The three major machines for turning raw cotton into a useable product were a machine to pick cotton, one to separate the cotton from the seeds (the gin), and a device to create the product (the loom). A persistent problem in American economic history is the explanation of the failure of the South to mechanize cotton production. After the invention of both the gin and the loom, picking became the bottleneck operation in cotton production during the antebellum period. Elimination of this constraint under the existing technology would have doubled or tripled the amount of cotton each person could cultivate. Additionally, there was further room for improvement through employment of implements already in use in the North. The history of inventions designed to mechanize the cotton harvest is peculiarly fascinating because of the great variety of approaches tried out at one time or another and the truly formidable technical, economic, and social obstacles which had to be overcome in order to find solutions.

Cotton, unlike grain crops whose simple characteristics permitted mechanization much earlier, is a difficult crop to harvest by a uniform mechanical method. The crop is grown under considerable diversity of soil and climatic conditions, and the resultant plant varies from a scrubby knee-high bush to a wide branching one taller than the average man. Also, as many as five hundred varieties of American upland cotton have been grown in this country simultaneously, with great variation in plant conformation, hairiness of leaf, tightness of boll, and other characteristics which affect the ease of harvesting. Much of the value of the fiber depends on its freedom from leaf trash, staining by foliage sap, and tangling with weeds. This factor, together with the waste entailed when the fully exposed fleece is readily knocked to the ground, makes picking a delicate operation. Perhaps the most troublesome aspect of the plant is that its bolls[30] do not ripen uniformly and the crop therefore cannot be gathered at once. Unripe bolls are likely to be injured by any crude mechanical device used to harvest the early crop. These were some of the technical factors with which would-be inventors of successful cotton harvesters had to contend.

Even under the conditions of slavery, some efforts were made to reduce the amount of hand labor in cotton production. As early as 1820, an imaginative Louisiana planter imported a cargo of Brazilian monkeys with the hope of training them to pick cotton.[31] Had this scheme worked, it is conceivable that monkey breeding might have replaced the slave trade and thus averted critical events leading to the Civil War.

The first recorded invention of a machine to harvest cotton was a mule-drawn picker patented by Samuel S, Rembert and Jedediah Prescott of Memphis in 1850.[32] This machine embraced two sets of rotating cylinders and disks studded with teeth to comb the cotton off the plants. Although it may be considered a simple prototype of the modern spindle picker, it was too crude to do an effective job. By 1864 there were twelve patents in effect on a variety of manual or mechanical picking aids and in nearly every succeeding year at least one patent was granted for some type of harvesting device; however it was not until the late 1930s that a successful cotton picker was invented by John Rust![33]

Most explanations of the failure to find a better way to harvest cotton fall into one or more of three categories: economic, the low cost of labor making mechanization unprofitable; technical, the solution being too complex for nineteenth century technology; and finally, structural, meaning structural forces impeded the chances for adoption and invention of accelerated harvesting techniques. Actually, such techniques, which were both profitable and technically feasible, were either available to cotton producers before the war or were within their conceptual grasp. This seems to indicate that both the economic and technological arguments are incorrect. As an example, in the 1860s an Arkansas farmer found that it was profitable to sickle his unpicked cotton at the end of the season and thresh it in the wagon in which it was collected.[34] Also during the period 1914–1926 farmers in the Texas Panhandle, apparently responding to depressed prices and high labor costs, developed an implement for harvesting cotton that they called a "sled." This instrument was a large wooden box with a wedge-shaped opening at the base; it was dragged over the plants, removing the cotton balls and foliage. Since it had no moving parts, it seemed well within the reach of antebellum technology.

If mechanical harvesting was both technically possible and profitable before the Civil War, how can the failure to mechanize be explained? In order for mechanical harvesting to occur, first, the process or machine must be invented; then it must be made available to potential users; and lastly it must be adopted by these users.

Another factor, which should have prompted the invention of a mechanical picker before the war, was the financial gain that would have accrued to the inventor. Another machine, the reaper, gave an indication of the usefulness of mechanical harvesting devices. Further, if a feasible solution to a problem that would bring a large financial gain exists, then it is more likely that the solution will be found. The reality was, however, that only a small portion of those engaged in cotton growing had an immediate interest in solving the harvesting problem. In the antebellum period there is no reason to believe that slaves had the time or incentive to develop a solution, although an incentive did exist for the owners. Finally, most experimentation involves risk. Time and materials must be invested and perhaps even part of the crop endangered. Also, the general poverty in the South probably had a discouraging effect on experimentation by operators of small units.

Such devices and processes as were invented, however, had to be made available to the farmer. Again, the southern economy reduced the chances for success. The retarded state of manufacturing tended to prohibit the local white population of small farmers from acquiring mechanical skills. Additionally, independence from England brought little prospect of improvement in acquiring farming implements. Both farmers and planters were generally compelled either to make their own machines or to rely on the small number of blacksmiths in the South. The blacksmith became a particularly important member of the community and rendered invaluable service to the farming interests by reproducing and repairing implements of all sorts. Some few acquired reputations for special skills, and their services were widely sought after.[35]

Notwithstanding the fact that many inferior and outmoded implements continued to be in use in southern agriculture, the better farmers were alert to the improvements being made and were improving their farming by using the best instruments produced. This is particularly true of the last years of the antebellum period. As an example, between the years 1850 and 1860, although not successful in the case of the cotton picker, the rate of increase in the capital invested in farm implements and machinery in North Carolina was greater than in the nation at large. North Carolinians were using more and better farm implements than ever before. Prejudice against innovations was gradually overcome and the foundation established for a widespread acceptance of new devices.[36]

The second machine used in the antebellum production of cotton was the power loom. Invented in England in 1769 by Richard Arkwright, his machine held the key to the problem of spinning cotton by power-driven machinery. This invention was so ingenious that it still forms the basis of the cotton-spinning industry today. His simple, yet remarkable, invention of using pairs of rollers to replace human fingers opened a new chapter in industrial and human history because Arkwright's cotton factories were an example of an industrial organization which gave rise to the factory based on the use of first waterpower and then steam power that soon revolutionized it. Arkwright's invention had immediate effects on the country in which it was first used. The English cotton industry ousted Indian calicos from the African trade as cheaper cloth from their mills began to be produced in large quantities.

The greatest impact of the power loom was in the British export market. This expanding market encouraged the growth of mills at home, so that more mills, power, waterwheels, steam engines, spinning machines, machinery manufacturers, and machine tool manufacturers were needed in ever increasing numbers. As a consequence, greater experience in designing machines cheapened production and boosted sales, so that the cotton industry expanded rapidly in spite of severe slumps in the industry.

As we will see when I discuss Eli Whitney and the cotton gin, Arkwright may not have created his invention from "thin air." In 1738 and 1758 two Englishmen, Lewis Paul and John Wyatt, patented the idea of using the power loom using rollers. Several mills were established using their machines, and although they were almost successful, eventually their businesses failed. Between this time and Arkwright's successful loom, several other inventors attempted to create spinning machines but not successfully. In his patent application, Arkwright claimed that he "had by great study and long application invented a new Piece of Machinery never before found out, practiced or used for the making of Weft or Yarn from Cotton, Flax, and Wool, which would be of great Utility to a great many Manufacturers in His Kingdom of England, as well as to his Subjects in general, by employing a great Number of Poor People in Working the said machinery, and by Making the said Weft[37] or Yarn much superior in Quality to any ever heretofore Manufactured or Made."[38]

Although the machine depicted in the patent would not have spun flax or wool. Arkwright was able to develop it successfully for spinning cotton. In the patent, he envisaged horses providing the motive power; but soon something on a much larger scale was necessary, which after experimentation led to the establishment of the first successful water-powered cotton-spinning mill in England. In 1787 Edmund Cartwright invented the power loom and also a wool-combing machine. His inventions, combined with those of Arkwright, were the most important steps in the British textile revolution.

Like Whitney, Arkwright became embroiled in another problem, this time dealing with patents. Arkwright's defense of his patents extended over a period of some four years, from late 1781 to 1785, from his first suit for infringement to loss of his surviving unexpired patent due to government action. Arwright lost all three suits and while the English patent system (before the

Nineteenth century cotton gin in Florence County, South Carolina (Library of Congress, Prints and Photographs Division, HAER SC, 21-JOHVI.V, 1—15).

19th century reforms) was notoriously complex, there is a strong possibility that his rise to riches and fame aroused considerable envy and hostility at the time, partly because it was thought that he had copied the inventions of others and partly because his patent held the key to the problem of spinning cotton by power-driven machinery.

Angered by the ill treatment he felt he had received from Parliament at the trials of his suits for patent infringement of his 1775 cotton machinery patent, Richard Arkwright told fellow manufacturer Josiah Wedgwood in 1785 that he intended to take revenge on an ungrateful Britain. Parliament had invalidated his patent rights to the extraordinarily productive cotton-spinning machine he had introduced ten years earlier; he would now invalidate England's jealously guarded monopoly of the whole technology, including both his 1769 and 1775 patents. He would, he said, "publish descriptions and copper plates of all the parts that it might be known to foreign nations as well as our own."[39] And six years later, on December 30, 1791, a United States patent was granted to William Pollard of Philadelphia, "ass[ignee] of Richard Arkwright," for a machine for "Spinning and Roving Cotton" that included components of both of Arkwright's patents. Although no evidence is available to establish a direct personal connection between Arkwright and Pollard, a considerable amount of information is available concerning the origin, use, and fate of Pollard's patent, the first known to have been issued by the United States for cotton manufacturing machinery.

Toward the end of 1788 or early 1789, Pollard had purchased a model of a machine for roving and spinning cotton. It was "sold to him," he averred, "as a model of Sir Richard Arkwright's machine and was brought into this Country at the risque of vessel and cargoe, heavy amercements on the Captain besides imprisonment etc."[40] The delay between Pollard's acquiring the model in 1788 or 1789 and the issuance of the patent in late 1791 was certainly not a lack of commitment on the part of the patent commissioners to the idea of American parity with England in mechanical invention. Information about the remarkable British invention in cotton machinery, news of which had been prevented by the war between England and her former colony from reaching the ears of American mechanics, was now beginning to filter across the Atlantic.[41]

Two other individuals became involved in the transference of British cotton spinning technology to the United States. The first was Francis Cabot Lowell. Lowell came from great wealth, but he was no rich man's son. In Scotland during 1811, ostensibly for his health, Lowell visited the newly built cotton spinning plants in Lancashire and Derbyshire, not as a vacationing visitor but as a spy.

Not surprisingly, His Majesty's government was determined to protect the sources of the industrial revolution from outsiders. By the end of the 18th century, the British had passed rigorous patent laws and banned the export of cotton weaving technology. When foreigners found loopholes by recruiting skilled workers and luring them abroad, this was made a crime. So were the acts of making and exporting drawings of the machinery in the mills. Fortress-like walls topped with spikes and broken glass quickly grew up around the mills, and workers were sworn to secrecy. Skilled technicians who went abroad under false pretenses had their property summarily confiscated by the Crown

Yankee ingenuity being what it was then, there were plenty of prominent Americans trying to steal secrets from Britain.[42] But none went so far as Lowell. His target was the Cartwright loom, the crown jewel of the British textile industry. Cartwright's loom was so powerful and efficient that the British Parliament later awarded him a bonus of 10,000 pounds. The importance of the Cartwright loom to Britain's booming economy placed it at the top of a pantheon of industrial secrets. We may never know how Lowell acquired the blueprints for the British loom, but since historians credit him with having a photographic memory, he probably carried the blueprints in his head. Additionally, he appears to have taken pains to make sure that his secrets would never emerge. He kept no diary, confined his letters to family matters, and shared the method of his great triumph with no one.[43]

The other individual who was responsible for the tremendous growth of the cotton weaving industry in the United States was Samuel Slater. An Englishman, Slater learned the textile trade from one of the most progressive British manufactures, Jedediah Stutt. In 1789, Slater immigrated to the United States and within a year formed a partnership with William Almy and Smith Brown to construct and operate a spinning mill based on the Arkwright model. Like Lowell, Slater had brought the blueprints for the machine in his head, and therefore, also like Lowell, he had thwarted the wishes of the British government. After the success of the first mill, Slater participated in a number of highly profitable textile manufacturing ventures in four states. While these mills were not the equal in size or capitalization to the Lowell mill, Slater's medium-sized holdings were successful for a long period of time. His estate of over one million dollars at the time of his death in 1835 reflected his mechanical and managerial accomplishments.

Both Lowell and Slater were at the heart of the development of the American factory system. By stealing Britain's most valuable secret, by analyzing it and acting quickly upon it, they brought the industrial revolution to the United States and built the economic engine that later helped drive the North to victory in the Civil War. That in turn laid the cornerstone for a level of prosperity that created the American Century and led to the formation of the world's largest and richest economy.

The last of the cotton machines was the best known, and that was the cotton gin. Eli Whitney, rather than inventing the cotton gin, developed the second of two types. The first type evolved from the *charkha*, which originated on the Indian subcontinent and consisted of a pair of wooden rollers mounted on a frame. As the rollers were turned with a hand crank, the cotton passed between them and the seeds were squeezed out. Roller gins that evolved from the charkha were used in North America at least as early as the 1740s.[44] The first North American roller gins were crude but effective. Their major disadvantage was a failure to work equally well in ginning the two types of cotton grown—black seed, or long staple, and green seed, or short staple.

During the 18th century numerous individuals attempted to create the best possible cotton gin. However, of all those who sought to perfect ginning Whitney is the one remembered. Rather than attempting to improve the roller method, he invented a new principle in 1793 for removing the seeds. Whitney's gin contained a cylinder filled with wire teeth set in annular rows. As the cylinder was turned, the teeth drew the cotton into a breastwork of transverse grooves through which the lint passed but not the seed.[45]

Development of the Whitney machine meant that there were two methods of ginning cotton, each with its advantages and disadvantages. The Whitney gin could easily clean either green-seed or black-seed cotton and its other advantage was speed: the larger, second, model Whitney gin reportedly could "clean ten times as much cotton as ... in any other way known."[46] Its disadvantage was that it shortened the staple by cutting many of the fibers and thereby lowered the price of cotton.

The reason that Whitney's machine had such a profound effect on the production of cotton was not only that it could clean large quantities of cotton, but also that it was copied and improved upon by local craftsmen almost from its introduction. Each artisan introduced slight innovations, and as time went by, certain manufacturers became famous for their improvements.[47] Most gins were used only in the vicinity of their manufacture. Others were widely sold. In 1860 there were fifty-seven manufacturers of cotton gins in the United States. All were small and all but three were in the cotton regions. Of the fifty-seven manufacturers, thirty-four employed fewer than ten workers and thirty-one sold less than $10,000 worth of cotton gins annually. The largest factory, operated by Daniel Pratt in Autauga County, Alabama, built more than 8,000 gins between 1833 and 1860. In 1860 his operation employed sixty-six workers and produced gins valued annually at $289,000.[48]

The effect of cotton on southern manufacturing was huge because the manufacture of the gins did not depend on highly skilled labor, which was not widely available in the South. By the Civil War, these manufacturers had expanded along with "King Cotton" from South Carolina to Texas. The reason for the growth of gin manufacturers in the South was due to the poor legal protection from the patent system that Eli Whitney received. His innovation was copied by many southern "ginwrights" who supplied nearby planters. Subsequent attempts to license the gins to local producers were too late to reverse his fortunes.[49]

Aside from the profits to be made in dealing in cotton, there was also money to be made in investing in the southern gin factories where the rates of return averaged 25 percent in 1850 and 28 percent in 1860, against 4 percent in the North during the same period. These returns were better than in agriculture and should have induced more rapid industrialization in the South. The reason that it did not was that the additional profits in the South were due to much lower labor costs owing to the fact that as much as two-thirds of the gin manufacturers' labor force was slaves. Another factor was that the transportation costs of delivering cotton gins gave small ginwright shops local monopolies when selling to nearby planters. Eli Whitney's early attempt to use northern factory production also suffered from the fact that his first machine was not of superior quality. So by copying the basic Whitney design, local craftsmen could make gins of similar quality that sold at lower prices.

Nevertheless, Whitney's cotton gin was the most significant invention during the years between 1790 and 1860. The growing dilemma of the South was that the demand for its traditional exports staples (e.g., tobacco and sugar) was no longer increasing and its heavy capital investment was in slaves. The concerted search for new export staples and the experiments with cotton all reflect the problems of the region; invention of the cotton gin can be viewed as a response to the dilemma rather than an independent accidental development. Had there been no cotton gin, it is certain that the resources directly and indirectly devoted to the cotton trade would have been at least partially absorbed in other types of economic activity. Given the social structure, attitudes and motivation of American society, and the rich quantity and quality of resources which made even the self-sufficient farmer well off as compared with his European counterpart, the economy of the United States would not have stagnated.[50]

The cotton textile industry remained central to the industrial revolution. Paramount in this industry was its technological progress, more especially the inventions that emerged towards the end of the 18th century. Innovations in this period precipitated an extraordinary acceleration in the growth of output and a steep decline in the cost of producing product from cotton. In the hundred years from 1660, the technical progress that propelled the textile industry on to higher and more variegated levels of output depended on a wave of macro inventions that transformed the process of cotton production. A period of improvement followed approximately from the 1790s, during which the commercial potential of these machines was realized. Virtually the entire body of advanced technology, which transformed textile production in the period from 1760, was initiated by British inventors and improved by British mechanics to the point at which it could be exploited commercially by British businessmen.

Britain's lead in the development of mechanized cotton production came about because of the growth of their substantial domestic market for cotton cloth provided by trade with India. By the 18th century, English taste for cotton cloth was well established and the potential for mixing cottons yarns with yarn spun from flax was fully realized. This domestic base of cotton usage coupled with an expansion of foreign markets prompted not only the number and sophistication of inventions to feed product to these markets but also the political decisions which attempted unsuccessfully to keep the wealth engendered by the use of cotton in British hands.

From the Revolutionary War to the Civil War, American engineering and invention continued to play an ever-increasing role in the interpretation of American civilization to the world. In reading the popular and technical press after 1820, it is easy to see a growing reputation abroad of American inventive abilities. European men of science, reported the *American Journal of Science* in 1822, were astonished at the rapidity of American discovery and improvement.[51] The flow of ideas was now moving in two directions, and in the 1840s a congressional committee could report proudly, "Formerly, we borrowed and copied much that was valuable from Europe. Now, Europe is borrowing and copying with no little advantage from us."[52] By mid-century, Americans were reading with immense satisfaction headlines announcing, for example, "Another American Triumph in England," as with Samuel Colt's revolvers.[53] Overshadowing all other American inventions, however, was the one that allowed the nation to expand its trade and wealth enormously: Eli Whitney's cotton gin.

2

Transportation

The nation possessed two main cotton belts during the antebellum period, with different transportation situations. The first, in the East, stretched from the southern edge of Virginia to central Alabama. Its outer edge could be reached by navigation upon a few of the larger rivers, but easy natural means of transportation within the belt itself was wholly lacking. The problem was to send cotton to the coast and to get supplies from across the pine barrens on the one hand or the mountains on the other. Initially, the planters shipped cotton on the rivers that crossed the barrens and also used a network of country roads when there was an absence of rivers. If the cotton was traveling to the North, the choice was to use Georgia and Carolina rivers or send the product down the Mississippi to the Gulf and from there to the Atlantic, either to the northern United States or Europe. The eastern cotton belt confronted by far the most difficult transportation problem in the South.

The western cotton belt, reaching from Alabama to Texas and as far north as the southern edge of Kentucky was similar to the eastern belt in that the plantations also produced short-staple cotton. But shipping was different. The West possessed a large number of navigable streams which flowed into nearly every area where the best cotton lands were located. The planters had only to haul their cotton to the nearest river and wait for the next boat bound for Mobile or New Orleans. The strategic trading points always had two features in common: access to the outside world and a river system connected to it. The most important were cities such as Charleston, Savannah, Mobile and New Orleans because they possessed both features. Next came Beaufort, South Carolina; Brunswick, Georgia; and Pensacola, Florida. These cities had good harbors but no river connection to the interior cotton plantations. Finally, there were cities such as Georgetown, South Carolina, and Apalachicola, Florida, which possessed river communication with the interior, but had no harbors.

2. Transportation

Aside from geography, the cotton belt had certain features of social economics which strongly influenced transportation and commerce. First, plantations in the South were widely scattered, limiting large amounts of traffic moving together. Second, it was difficult for a common carrier (such as a steamboat or railroad) to make money on cotton during any months other than after the cotton harvest between September and January. Third, with the large investment in the South in slaves and cotton, there were little funds left to invest in transportation. Fourth, the southern inclination toward agriculture diminished the supply of native white labor for any other purpose and the plantations monopolized the supply of black laborers. Fifth, the plantation system, dominating the whole industrial life of the South, attracted nearly all the men of ability into agricultural management, which caused a shortage of efficient managers and promoters in other areas.

In the early years of cotton cultivation in the Southeast, the new staple merely continued what tobacco had begun. Two-thirds of the cotton crop was raised within five miles of some river, and the remainder not more than ten miles from water which could be considered navigable.[1] The road systems were mainly used to supplement the rivers, but in both cases, whether the shipments were made by land or water, there were problems. As far as the roads were concerned, not only were they usually in poor condition but also, legally, the responsibility for maintaining them was up to the local community. Since this was the case, there was less concern in repairing roads used by planters on their way to market than in repairing those used by the community.[2] To remedy this situation somewhat, local legislatures would give an individual or company the opportunity to create a causeway, a bridge, or a turnpike and charge for its use. As an example, in 1803, the Georgia legislature signed a contract with Ebenezer Jenckes to maintain a road from Savannah towards the coast for a distance of twenty-one miles and to charge a toll provided for in the contract for a term of thirty years.[3] The waterways were cared for in much the same way. In 1799, the Georgia legislature contracted with a stock company to keep the Savannah River navigable from the cities of Augusta to Petersburg and to collect tolls on the traffic.[4]

Both river and road traffic was too light before 1815 to make effective demands for expensive systems of improvements. Cotton prices were high and labor scarce. Most of the people in the Southeast were eager to take advantage of the cotton profits, which were high enough to overcome any expenses incurred in getting the product to market. After the War of 1812, competition by western producers of cotton became a spur to cheapen the cost of marketing in the East through the improvement of the means of transporting the crop. Aside from getting cotton to market, the other problem was in getting supplies to the plantations. The country stores in the region were very thinly distributed and had exceedingly light stocks of merchandise. If the supplies were brought by wagon, it was over poor roads, and if by river the pole-boats moving upstream took an inordinate amount of time to reach their destination. As examples, the pole-boats required at least fourteen days to ascend from Savannah to Augusta, and five to seven days to make the same journey downstream. Wagons could make the trip between the same points in about a week, barring accidents, and stagecoaches in three to four days. So long as the motive power was the labor of men and horses, the northbound freight charges were prohibitive on all but expensive articles.

To overcome these problems, the state legislatures began to look for new ways to transport both cotton and supplies. In 1807, Robert Fulton had created a workable steamboat, which had been improved to the extent that by the end of the War of 1812 there existed a steamboat that could be used for commercial traffic. In 1816, the Georgia legislature granted Samuel Howard and his Steam Boat Company of Georgia a monopoly to navigate all of the rivers of the state of Georgia exclusively for a period of twenty years. The service began on April 17, 1816, and was described by the *Savannah Republican* as follows:

> The Steamboat, *Enterprise*, with a numerous concourse of citizens on board, started from Howard's wharf yesterday morning at 12 o'clock on a party of pleasure. She moved beautifully through the water and was certainly an interesting curiosity to those who have not seen steam vessels elsewhere. To behold a large and apparently unwieldy machine, without oars or sails propelled through the element by an invisible agency at a rate of four miles an hour, is indeed a novel spectacle. We understand from the proprietors that the *Enterprise* fully meets their expectations and behaved very well yesterday. Our enterprising townsmen have our very best wishes for so laudable an undertaking.[5]

By 1821, the company had become insolvent and was sold to a group of investors in Charleston. The monopoly also ceased when the Supreme Court ruled that a similar control of the Hudson River in New York was unconstitutional, the ruling also applying to Georgia, thus allowing competition on Georgia's rivers once again.

The agitation for public works in Georgia did not abate, however, and came to include not only river and turnpike improvements, but also a great canal from Savannah into the interior which would gain the same benefits for Georgia as the Erie Canal had for New York. Those who were in favor of the canal project argued that once the canal was completed the worth of the interior land would rise to that of Savannah. They were forgetting that the situation in Georgia was not analogous to New York; in Georgia the canal may have increased cotton production to the extent that cotton prices and profits would fall, balancing any rise in the price of the interior land. On the whole, all the efforts to develop long-distance commercial transportation on roads and rivers in Georgia failed. In retrospect this may have been a benefit, because in virtually every instance the railroad accomplished the task to a far better degree.

In South Carolina, the transportation situation was worse than in Georgia. The state appropriations for "improvements" in the building of a few poorly constructed turnpikes and the removal of some river obstructions were simply an attempt to transform a totally inefficient system into an efficient one by means of patching over the numerous problem areas. If shipment was by water, the rivers were too small in volume and contained numerous rapids; by land, the distances were too great to be traveled if horses were used. Aside from sporadic instances of bridge building by private companies, the construction of railroads took practically all of the capital and legislative support available for transportation improvements after 1829. The care of turnpikes, causeways, and canals was left to those companies and individuals who leased them from the state and charged a toll. As a consequence, these structures were usually greatly neglected. The care of common roads and rivers continued to be in the hands of local authorities.

A view of the general system of transportation in South Carolina just prior to the railroad era (about 1830) would show that, except for the introduction of steamboats on the major rivers, there was little change in the ability to move either cotton or supplies on the roads or streams. On the whole, the cotton belt was so far removed from the sea and transportation so costly that only vehicles and boats carrying essential items used the roads and rivers. Practically nothing but cotton was sent to market and only supplies that could not be produced at home were imported. As an example, the cotton planters would have been glad to use their land to grow more cotton and bring in their grain and meat supplies at moderate prices. But the long and roundabout transit for these items—from the northwest to the Ohio River, down the Mississippi, transshipped to Savannah or Charleston, from there to the edge of the cotton belt, and finally to the plantation—with freight charges and numerous middlemen's profits along with delays and risk of loss made the cost too great for the planters to afford except in emergencies. A characteristic of the period was the predominance of individual enterprise and self-reliance. Transportation of both cotton and supplies was mostly informal, irregular, expensive, and inefficient; common carriers were not yet predominant, thus making every planter his own carrier, boatman, and road repairer.

This situation in South Carolina, especially in Charleston, became of grave public concern especially in the 1820s when the community realized that it was not recovering as rapidly as the rest of the country from the panic of 1819. As a result both the cotton planters and the local merchants were losing business, while on the other hand Savannah was prospering. In 1822, the legislature in Charleston began discussions on building either a canal or a railroad from Charleston to the interior. On January 30, 1828, after much discussion, the legislature enacted a new law chartering the South Carolina Canal and Railroad Company connecting Charleston with the city of Hamburg, South Carolina. The work was completed in 1833 and the effect on cotton transportation was immediate, as can be ascertained from this item printed in the *Charleston Courier*: "A most unprecedented and pleasing circumstance was witnessed on Sunday last, at the Railroad Depository, being the arrival of three locomotives at one time, having at their train sixty freight cars laden with nine hundred and eighty bales of cotton."[6]

The railroad did fairly well during its first few years of operation. The bales of cotton carried during the years 1834–1839 were as follows: 1834: 24,567; 1835: 34,760; 1836: 28,497; 1837: 34,395; 1838: 35,345; and 1839: 52,585. These volumes allowed the line to return enough profit to its investors so that an expansion program was planned. The expansion became the Louisville, Cincinnati, and Charleston Railroad, running from Charleston on west. Colonel Robert Y. Hayne, a former senator and governor of South Carolina, was in charge of a committee to explore building the road. He reported that, first, it was essential to the prosperity of the southern and western states that they be connected by a railroad from the Ohio River to the Atlantic; second, that such a highway would allow an inconceivably large volume of traffic; and third that it terminate at Charleston. The main point of this railroad was not only in moving cotton. Just as important was moving the planter's supplies from the West to the plantations, supplies without which the plantations could not operate. The proposed railroad from Charleston, Colonel Hayne went on to say, would have a monopoly for much of its route and would compete favorably with the Mississippi River in the long-distance traffic in foodstuffs. Anyone traveling in the mountains at that time, he said, would see long lines of six-horse teams constantly employed on almost impassable roads, hauling bacon and other heavy articles to the southern states. Hayne even convinced the planters to pay for extending the railroad through their plantations. Hayne died in 1839 and with him died the company's dreams. Not only that, but in the same year the "cotton crisis" began when the price of cotton crashed and did not regain its past position until 1844.

Outside of South Carolina and Georgia, especially into the Southwest, prior to the steamboat era, keelboats and flatboats[7] were the primary means by which cotton reached outside markets (especially through New

Orleans).[8] Although flatboating persisted, keelboating was quickly eclipsed with the introduction of the steamboat. This contrast is explained in part by the differential impact of the steamboat on upstream and downstream rates. Successful keelboat operations depended primarily on upstream revenues, and it was on the upstream rates that the steamboat had its most dramatic effect. Flatboating not only survived but even expanded in the face of the new technology; for instance in 1816, the year before the first successful navigation of the western rivers, 1287 flatboats arrived in New Orleans. By the year 1847, the number of arrivals had increase to a peak of 2792.[9] This longevity of flatboating occurred despite the fact that flatboats underwent no changes in their physical characteristics. Neither were there any apparent technical advances in their handling or navigation. Steamboats, when they came on the scene, aided flatboats and cotton planters because now flatboatmen who were usually plantation employees or slaves were saved the arduous return journey by land. There is general agreement among historians that the steamboat produced other savings for the planters. The return journey, which previously took several months, could be made in about a week by the 1840s.[10] This was particularly important, as the planter's flatboatmen were able to avoid absences during critical seasons such as planting time, which lowered the cost of labor.[11]

Steamboats for the short time that they lasted as a transportation factor altered the shape of the southern economy. By the 1830s, steamboats had become the workhorses of the South in the areas in which they could operate. They enhanced the value of slaves, raised plantation productivity, and provided new sources of revenue for the planters. These planters now became increasingly enmeshed in a global system of commerce that cotton came to define. As riverboats connected merchants to regional, national, and international markets, they brought wealth, population, and political power to the Southwest. Steamboats also created new markets in the interior part of the Southeast. Because of the steamboat's huge impact on the production of cotton, *De Bow's Review*, the leading southern magazine on commercial matters, featured a riverboat as one of the images on its cover. When a foreign observer noted "the circulation of steamboats is as important to the welfare of the west, as the circulation of blood is to the human frame," he demonstrated that he understood how riverboats helped create a cotton-dominated southern economy.[12] No section of the country was so completely dependent upon steam for effective transportation, and in no other part of the world were so many steamboats built and operated.[13]

The steamboats, however, had a number of deficiencies, the main one being operating in low water. From mid to late summer, streams evaporated and sandbars shifted irregularly, particularly on the Mississippi River's tribu-

An 1830s steamboat (Library of Congress, Prints & Photographs Division, Theodor Horydczak Collection, LC-H812-T-2338–012).

taries. Groundings were so common in the dry season that John James Audubon, who was floating down the Ohio River on a flatboat, nonchalantly remarked at "having Seen Steamboats almost every day fast on Sand Barrs I have taken no particular Notice of their Names and Positions."[14]

As the rivers dried up, so did business in the river towns. The "absence of steamboats at the wharfs—the scarcity of cotton, the unemployed draymen to be seen in the shade, quietly waiting for a job—and at night the unlighted counting rooms, all gave indication that the business season was over," concluded one small-town newspaper. As an example of the effect of the water level on first steamboats and then on cotton prices, when an 1855 drought reduced the Alabama River to a mere stream, shipping prices spiked to $5 a bale, tempting desperate planters to build flatboats to get their product to market. The paralyzed riverboat trade brought financial ruin to overextended southerners like the financier W.N. Smith, who had given the cotton planter William P. Gould generous terms for a loan. When the drought struck, Smith called in his loan, apologetically explaining that those "extra-ordinary times of low rivers have caused an oppressive demand for money," but Gould was unable to pay up. By contrast, planters had to act quickly when the rains came. A rapid rise in river levels could undercut cotton prices, as one cotton factor, McDowell, Withers, and Company, warned cotton planter Hugh Davis: "sell now before the rivers get up and large quantities [of cotton] arrive with its restless owners." Planters like Davis, who once saw the steamboat as their economic savior, grew weary of being a slave to natural conditions.[15]

Another problem with the steamboat was profitability. In 1818, Estwick Evans, a historian, wrote that "the profits attending the business of steamboats upon the western waters are beyond belief; but the competition arising from this circumstance is daily lessening them."[16] In 1834, another historian, Morgan Neville, wrote that "although the benefit conferred on our country, by steam navigation, was incalculable, the stock invested in boats was, as a general rule, a losing investment. In a few cases, owing to fortuitous events, or to the exercise of more than usual prudence, money has been made; but the instances are as few as not to affect the rule."[17] Steamboat losses were the result of explosions, fires, snaggings or some less common hazard, and the short lifespan and hazardous conditions under which they operated were reflected in their insurance rates. Many steamboat operators carried no insurance and those who did purchase commercial insurance could do so only up to two-thirds or three-quarters of the value of the boat.[18] Given the competitive character of the market for steamboat services and the attendant losses, it is quite clear why the steamboat transport industry did not produce a class of financial and industrial tycoons as the railroad era did.

Throughout the South, the inconveniences associated with steamboats made it clear that another technology was necessary to move the cotton to market and supplies to the plantations. As we have seen, the Southeast had already turned to railroads to overcome the liabilities of other forms of transportation, in the more densely populated areas along the Atlantic coast, especially Charleston. Because of this, planters in the southern interior also became interested in the new technology. For these cotton growers, railroads seemed be the answer because they did not depend on the vagaries of the rivers or poor wagon trails. Additionally, they could extend into regions untouched by steamboat traffic and travel to wherever they were needed instead of depending on winding rivers and streams. Also, "ice in winter, low water in summer, [and] a circuitous and tedious route at times, interfere with [the] precision and accuracy" of riverboat travel. Railroads held out the promise of mastering the environment rather than working within its constraints.[19]

Given the obvious inadequacies of steamboats, one might think that railroads garnered enthusiastic support, especially among the cotton planters in the interior. Added to that, southerners along the Atlantic seaboard were capable of promoting, funding, and building railroads. In 1840, the seven slave states bordering the Atlantic Ocean had 28 percent of the nation's track, while the southern interior had a woeful 5 percent. Ten years later, the picture had hardly changed, Coastal southern railroads accounted for 22.3 percent of the nation's track, and the interior 4.7 percent. Judging from these figures, residents of the Southeast had the capacity to build railroads; they just chose not to do so.[20]

Perhaps the reason for this aversion to railroad building in the South in the early part of the century had to do with the fact that railroad construction as it finally emerged ran parallel to the area's rivers, which were in effect competitors of the railroads, albeit of varying degrees of efficiency. The direct benefits provided by southern railroads were limited not only by the relatively large amounts of freight that could be transported by water, but also by the small difference between water and rail rates. As an example, the following report was issued by the President of the Mississippi Central Railroad in 1860: "The quantity of cotton that has been transported on the road since the first train started, has been 400,000 bales. The amount saved to the producers of this cotton, by a reduction of the cost of transporting it to market, together with a reduction in the cost in return freights, during the same period of time, had exceeded one-tenth of the cost of the road and its equipments."[21]

Another alternative to the railroads were turnpikes. Before the inauguration of the "cotton triangle," the only effective means of communication between the North and South after the Revolution was by means of sailing along the Atlantic coast. However, reliance upon water alone was not wholly satisfactory. Secretary of the Treasury Albert Gallatin made a recommendation in his report of 1808 to construct a turnpike paralleling the coast from Maine to Georgia: "It is sufficiently evident that whatever the annual expense of transportation on a certain route in its natural state exceeds the interest on the capital employed in improving the communication and the annual expense of transportation (exclusive of the tolls) by the improved route, the difference is an annual additional income to the nation."[22]

Not until the railroad era was a continuous overland route completed, however, and then only by a variety of poorly coordinated independent roads which were chartered separately to serve existing traffic. While passenger earnings justified construction of railroads, freight revenues from the transport of cotton north were scant; therefore the most economical methods proved to be a combination of ship and rail. The railroad served for the shorter distances and the coastal packets for the longer trades.

Given the problems associated with turnpikes, and because of the readily available rivers, southerners retained a stubborn loyalty to steamboats and originally envisioned railroads west of the Appalachian Mountains as complementing river traffic rather than competing with it. The first southern railroad west of the Alleghany Mountains wasn't completed until 1832. Its purpose was to move cotton out of the Alabama interior in the absence of a water route. In the 1840s, southerners completed other lines into the back country, all of them to augment steamboat service. One Mississippi resident argued that it was "common sense" to build a railroad into the interior "for the conveyance of cotton bales to the river, merchandize [sic] to the country, and passengers to and fro." As late as 1850, residents of the southern interior continued to envision a transportation network with steamboats as the dominant partner.

Before the advent of the railroads, the last large expenditure to complement the steamboats were canals. Just as the financial success of the Erie Canal had led to enthusiasm over a canal's ability to create a great transportation system, the financial crises of 1837 and 1839 showed that canals were costing huge sums and producing so little revenue that public credit was threatened. No canals of major size were begun between 1840 and 1860. In the 1840s less than 400 miles of canals were constructed nationwide and by 1850 abandonments exceeded new construction.[23] Finally, it was the misfortune of most canals to become obsolete even before they were opened for traffic. The advantages of the railroads were so great that even the strongest canals could not retain a profitable share of the transportation business.

Beginning in the 1850s, the direction of the railroads changed. Previously they had been almost exclusively east-west lines, moving cotton to the coast; now the belief was that north-south lines would be more profitable. These new railroads were designed primarily not as supplements to the rivers or as substitutes for them, but rather they depended for their prosperity more on the regions through which they passed than on the terminals. Cotton shipments from the upper Mississippi River, at one time securely bound for New Orleans, were moving directly eastward. New Orleans' need for railroads became acute as the Atlantic cities built their railroads deeper and deeper into the West. She had to hold the hinterland and at the same time develop new trading areas in western Louisiana, eastern Texas, and Arkansas.[24] When these new railroads were built, both the Mississippi River and the Atlantic coast would be paralleled by railroads, which then began to secure an increasing volume of both local and through cotton traffic. This indicated that the time was near when the river and coast trade would be relegated to an inferior position.[25] The other difference was that now the states in the eastern cotton belt, mainly Alabama, Mississippi, Tennessee, and Louisiana, began to finance the building of railroads themselves as well as look for outside money in order to open up their isolated areas. These states gave direct aid to the roads as well as loans and bond issues. Loans were difficult to obtain in Europe at this time due to poor harvests and the approach of the Crimean War. Also, the London banks had not forgotten a former repudiation of debts by the state of Mississippi. However, after the Crimean War, European borrowing became easier.

Using Louisiana as an example, we can see that railroad development in that state before the Civil War followed the general pattern. Since railroad finance and construction proved to be a tremendous task even for an advanced industrial state like England, it was usually too great an undertaking for private enterprise in underdeveloped America. Therefore aid from the state and local governments was so important that when the state withheld assistance during the decade of the 1840s only a few miles of railroad were constructed and only one railroad company was chartered. The reason for the states' curtailing aid to the railroads was because, since the 1820s, the state had used a land-bank system through its banks to provide capital for internal improvements. By 1844, however, the state's indebtedness to the banks had risen to $16,500,000. The banks were also using the funds for risky but lucrative speculation in cotton. Occasionally, voices of protest like those in the *New Orleans Bee* lashed out at the legislature for its "bastard ardor" in chartering so many "gambling speculations" and at the bankers for making "large advances" to cotton planters while the railroads starved for capital. But these attacks went unheeded. Although the speculation ended with the Panic of 1837, it was little consolation because the panic nearly ruined the railroads as well.[26]

The ocean part of the cotton trade concerned New York City because of that city's invention of the packet system of shipping. Simply put, an ocean packet system consisted of taking regular trading ships and operating them on a fixed schedule, as other services such as railroads and steamships did. This radical alteration of the usual haphazard sailing schedules contained risks as well as the prospects of profit. The ships in the packet line were pledged to sail on their scheduled date—"full or not full," as an advertisement for their services declared. That involved the risk of running the ships at only a fraction of their freight-earning capacity. The announced schedule of sailings meant that each ship would make three round-trips to Europe each year instead of the usual two. The third voyage had to fall in the winter months when the North Atlantic was at its worst because of gales that would strain both men and ships. The winter westbound trip of the packets was one of the most grueling sailings in the early nineteenth century. On the other hand, the third trip meant that 50 percent more service would be derived from the capital invested in the ships and the extra income from the third trip would more than compensate for the wear and tear from the winter crossing. By inaugurating this packet service, one of New York's most profitable and original achievements, the city was able to create a three-cornered trade known as the "cotton triangle." At the three corners were the cotton port—Charleston, Savannah, Mobile, or New Orleans—the European port—generally Liverpool or Le Havre—and New York.

Previously, the majority of sailings were from the southern port that sent cotton directly to Europe. Most of the ships then returned to New York with general freight or immigrants, and finally turned southward on a coastal run to pick up more cotton. With the packet system in place, New York eliminated the direct run between the South and Europe. Now, the cotton was carried to Europe via New York, even though that involved some two hundred extra miles of sailing and the extra charges for unloading and reloading that gave the packets on the Atlantic shuttle their eastbound cargo. In return, an even larger proportion of European goods reached the South via New York.

Looking at this "cotton triangle" objectively, it would seem that there was no logical reason for it. Given the European need for raw cotton and the American need for European manufactured goods, the trading business between Europe and America would have happened anyway, whether or not New York had created its packet idea. The South, on the other hand, could have still shipped cotton directly to Europe. New York, however, had very good reasons for interfering. Without the cotton, New York would have been hard-pressed to provide return cargoes for the vessels which brought imports from overseas. The reason for allowing the "cotton triangle" to exist may have been one of default: the planters did not wish to become involved in the commercial aspects of marketing and shipping their cotton, allowing New York companies to become involved and to take the lion's share of the business. Given this situation, it is no wonder that New York was eager to participate in this grand prize of American commerce, the cotton trade.

It is interesting to note how the "cotton triangle" began. Its creation was a very gradual and quiet affair so as not to alarm the South lest they then safeguard their direct trade with Europe. The triangle began just before the War of 1812. In 1811, as an example, the port of New York shipped 15,000 bales of cotton to Europe spread among forty different cargoes, so nearly every ship bound for Europe had at least a few bales. With that experience, as soon as peace came New York was in position to perfect the triangle. In 1822, for instance, cotton was far and away the most valuable of New York's domestic exports. The total value of these exports was $9,228,000, with cotton accounting for 40 percent of the total. This preponderance of cotton shipments from New York to Europe had become so common that when, in 1843, the new packet *Queen of the West* sailed on her maiden trip without cotton, New York City mayor Philip Hone wrote the following in his diary:

> Saturday, Sept. 16—A state of things exists in the commerce of this country unprecedented and worthy to be noted down among the memorabilia of the day. This ship has taken out to England a cargo consisting of articles all (with the exception of naval stores) of Northern production, and the *Ashburton*, which sailed a day or two since, has not a southern article on board. Not a single bale of cotton in both cargoes. The *Stephen Whitney* has only 119 bales of cotton.... The large shipments of provisions may be accounted for by Sir Robert Peel's new tariff. Cotton is higher in the United States than in England, and rising.[27]

By the time the Erie Canal was finished in 1825, the "cotton triangle" was a well established and strongly functioning business. Even after the canal was finished, the cotton brought north to New York far exceeded in value the flour and other western products carried east by the canal boats.

Of the four major cotton ports involved in the triangle, the business at first centered on the two old and well-established seaboard cities of Charleston and Savannah. Gradually they were overtaken in volume by the Gulf ports of Mobile and New Orleans. Charleston, the oldest of the cotton ports, was the most difficult for the Yankee traders to penetrate. Nevertheless, enough of them were there in 1819 to form a New England Society. The next city, Savannah, had a mercantile community that was not as large or as wealthy or as exclusive as Charleston's and consequently offered better openings to the ubiquitous northerners, who also swarmed up the river to Augusta, the chief gathering point for Savannah's cotton cargoes. More than any of the other cotton ports, Mobile depended on New York for its imports, developing almost no direct trade with Europe.

The final cotton port, New Orleans, has already been covered. The commercial potentialities of the city were not realized under the French or Spanish regimes, but by 1803, when the Louisiana Purchase brought it into the United States, the opening of the West meant an almost immediate stimulus to the business community. As the port expanded, this business community was joined by financial adventurers from the North whose numbers grew rapidly even though the newspapers carried long casualty lists of northerners dying of yellow fever, most of the victims being in their twenties and thirties.

During the 1820s, the success of the packet line service to Europe led to the organization of similar packet lines to the cotton ports. The operators of these lines began sending cotton northward and shipping general cargo southward, believing that regular service would bring them additional profits. As for shipping between New York and these ports, while statistics are available for foreign commerce the customs authorities were not required to keep records for the even larger volume of traffic which passed between the ports of the American coastline. Altogether, New York's coastal packet fleet was an invaluable adjunct to its ocean packets and the fact that these were mere "coasters" should not obscure the fact that in size, performance, and earnings the ships plying the cotton ports were among the finest afloat.

Even without verifiable statistics, it seems likely that the South received only a small amount of its imports directly from Europe, with the majority coming from the North in the form of domestically manufactured goods. Southern industry was in its infancy, so much so that northern manufacturers made up for much of the region's needs. Since the South was essentially a one-crop region, specializing as it did in cotton, it received the bulk of its foodstuffs from the West and the remaining portion of its outside needs from New York.

The cotton season extended from early autumn until late spring. By October, the season was in full swing until it began to taper off after April. During the summer, cotton shipments were almost at a standstill. In 1835, for instance, the receipts of cotton at New York by coastal packets from New Orleans dropped from 2577 bales in April to 119 in September. The major portion of the cotton brought northward to New York was simply shifted from one wharf to another on South Street and carried to Liverpool or Le Havre on an ocean packet. The ports of New Orleans, Charleston, and Savannah sent enough cotton North to fill the Liverpool packets for a year, while the port of Mobile sent enough cotton North yearly to fill the packets sailing to Le Havre.

As time went on a new inland triangle developed, complementary to the cotton triangle. The two had a common base in the sea route between New York and New Orleans, but the other anchor of the triangle became Cincinnati or some other western city in place of Liverpool or Le Havre. The question now was how the western suppliers of foodstuffs needed on the plantations would replenish their stocks, either from New York by packet to New Orleans and then up the Mississippi, Ohio, or Cumberland rivers or by way of the Erie Canal and then down the Ohio or Cumberland rivers. Either way, much of the westbound goods destined for country stores and thus the plantations came from New York, which took its profits in either case. Even the foodstuffs sent directly from the West to the South directly helped New York indirectly, for it enabled inland farmers to purchase imports and domestic goods from New York. Since this was the case, Wall Street profited whichever route the freight might follow to and from the backcountry.

In 1836, the South began to take steps to sever the dependence on New

York when Charleston attempted unsuccessfully to establish a packet line to Liverpool. In 1839, southerners held a convention in Charleston and drew up a report attacking New York's position in their trade. It was bad enough, the report said, to have a national tariff which discriminated against the South. In addition, "the direct trade, which was her own by every law of commerce and nature, and which should have grown and increased every year, grew less and less until it almost disappeared, being by this unpropitious policy transferred to the northern ports and people...The importing merchants of the South became an almost extinct race, and her direct trade, once so great, flourishing and rich, dwindled down to insignificance." The report included a detailed analysis which attempted to prove that the southern shopkeepers could procure their imports more cheaply and directly through Charleston than going by way of New York. It ended with these words: "The South thus stands in the attitude of feeding from her own bosom a vast population of merchants, ship owners, capitalists, and others, who without the claims of her progeny, drink up the life-blood of her trade."[28] Though European manufacturers and merchants showed an inclination to go halfway in developing a direct route with the South and a few short-lived attempts were made to establish packet or steamship lines, the southerners continued to deal with New York for their supplies. When the Civil War broke out the cotton triangle was still one of the major features of American commerce.

The other transportation question before the Civil War was how to deal most effectively with the commerce of the Middle West as far as the railroads were concerned. J.D.B. De Bow declared in a speech at Nashville in 1850 that northern "energy, enterprise, and an indomitable spirit had rolled back the mighty tide of the Mississippi and its ten thousand tributary streams until their mouth, practically and commercially is more at New York and Boston than at New Orleans."[29] The advantages in favor of the eastern routes as reported in 1860 were these:

> The uncertainties of river navigation and the vexations and ruinous delays that occurred in consequence; the risk of damage to plantation products shipped during the summer months through the southern latitudes; the speedy transportation by the safer and more economical canals and railroads as compared with transportation by river to New Orleans, and thence by ocean ships around the Atlantic Coast; the superior advantages of New York City as an importing and exporting center; and the rapid growth of the cotton trade of New Orleans to the exclusion of almost every branch of commerce.[30]

The old theory that "trade will follow the rivers" was disproved. Southern leaders became keenly conscious of this fact and urged that the South realize the situation. The Memphis Convention of 1845, presided over by John C.

Calhoun, emphasized the importance of the river trade and urged that the improvement of the navigation of the western rivers was a proper subject for federal legislation.[31] New Orleans launched an educational campaign to attempt to keep the trade of the Upper Mississippi Valley.[32] Railroads linking the seaboard South with the Middle West were proposed, and direct trade with Europe was demanded. De Bow and others urged the South to industrialize and to patronize home industry.[33] Some progress was made in these directions, but it was slow compared to the transportation advancements in the North. Any progress in the South was postponed by the Civil War and its aftermath to the end of the century.

The southern railroads were prostrated by the depression beginning in 1839, and by 1850 the mileage in Mississippi and Alabama barely exceeded 100 miles, although almost a thousand had been projected. Yet, by 1849, without the benefit of improved overland transport, these two states produced almost half the cotton crop. By contrast, the two southern states that early succeeded in completing good-sized portions of their rail systems, Georgia and South Carolina, increased their production by lesser amounts. The reduction in the price of cotton in the 1840s was not due to improved transport but to a slower rate of growth of foreign demand. Western railroads were sufficiently few and isolated that there were no trunk line connections until the 1850s.

The vigorous growth of the cotton industry in the 1820s is evidence that railroad expansion was not a necessary factor at its inception. By 1860, the situation was unchanged. The total amount of cotton arriving in Boston in that year was 382,000 bales, and less than 23,000 arrived by rail.[34] The Pepperell mills at Biddeford, in spite of a direct rail connection to Boston, continued to obtain their cotton by schooner until 1859.[35]

While railroads were important in short-haul movements of raw cotton rather than long-haul, it is very likely that in the absence of railroads the cotton South would have developed as it did. Cheap transportation rather than railroads was the necessary condition for the emergence of cotton as the nation's chief export crop. The railroad was undoubtedly the most efficient form of transportation available to the planters, but the combination of wagon and water transportation could have provided a relatively good substitute.

3

The Founding Fathers

With the Revolution over, information about the British cotton machines began to filter across the Atlantic. National pride, military self-interest, and a balance of payments problem made acquisition of the new industrial techniques a matter of federal concern. For some federal officials, including Alexander Hamilton and his economic advisor Tench Coxe, the vision of an urban industrial America competing with Europe economically, as opposed to the conception of an agrarian America dependent for finished products on an industrial Europe, was already a compelling idea.

The design of Samuel Slater's machine was known at the time, but there was a delay in issuing a patent for it because of the delicate condition of American relations with England. For the patent commissioner, Thomas Jefferson, who was also secretary of state, to reward the violation of British law by issuing a patent for a stolen invention (it was a serious breach of British law to export textile machinery) and thus to encourage similar adventures by other industrial spies would hardly be considered a friendly act. Moreover, the issuance of an American patent for those parts of Arkwright's machine covered by the voided patent of 1775 might have been regarded as questionable in American patent procedure.[1] On March 24, 1791, an announcement appeared in the *Philadelphia Federal Gazette*. One George Parkinson, of that city, advertised that he had recently obtained a United States patent for a version of Arkwright's machine. Why was this version, which only marginally improved on the original, accepted? It was because "machinery with the original mechanism [was] of the utmost value to the United States."[2]

Jefferson approved Parkinson's patent application and helped to arrange the migration of Parkinson's family to America.[3] The patent commissioner and secretary of state thus sanctioned an overt violation of British restrictions on the diffusion of industrial technology. But Jefferson, staunch foe of Great Britain that he was, held conflicting views about technology piracy.[4] He lent a hand to Parkinson's family, but not to Parkinson himself; as Julian P. Bond writes, he "took no part in aiding the immigration of British artisans because it was forbidden by law." A year earlier, Jefferson had been reluctant to support William Pollard's application for a patent on another version of Arkwright's machine.[5]

Deliberate and semiofficial, if secret, American efforts to lay hands on the Arkwright machine had begun as early as 1787. (An even earlier attempt in 1783 to introduce English carding and spinning machinery into America had proved abortive when two loyal Englishmen purchased an illegally imported carding machine and a forty-four spindle spinning machine and shipped them back to England).[6] In 1787 Coxe, eager both to gain wealth for himself and to see the United States develop cotton machinery, sent an agent to England to procure models and patterns of Arkwright's machinery. The agent was Andrew Mitchell, with whom Coxe entered into a partnership to share equally in the profits of the venture. Mitchell was to go to England, purchase the models and patents, and carry them to France. There he was to make copies and sell them to French entrepreneurs. Finally, after satisfying the French market, he was to bring the original models back to the United States. Using a letter of introduction from James Madison—who had told Coxe in 1786 to devise a means to bolster the industrial output of the country using cotton because "there is not reason to doubt that the United States would one day become a great cotton producing country"[7]—Coxe wrote to Jefferson, then serving as American ambassador to France,[8] to ask his aid in this delicate business. In England in 1788, Mitchell spent $560 of Coxe's money successfully procuring the models and drawings; he also made plans to secure the new British method of bleaching cotton chemically and schemed to lure unemployed Manchester mechanics to America. However, he was caught by the British and convicted of intention to transport prohibited items out of the country. As a result, he paid a fine and was expelled from the country without his cache of secrets, which remained behind in a box stored in a friend's house and inaccessible to Coxe.[9]

Although Mitchell's mission failed, Coxe kept on trying to steal British secrets dealing with cotton machines. By January 1790 he was writing to George Clymer—an associate in the Pennsylvania Society for Promoting Manufactures and the Useful Arts[10]—that "we" were about to apply for a patent on various items of Arkwright's machinery:

> 1st We shall produce a drawing and model of Arkwright's two first and main movements for *spinning* by Water, applicable as we shall shew as well [to] our branches of *wool, flax,* and *hemp* as to his branch of cotton, and to silk of which first movements we are not the *inventors*, but the *introducers* there being no model or drawing of these invaluable movements in the United States—

2dly We shall produce a drawing and model of certain supple-mentary movements and apparatus for spinning of worsted, and of flaxen and hempen yarn in a manner *invented* by Us, and differing from any machine in the world—

These two form the Machinery for those Branches complete. Viz worsted and hempen and flaxen yarn—

3dly We think we can (tho not immediately) produce a drawing or model of another set of *supplementary* movements and apparatus; which in addition to those specified in No. 1, was equal to the manufactory of cotton goods after the Manner of Arkwrights, and which we consider him as the Inventor and ourselves as the *introducers*.

4thly The supplementary movements and apparatus for the silk manufactory, tho possessed by people in England we have not yet decided on but we do not consider our prospects of either discovering or obtaining it as hopeless, having a person of very great information and capacity in that line, and having trains of information laid for the purpose of obtaining them—

In this correspondence, Coxe was explicit in denying that "we" were making any claim to original invention of the cotton machinery, and he urged Clymer to use his influence in amending the patent bill before Congress in order to allow patent privileges to those who "introduced" valuable foreign machinery.[11]

While the patent commissioners marked time, the British government became aware of the applications. British intelligence agent George Beckwith reported to his superior in England that a model of Arkwright's machine stood in Jefferson's office; six months later he reported that Alexander Hamilton, as a promoter of an ambitious industrial corporation located in Passaic, New Jersey, possessed several models of spinning machinery.[12] By this time—mid 1791—there were in fact a number of more or less accurate copies of Arkwright's machine already at work or under construction in America, and the British were mounting, and losing, a clandestine counterintelligence operation to recover them. Several British agents or patriotic merchants were buying the American machines and shipping them back to England, and, in some instances, when the machines could not be procured, allegedly burning down the factories that contained them. And American agents—some of them secretly financed by the secretary of the treasury—kept on bringing in more plans, more models, and more English mechanics.[13]

It was in this context of industrial espionage, theft, sabotage, and arson that the petitions for patents were finally granted. The decisions may, in fact, have been motivated by a desire to terminate the escalating competition of spy and counterspy, with its attendant risks to relations between the United States and Great Britain, by actually publishing the information that specifications and drawings of Arkwright's machinery were in the possession and under the protection of the United States government. With the patents granted, unlicensed copying of Arkwright machinery would now be a violation of both British and American law. It was Alexander Hamilton, the preeminent neomercantilist in the United States, who drove the idea of the United States as a strong egocentric competing power to Great Britain. It would be done by liberalization of trade, development of the domestic economy, and government sponsorship of domestic manufacturers.[14]

On January 15, 1790, the House of Representatives asked the secretary of the treasury to prepare a report on the state of American manufacturers and devise a plan for their encouragement. Hamilton turned for information to manufacturing societies that had appeared in many cities in the 1780s. The responses had much in common: they described growing industrial activities and at the same time elaborated on the obstacles to manufacturing in the United States. Overcoming technological backwardness was seen as the key to success. Correspondents from states unable to attract foreign workers, such as South Carolina, blamed their industrial underdevelopment on the shortage of skilled labor.[15] Textile manufacturing in Massachusetts was "destitute of the necessary information," as local investors were "misled by every pretender to knowledge."[16]

Hamilton's queries to manufacturers who had successfully established factories brought basically the same answer: their success depended on their ability to pirate British technology, primarily by enticing skilled artisans to emigrate. A famous example was that of Moses Brown, an entrepreneur in Providence, Rhode Island, whose repeated technological failures had halted his attempts to create a textile mill until he was approached by "a young Man then lately arrived at Newyork from Arkwrights works in England." Brown had to pay a steep price for this man's services. The young man, Samuel Slater, demanded and got complete control of the mill's operation. The venture became a huge success.[17]

Hamilton believed that technological deficiencies accounted for the great disparity between American and European manufacturing and that the gap would be "diminished in proportion to the use which can be made of machinery."[18] With modern technology, American manufacturing would catch up. The process need not take long. The great technological advances of the preceding twenty years, for example, were responsible for "the immense progress" of British textile industrial output. This output was all the more remarkable because it was achieved without drawing on the agricultural labor supply,[19] which was critical to the United States, since this was the era before the huge migrations from Europe to America.

Technology could be acquired by smuggling up-to-date machinery out of England and by inducing skilled workers to move to the United States and build the machines they had operated in Europe. Hamilton also believed that "machinery forms an item of great importance in the general mass of national industry."[20] He warned that to procure all such machines as were known in any part of Europe, could only require a proper provision and due pains. He explained that America had an advantage over Europe in its abundant supplies of raw materials and energy sources needed to construct and operate advanced machinery. Moreover, modern machinery required fewer operators, a boon for a young country with a chronic labor shortage.[21]

Hamilton also realized what American textile manufacturers had already experienced, that machine importation was problematic. Americans could not build machines from European manuals because the blueprints for these machines were never published. Even those published in magazines were not translatable into actual machines, because the descriptions and drawings lacked specificity and clarity.[22] In theory, patented English inventions could be examined by the public in the London patent office during the term of the patent, but the knowledge required to conduct an effective search rendered copying specifications all but impossible.[23] Additionally, seventeenth and eighteenth century technical improvements were more of a knack than an invention. When a machine was taken apart and sent to the United States, only those who had operated it in England could put it back together and make it work.[24]

Hamilton, writing in a prospectus for the Society for Establishing Useful Manufacturers, laid out his vision for competing with the British textile industry: Americans must have a better qualified work force, competitive pricing, and capital for investment. His two reports on public credit addressed these last two needs. Skilled workers were "an essential ingredient" of American industrialization, yet thus far efforts "employed have not generally been adequate to the purpose of procuring them from abroad."[25] In his "Report on Manufacturers" (ROM), Hamilton explained that "progress of particular manufacturers has been much retarded by the want of skillful workmen." Leaving it to individual entrepreneurs to rectify this imbalance would not produce the desired results, because "the capitals employed here are not equal to the purposes of bringing from abroad workmen of a serious kind." The federal government through some "auxiliary agency" must manage this "source of valuable acquisitions to the country."[26]

Since Hamilton understood the larger domestic and international ramifications of an enticement program, he used the ROM to explain and advocate his position. He realized that the dominant agricultural sector would resist government sponsorship of competing manufacturing. Former physician-in-chief of the Continental army John Morgan, for example, wrote in 1789 that manufacturing was suited to a country "fully stocked with inhabitants." America's labor shortage meant to Morgan that industrialization would come at the expense of agriculture, which was the real source of national wealth.[27] To counter "dearness of labour" objections, Hamilton played on the national mood favoring population growth. He promised that manufacturers "will have the strongest tendency to multiply the inducements" to foreign emigration.[28] To further alleviate the widespread fears that industrialization would further deplete the already labor-starved agricultural sector, he elaborated: the advantage of manufacturing is its "tendency to draw emigrants from foreign countries."

Artisans would not come unless they could find employment in their familiar line of work as "men are commonly reluctant to quit one course of occupation and livelihood for another." In addition, America had much to offer: higher wages, cheaper raw materials, and political liberty. European migrants, Hamilton promised, would industrialize America. They had already become a reliable source of labor and innovation. Go through the towns of America, he said, and see the "large proportion of ingenious and valuable workmen, in different arts and trades, who, by expatriating from Europe, have improved their own condition, and added to the industry and wealth of the United States. It is a natural inference from the experience, we have already had, that as soon as the United States shall present the countenance of serious prosecution of Manufactures—as soon as foreign artists be made sensible that the state of things here affords a moral certainty of employment and encouragement—competent numbers of European workmen will transplant themselves, effectually to ensure the success of design." In sum, American manufacturers would "in a great measure trade upon a foreign Stock."[29] The agricultural and commercial sectors would also benefit, as this "fruitful means of augmenting the population" would result in higher prices for agricultural products without "deducting from the hands, which might otherwise be drawn to tillage."[30]

Hamilton's efforts to increase manufacturing in the United States through support of manufacturers of textile machines depended basically on the issuing of patents. His emigration inducing proposals, such as travel subsidies for artisans and customs exemptions for their tools, implements of trade and household furniture, were not enough. What was most important, in order to spark textile manufacturing in the United States, he came out strongly in favor of granting an inventor monopoly to introducers of technology. That issue had surfaced the year before during debate on the Patent Act that Congress passed in 1790. The president had asked Congress in his annual message of January of that year to enact legislation encouraging "the introduction of new and useful invention from abroad."[31] The House of Representatives' version of the bill followed English law in giving to the first importer of technology the monopoly privileges accorded to original inventors.[32] But the Senate amended the bill to grant patent monopolies only to inventors of machines "not before known or used" and deleted the location qualifier "within the United States."[33] In the ROM, Hamilton urged Congress to revise the Patent Act of 1790, explaining that the United States must employ the same methods "which have been employed with success in other Countries."[34]

Hamilton's two inducements to attract foreign mechanics—patents and land—were both in jeopardy. Without being able to grant patents unless the invention was "not before known or used," the foreigners could not protect their inventions; and giving land as an incentive would not, Hamilton thought, be successful, because, he believed, men were naturally inclined to become farmers. He feared that immigrant artisans would yield to the temptation of bucolic life and not remain in urban centers to develop their trades: "The desire of being a proprietor of lands depends upon such strong principles in the human breast, that where the opportunity of acquiring it is so easy as it is in the United States the proportion must be small of those, whose circumstances would otherwise lead to it, that would be diverted from the pursuit toward manufacturers."[35]

Population and migration patterns in the second half of the eighteenth century lent some credence to Hamilton's observation. The South and the Southwest were growing so rapidly due to immigration that North Carolina, for example, which in 1760 had roughly the same population as New York, had gone ahead of that city by sixty thousand twenty years later. Contemporaries assumed that the trend would continue and that immigrants, even skilled artisans, would become farmers. In not supporting a land grant program to attract immigrants, Hamilton was not driven by a reluctance to confront Great Britain. Rather, he feared that skilled immigrants would move to the South and Southwest without sharing their trade secrets with their new countrymen.[36]

Hamilton's solution to the problem of encouraging textile manufacturing in the United States was through the use of a federally funded board which would "defray the expenses of the emigration of Artists and Manufacturers in particular branches of extraordinary importance" and promote "the prosecution and introduction of useful discoveries, inventions, & improvements by proportionate rewards judiciously held out and applied." American manufacturing was hampered by "the want of skillful workmen," and the federal government should subsidize the numerous "workmen, in every branch, who are prevented from emigrating solely by the want of means." The very same fund could also be used to "procure and import foreign improvements"—that is, machines.[37]

This idea of Hamilton's that the federal government should support the emigration of foreigners who would further America's domestic cotton industry and therefore industry as a whole became central to his vision. He explained in the ROM that organizations like the Pennsylvania Society for the Encouragement of Manufacturers and Useful Arts were "truly invaluable." "There is scarcely anything," he wrote, "which has been devised, better calculated to excite a general spirit of improvement." But the funds of such voluntary organizations had "been too contracted" to launch an adequate incentive campaign. According to Hamilton, the United States could not wait for patriotic private entrepreneurs to undertake the costly effort of bringing over machines and artisans from Europe.[38]

This federal support of American industry extended, under Hamilton, to an organization known as the Society for Establishing Useful Manufactures. Essentially, it was a private state-sponsored corporation founded in 1791 to promote industrial development along the Passaic River in New Jersey using the "Great Falls" of the river as a source of mechanical power. The society was the brainchild of Hamilton's assistant, Tench Coxe, who convinced Hamilton to support the creation of a quasi-public manufacturing town. By 1796, the society's efforts to build its own mills had failed, largely because the slow profits generated were not enough to cover start-up costs. Nevertheless the society successfully promoted real estate development in the area, leasing sites to other private ventures to establish their own mills while maintaining control of the power that supplied the factories. The society's management of the falls subsequently became a lucrative source of profits as the area became the nucleus for the textile industry. By 1815, thirteen water-powered cotton mills were operating beside the falls and employing over 2,000 workers.

The society was a determined effort on Hamilton's part to integrate manufacturing into his overall plan to stabilize both the nation's finances and its manufacturing. If the society had been successful it would have constituted a very large amount of cotton goods. Its size and advanced machinery would have allowed it to compete with foreign imports, particularly in providing cotton for export. In keeping with Hamilton's overall ideas, the society would stabilize prices and lessen speculation. As he noted in the ROM, the society would be eligible for government bounties if such a program were enacted. Also, protective tariffs that endangered import revenues would not be needed. Finally, the owners and directors of the society were to be its creditors and merchants, not the federal government.

Emigration from England to America had been continuous during the nineteen century because of the opportunity to acquire land cheaply and because of the means to sail to the New World through the use of indentured servitude. The British had become concerned over the depopulation of the English countryside by the 1760s and now Hamilton had a plan which targeted the men the British most wanted to keep. The British were alarmed on two levels. First, this plan meant state sanctioned flouting of British law and on a second level the economic consequences of the emigration of skilled workers would have heightened foreign competition.

When the ROM became public, British officials immediately understood its explosiveness. If Hamilton's industrialization plan had proved as successful as his stabilization of American finances, Britain could have lost much of its export trade—worth more than 15 million dollars in 1791 alone—to the United States.[39] The British minister in Philadelphia, George Hammond, expected the American government to support fully the proposed program because "Mr. Hamilton's reputation is so materially involved in the result of the experiment."[40] England must now energetically enforce the prohibitions on technology exports, he wrote to Grenville, "to prevent the emigration and exportation of machines necessary to the different branches of manufacturers."[41]

During 1791 Hamilton sought those foreigners who could introduce English technology by interviewing immigrants. He sent a stocking weaver back home to recruit men for a factory in America. English artisans heard of the secretary's interest in English technology and expected assistance upon arrival. Roger Newberry, a British machinist, for example, believed that Hamilton should help him find a job in America because he possessed plans for two "most ingenious & *very beneficial*" new English textile machines.[42] In December, Hamilton reported his understanding with one Mr. Mort, who agreed to "go to Europe, to bring over Workman, at his own Expense in the first instance, but with the assurance of reimbursement and indemnification." This action of Hamilton's was supported by his Society for Establishing Useful Manufactures, an organization very much in agreement with the idea of importing technical knowledge.

European correspondents such as Samuel Paterson of Edinburgh, aware of Hamilton's support for travel subsidies, reported that thousands of eager-to-emigrate skilled artisans were not coming because "they are Utterly unable to pay for a Passage to America." Paterson begged Hamilton "to procure a Grant of Some Bounty or Relaxation of the Duties, to European Shipping bringing over Poor Industrious workmen to America."[43] A year earlier, Congress had debated such a subsidy and turned it down.[44]

When Hamilton suggested defraying the expenses of artisan's emigration, he knew he was aiding in the violation of the central codes of English economic policy and hence challenging British power. To Hamilton, the idea was to circumvent British authority to benefit the United States. As an example, when his European correspondents informed him that in "Britain the Penalties are 500 pounds Str & 6 Mo imprisonment for every person Indented to goe out of the Kings Dominions," Hamilton suggested that bounties for smuggling artisans be given to European shippers because the "Penalties and Forfeitures are so very heavy & so easily incurred, that No person Unacquaint[ed] with the Laws durst Venture upon Such a Measure—But the European Captain & owners know how to agree with Passengers so as to Escape the Penalties."[45] In the ROM, Hamilton acknowledged that most manufacturing nations "prohibit, under severe penalties, the exportation of implements and machines, which they have either invented or improved." In spite of this, Hamilton believed that the United States government must circumvent the efforts of industrially advanced nations to frustrate and prohibit the international diffusion of industrial know-how.[46]

It is interesting to compare Hamilton's ideas on the protection of inventions with that of Benjamin Franklin. Franklin did not believe that knowledge and skill should be viewed as property. He believed rather that "science must be an international pursuit" for "the improvement of humanity's estate."[47] He had actively sponsored the dissemination of European technology in America since the early 1750s, and he shared his scientific findings and technological innovations with friends and rivals.[48] He never sought to profit from the implementation of useful inventions such as the lightning rod and the Franklin stove. But his position was rapidly becoming anachronistic. Invention was now taken to be the fruit of the labor of the inventor, and by the time of the Revolution, the American consensus was that "only an individual's labor created property, and therefore the individual had sole right to possession and disposition of that property.[49]

Hamilton did not share Franklin's views, nor did he subscribe to Enlightenment views about universal access to knowledge. He was more swayed by William Barton's *The True Interest of the United States,* which declared that nations should "spare no expense in procuring the ablest masters in every branch of industry, nor any cost in making the first establishments; providing machines, and every other necessary or useful [thing] to make the undertaking succeed."[50] In the ROM, after a few paragraphs suggesting ways to bring knowledge across the Atlantic, Hamilton, deciding that he wanted it both ways, called for prohibiting European-bound transmission of American innovations by imposing stiff penalties against the export of technology invented or acquired by Americans, and at the same time openly campaigned for the violation of British patents.

Hamilton's position was in line with international law in the sense that such law was "not ordained by nature, but established through international behavior," most notably in treaties among nations.[51] Prohibitions on technological piracy were not defined by any international agreements until well into the nineteenth century. It is interesting to note that even before Hamilton's actions on the importation of British cotton manufacturing information, the British were using their patent law to encourage foreign artisans to come to England and teach apprentices their trade. The policy was highly successful, changing the country from a technologically debtor nation in 1700 to one of creditor just half a century later. It continued to draw on continental technology throughout the Industrial Revolution.[52] Also, before Hamilton's involvement in the controversy, the French spied on British innovations for their own industrialization efforts. Jacques Necker, Louis XVI's chief advisor, explained that acquisition and exploitation of foreign industrial technology was the surest way to national economic independence. Industrial espionage was practiced "on a very wide scale by all western countries of any industrial significance."[53]

Hamilton's action's, then, contravened English domestic prohibitions, not the law of nations. Other members of Washington's cabinet, however, felt the United States should avoid promoting direct violations of British laws. Jefferson and attorney general Edmund Randolph advised the president in 1791 not to support a proposed cotton textile factory in Virginia because it would be equipped with machines feloniously imported from England. Washington agreed, explaining that "it certainly would not carry an aspect very favorable to the dignity of the United States for the President in a clandestine manner to entice the subjects of another Nation to violate its Laws."[54] The issue was resolved by France's decision to export its revolution, which forced Hamilton to move away from programs that could adversely affect Anglo-American relations. The European war made Hamilton "absolutely determined that nothing should be done which might directly benefit France."[55] The French Revolution had changed his priorities. United States technological deficiencies did not justify alienating the nation he believed was America's sole protector from France.

These developments must not obscure the fact that before the French Revolution, the manufacture of cotton gave Hamilton the opportunity to publicly urge the United States government to sponsor large-scale violations of Britain's laws and that this technology piracy threatened the perceived source of Britain's premier position in the world—its superior industrial base.[56] By 1791, Hamilton could say with confidence, in his ROM, "The expediency of encouraging manufacturers in the United States, which was not long since

3. *The Founding Fathers* 57

Thomas Jefferson's Poplar Forest in Bedford County, Virginia (Library of Congress, Prints & Photographs Division, HABS VA, 10-BED.V, 1—79 [CT]).

deemed very questionable, appears at this time to be pretty generally admitted."[57]

The views of Thomas Jefferson on American manufacturing in general and the use of cotton as a manufactured product specifically are far less straightforward than Hamilton's. Profound concerns, both personal and international in scope, led to Jefferson's embrace of manufacturing late in his life. His earliest writings—most elaborately expressed in the *Notes on Virginia*—demonstrate his distain for British-style industrial manufacturing in the United States. Jefferson remained, throughout his early political career and public life, beholden to the agrarian ideal of the farmer-citizen in a predominantly rural republic. The nobility of the *husbandman's* lifestyle—to utilize one of Jefferson's preferred terms—would work to cultivate virtue and help to insulate against vice. Large-scale, machine-driven industrialization brought with it, in Jeffersonian political economy, the specter of powerful private interests often at odds with public good, a permanent proletariat work force, and the gradual despoiling of nature. In his *Notes on Virginia*, he emphasized that "those who labor in the earth are the chosen people of God, if ever He had a chosen people, whose breasts He has made his peculiar deposit for substantial and genuine virtue."[58]

Fearing that industrialization was the disease that would destroy democracy, Jefferson was determined to have the United States remain an agricultural society, growing its own foodstuffs but not producing its own manufactured products. He wrote as follows in his *Notes on Virginia:*

> While we have land to labor then, let us never wish to see our citizens occupied at a workbench, or twirling a distaff. Carpenters, masons, smiths, are wanting in husbandry; but for the general operations of manufacture, let our workshops remain in Europe. It is better to carry provisions and materials to workmen there than bring them to the provisions and materials, and with them their manners and principles. The loss by the transportation of commodities across the Atlantic will be made up in happiness and permanence of government. The mobs of great cities add just so much to the support of pure government, as sores do to the strength of the human body. It is the manners and spirit of a people which preserve a republic in vigor. A degeneracy in these is a canker which soon eats to the heart of its laws and constitution.[59]

Over the course of his life this view would be basically unchanged except that Hamilton's corporate industry would now be at home and its purpose would be not to change America into a British-style industrial giant, but rather that machinery would become an assistance to the household economy. Jefferson modified his views on industrialism a few years before the War of 1812. The devastating effect of the Napoleonic Wars on American shipping convinced him of the expediency of domestic manufacturing. Writing to John Jay in 1809, he said:

> An equilibrium of agriculture, manufactures, and commerce, is certainly become essential to our independence. Manufactures, sufficient for our own consumption of what we raise the raw materials, (and no more). Commerce sufficient to carry the surplus produce of agriculture, beyond our own consumption, to a market for exchanging it for articles we cannot raise (and no more). These are the true limits of manufactures and commerce. To go beyond them is to increase our dependence on foreign nations, and our ability to war.[60]

At Monticello, this meant the establishment of a nail manufactory, which operated for twenty years. After ceasing to operate it was replaced by a textile factory, which employed "a few women, children and invalids who could do little in the farm."[61] To Jefferson, this cotton factory became a solution to a standard problem on any southern plantation: how best to employ those too young, too old, or too infirm to profitably work the fields.

This manufacturing, however, had a much greater use: to replace slave labor with machinery, exchanging, in effect, human property for the mechanical kind. Laborsaving technology was not simply about efficiency but also reflected Jefferson's veiled desire to eradicate the problem of the slave from the plantation economy, to render invisible, as it were, a type of disreputable labor.[62]

The idea of using cotton for home manufacture had been in Jefferson's mind as early as 1774 when he first purchased three pounds for his large family. He told his Charlottesville neighbor Nicholas Lewis in 1790, "It is vastly desirable to be getting underway with our domestic cultivation & manufacture of hemp, cotton & Wool for the Negroes."[63] Based on his personal experience, Jefferson knew that cotton could only be a home-manufactured item in the North. He spelled this out in a letter, written in 1808, concerning the crop's limitation in which he said that cotton could be cultivated satisfactorily only south of the Rappahannock River and east of the Blue Ridge Mountains. He observed that from the Rappahannock to the Roanoke cotton could not compete with the yields further south and it therefore was grown in the north only for family use.[64] This was borne out in a letter from Paris in 1789 to Edward Rutledge of South Carolina: "Cotton is a precious resource, and which cannot fail with you."[65] Also, on the same subject of cotton being produced in the South and used in both the North and South he said,

> The four southernmost States make a great deal of cotton. The poor are almost entirely clothed in it in both winter and summer. In winter they wear shirts of it and outer clothing of cotton and wool mixed. In summer their shirts are of linen, but their outer clothing cotton. The dress of women is almost entirely of cotton manufactured by themselves, except the richer classes, and even many of these wear a good deal of homespun cotton. It is as well manufactured as the calicos of Europe. Those four Southern states furnish a great deal of cotton to the States north of them, who cannot make it as being too cold.[66]

As far as using cotton for home manufacture, before retiring as secretary of state Jefferson, as head of the Patent Office, issued a patent to Eli Whitney for his cotton gin, "as I [manufacture cotton] myself, and as one of our greatest embarrassments is the cleaning of the cotton of the seed, I feel a considerable interest in the success of your invention, for family use."[67] Jefferson's perspicacity in appreciating the value of this invention, which was to revolutionize agriculture, is clearly demonstrated by the questions he raised in his official communication to Whitney:

> Permit me therefore to ask information from you on these points. Has the machine been thoroughly tried in the ginning of cotton, or is it as yet but a machine of theory? What quantity of cotton has it cleaned on an average of several days, & worked by hand, & by how many hands? What will be the cost of

one of them made to be worked by hand? Favorable answers to these questions would induce me to engage one of them to be forwarded to Richmond for me.[68]

Embracing domestic manufacturing, Jefferson argued, would free the United States from both the economic tyranny and the military power of England. But he might also have been exploring the potential for preserving the plantation economy within the rapidly emerging cultures of industrial capitalism. There were, for example, Jefferson's attempts as president to find new markets for American produce, especially cotton. "Bring the factory to the farm," cried Henry Clay in his 1824 tariff speech before the House of Representatives. Clay, a Kentucky blueblood, saw this as a way both to modernize and to preserve the southern agrarian ideal.[69]

At the beginning of 1813, cotton again became a topic for Jefferson. Writing to John Melish[70] he outlined the necessity of domestic manufacturing. Noting the surprising "number of carding and spinning machines dispersed" throughout the "Western States," he claimed Monticello as a model for American society:

> We are but beginning here [Virginia] to have them [machines] in our private families. Small spinning jennies of from half a dozen to twenty pindles [sic], will soon, however, make their way into the humblest cottages, as well as the richest houses; and nothing is more certain than that the coarse and middling clothing of our families, will forever hereafter continue to be made within ourselves. I have hitherto myself depended entirely upon foreign manufacturers; but I now have thirty-five spindles agoing, a hand carding machine, and looms with the flying shuttle, for the supply of my own farms, which will never be relinquished in my time.[71]

Jefferson's dream of a rural republic, isolated from the commercialism and industrialization of Europe and composed entirely of self-governing farmers, had begun to fade before it was full-blown. As the intransigent John Taylor[72] lamented to James Monroe in 1810, "There were a number of people who soon thought, and said to one another, that Mr. Jefferson did many good things, but neglected some better things; and who now view his policy as very like a compromise with Mr. Hamilton's."[73] Taylor continued to prompt Hamilton with such sentiments as "the divine intelligence which selected an agricultural state as a paradise for its first favourites, has ... prescribed the agricultural virtues as the means for the admission of their posterity into heaven,"[74] but both Hamilton and Jefferson saw that the rising tide of commerce and industry could not be held in check. European industrialism had now visited America. Also, it is hard to believe that Jefferson foresaw that cotton growing would enrich only a few at the expense of the land of the region as a whole, as he wrote to Edward Rutledge. While he assigned cotton culture on his own land to the old and infirm, further south where cotton could be grown profitably the crop began the process of pitting one section of the nation against another.

George Washington also not only knew of cotton, but also had his own ideas of its uses apart from those of Hamilton and Jefferson. At Mount Vernon he spun and wove it and other clothing goods for twenty-eight persons in addition to his wife, Martha. In his 1768 business summary, Washington noted that about three hundred of the 1,556 yards of cloth were used for "cotton striped, cotton plain, cotton filled, cotton birdseye ... and Cotton India dimity." For his own use he spun and wove linen, wool, linsey, and "forty yards of cotton," in an effort to free himself and his family from English dependence.[75]

Washington had also seen the beginning of cotton manufacturing away from the home. When John Cabot in 1788 built the nation's first cotton factory in Massachusetts near Boston, on the Bass River at Beverly, a Virginia weaver— President George Washington—soon showed up to take a tour. "In this manufactory, they have the new invented spinning and carding machines," he wrote in his diary, "one of which spins eighty-four threads at one time by one person.... In short, the whole seemed perfect, and the cotton stuffs they turn out excellent of their kind...."[76] Washington wasn't just a tourist, he was trying to bolster an independent economy for a new nation that was struggling to become self-sufficient. Cotton, cultivated domestically on only small acreage, might have seemed like an appendage at best, but to our first leaders it also represented an investment of hope in the country's future.[77]

4

Slavery

Tracing the advent of slavery in the new world shows that 80 percent of all slaves were imported into America between 1451 and 1810. Since this was the case, cotton, which as a crop was in its infancy in 1810, was not the reason for the slave traffic. Nor was tobacco the cause. The number of slaves was more than 9,500,000 in those years and this number was far more than was needed for processing tobacco. Surprisingly, it was Europe's sweet tooth that initially determined the extent of the Atlantic slave trade. The early sugar economy prefigured that of the modern New World economies in general and the plantation-slave economies in particular. As early as the period 1670–1690, overproduction plunged the sugar economies of Brazil and the Caribbean into crisis that ruined both the planters and their creditors.

The plantation slave economies in the New World received a new lease on life after the Revolutionary War in America. Cuba became a major producer of sugar and coffee. Plantation output also increased in both the British and French Caribbean. In response, the slave trade increased beyond prewar levels. Even the smallest slaving nation, Denmark, carried more slaves than it had earlier in the 18th century. "Aggregate slave imports into the Americas," it has been argued, "reached an all time decadal high between 1781 and 1790.... Peacetime prices of sugar, cotton, indigo and tobacco continued to rise.... Clearly, the increase in demand exceeded the increase in supply, and demand pressures, previously felt by non–British and non–French areas only in time of war, now became steady and permanent."[1]

In the sparsely peopled British colonies in America, with their continual shortage of workers, slave labor was mainly used in the South in the production of tobacco, rice, and indigo. By 1787, slavery had proven to be unprofitable in the northern states where staple crops were not grown. Of the 9,500,000 slaves in the western hemisphere, there were approximately 700,000 in the United States. Of that number, 642,000 lived in the South and 42,000 in the North.

In addition, there were 59,466 "free colored" persons. Slaves accounted for about 17 percent of the total U.S., population at the time of the Revolution. A disproportionate 396,463 slaves, or 60 percent of the slave population, lived in the two primary tobacco growing states of Maryland and Virginia.[2]

Southern slaveholders, no matter their views on the morality of human bondage, were chained to their slaves by economic necessity. George Mason, the Virginia delegate to the Constitutional Convention who excoriated slavery and the slave trade, owned more than two hundred slaves. Slaves, he thundered, "produce the most pernicious effect on manners. Every master of slaves is born a petty tyrant; they bring the judgment of heaven on a country.... Slavery discourages arts and manufacturers. The poor despise labor when they see it performed by slaves." Mason, a resident of the largest slave state, blamed the British for introducing the slave trade and also New England, whose "lust for gain embarked on this nefarious traffic."[3]

Yet by 1787, the belief was common that slavery would wither away of its own accord, since the health of the slave grown tobacco business was in doubt, mainly due to lower prices and a depletion of the soil by overuse. Also, the other slave-produced crops, rice and indigo, were far smaller markets than tobacco and would not therefore replace it as a profitable crop. While there was nothing on the economic horizon in 1787 to suggest a demand for slave labor, and while slave prices showed some weakness after the Revolution, they rebounded to roughly the pre–Revolutionary level by the mid 1780s and remained on a fairly high plateau for the rest of that decade.

During the 1790s, the slave population in the United states increased at a higher rare than in any other previous decade. While George Washington had advised a friend in 1794 to convert his slaves into other forms of property, other slaveholders were increasing rather than decreasing their holdings of slaves. Even in 1796, when prices were at their lowest point in the post–Revolutionary era, the demand for slaves was over 50 percent higher than it had been in 1792. The conclusion is that since there was a heavy flow of slaves into the United States after the war, it was profitable to keep them. Otherwise the United States would have become an exporter of slaves, rather than an importer.[4]

Probably the first of the Founding Fathers to see the connection between slavery and cotton was Alexander Hamilton. As a founder of the New York Society for Promoting the Manumission of Slaves, he attempted to pass a rule that required abolitionist members of the society to free their slaves. Yet when Hamilton was forced to choose between his financial system and slavery, the choice, like that of his fellow Americans, was nearly always the former. By 1792 Hamilton realized that the cotton textiles industry should be promoted in

America, not the "rapidly rising Cotton" manufacturing in England. In 1795 he recognized the potential of cotton as an export commodity:

> [Cotton] ... has not been cultivated except in a limited degree, and as an article of export rather, in the manner of Experiment than otherwise.... From the Experience and Difficulty of separating the Seeds, from the Cotton, we have been [hardly] able ... to class Cotton among our exports. Its cultivation is said latterly to have become an object of attention in Georgia & South Carolina—still however it cannot yet be considered as a staple commodity. But from the recent Invention of an ingenious & simple, Machine, for ginning Cotton. It is hoped that the cultivation may be extended, so that not only our own Domestic manufacturers may be relieved from a Dependence on foreign supply, but the catalogue of our valuable Exports enriched by the addition of this inestimable production.[5]

Unwittingly, Hamilton, who opposed slavery, facilitated its expansion along with cotton. Through his efforts, the young American nation had established a stable financial system that enabled the country, using credit, to double its size and gain control of the Mississippi River, a prime boulevard for the transportation of cotton, with the purchase of the Louisiana Territory. Cotton was the impetus for the stampede to settle the fertile lands that became known as the Old Southwest, a territory that included present-day western Georgia, Alabama, Louisiana, Mississippi, and parts of Arkansas and Texas. The Indians who occupied the land were simply removed. Their forced migration, of which much has been written, occurred simultaneously with the cotton induced migrations of whites and slaves.

By the 1820s, slavery, the "peculiar institution," was firmly linked with cotton, and it expanded only to those areas in which cotton could be grown. The historian Frederick Jackson Turner acknowledged that "never in history, perhaps, was an economic force more influential upon the life of a people. This economic transformation resuscitated slavery from a moribund condition to a vigorous and aggressive life." As demand for cotton grew, slavery was considered indispensable as a means of maximizing profit for this labor-intensive crop. Of equal importance, slaves could be financed—that is, purchased on credit. Planters had one objective: increased cotton production, which demanded an endless supply of slaves as long as the price of cotton permitted financing.

One historian of cotton, W.B. Hammond, believed, "the expanding geographical distribution of slaves and of cotton cultivation affords the most striking evidence of the close connection of the two institutions that can be had; for the gradual spread of slavery over the map coinciding almost exactly with those suitable for the extension of cotton: as if this plant-king were literally leading the human captives in his train."[6] But because the importation of slaves into the United States had been banned in 1808, this "expanding geographical distribution of slaves" had to come from inside the United States. The result was a migration of whites and slaves principally from the tobacco growing regions of the upper South to the cotton fields of the Southwest.

Planters in the eastern slave states that did not produce cotton began selling their slaves to the states in the Deep South. By 1823, Delaware, Maryland and Virginia were selling between 10,000 and 15,000 slaves per year to the cotton states. In 1836, Virginia, according to one "probably exaggerated" source, sent 120,000 slaves south. Virginia's cotton production, always negligible, had peaked by 1826. By 1850, there were 74,031 plantations in the United States that raised five or more bales of cotton; only 198 of these farms were in Virginia. So it should come as no surprise that Virginia, like other non-cotton states recognized the unprofitability of keeping slaves and so began selling them instead.[7] The historian James Scherer quotes a Virginia academic, Professor Thomas Drew, who noted in 1832 that "Virginia is, in fact, a negro raising state for other States."[8]

Between 1830 and 1850, while the slave population of Maryland declined, Louisiana's more than doubled, Alabama's nearly trebled, and Mississippi quintupled its number of slaves. The slave migrations to Alabama, Mississippi, and Louisiana combined were huge: 155,000 in the 1820s, 288,000 in the 1830s, 189,000 in the 1840s, and 250,000 in the 1850s.[9] In the short span of time between 1817 and 1860, Mississippi became the largest cotton producing state in the nation. Mississippi's population rose in lockstep with its expanding cotton production. The white population of the state grew from 5,179 in 1800 to 354,000 in 1860; during the same time, the slave population went from 3,500 to 436,631. Slaves outnumbered whites 55 percent to 45 percent. Cotton production in Mississippi exploded from nothing in 1800 to 535.1 million pounds in 1859. Alabama's development was similar and on the eve of the Civil War ranked second in cotton production with 440.5 million pounds.[10]

By 1860 the slave population of the South had grown to 4 million, comprising one-third of the region's 12 million inhabitants (in 1790 the population of the United States had been 12 million, 700,000 of that number slaves). Estimates vary as to the number of slaves in cotton agriculture. One source calculates that by 1850 three-quarters of the slave population was involved in cotton; another suggests 64 percent. The 1850 census broke down the types of farms using slaves: cotton 75 percent, tobacco 14 percent, sugar 6 percent, rice 5 percent, and hemp 2 percent. Of the 75 percent involved in cotton production, only 38 percent were used in the actual production. The remainder were employed in ancillary functions which supported the cotton plantation such as corn and livestock production, land improvement chores, other crops, and home manufacturing.¹¹ Cotton, the money crop, was the raison d'etre of these farms. Within a half-century, an insignificant crop had become the driving force behind America's most horrific institution.¹²

As cotton demanded a greater and greater share of America's slaves, the general price of slave men and women increased substantially from 1800 to the eve of the Civil War. Periodically prices declined, usually because the price of cotton had fallen, but the trend was continually higher. In 1790 the approximate price for a prime slave to be used as a field hand was $200; by 1850 it was $1,200 and in 1860 it was $1,800. There were large price swings. In 1810 the price of field hands in New Orleans rose to $900 before collapsing during the War of 1812. Field hands brought $1,700 to $2,000 in that city in 1819 before falling below $700 in 1823, and the financial panic of 1837 dropped these prices down to $500. They remained low until the late 1840s, when an upward trend resumed.¹³

Since the price of a slave was usually pegged to the price of cotton, a ratio was generally used. The price of a slave was thought to be ten thousand times the price of a pound of cotton. Thus 10 cents per pound for cotton would yield a slave value of $1,000. In the 1850s speculative fervor prompted higher slave prices that ignored this ratio. A Georgian noticed the change and predicted a price decline, "the old rule of pricing a negro by the price of cotton by the pound ... does not seem to be regarded. Negroes are 25 per cent higher now with cotton at ten and a half cents than they were two or three years ago when it was worth fifteen and sixteen cents.... A reversal will come soon." The price of a slave in Virginia was lower than that for a slave in New Orleans, reflecting the proximity of the slave to actual cotton production.¹⁴

The number of slaves in the Southwest grew with each decade of the nineteenth century. With that growth and the increased importance of cotton came a gradual shift in the rhetoric of slavery. Nowhere is this more apparent than during the pivotal decade of the 1830s, during the cotton and land boom. Nat Turner's Rebellion in 1831 and the growing antislavery movement in the North exacerbated southern racial and political fears. In 1831, the Mississippi lawyer and politician Sergeant S. Prentiss expressed a commonly held belief: "That slavery is a great evil, there can be no doubt—and this is an unfortunate circumstance that is was ever introduced into this or any other country. At present however, it is a necessary evil, and I do not think admits of a remedy." However, five years later in a recommendation to his state legislature, Prentiss's views had changed: "Resolved that the people of the state of Mississippi look upon the institution of domestic slavery ... not as curse, but as a blessing, as the legitimate condition of the African race, as authorized both by the laws of

God and the dictates of reason and humanity.... We will allow no present change, or hope of future alteration in this matter."[15] The English historian and traveler Robert Russell had this to say on the necessity of having the combination of slavery and cotton:

> If the climate had admitted of the growing of cotton on the banks of the Ohio, we should have seen that slavery possessed of great advantages over free labour in the raising of this crop as it does in that of tobacco.[16]

By the 1850s, idealistic northerners like Frederick Law Olmsted thought that free white labor could replace slave labor in the cotton fields. Olmsted used the example of successful German immigrants who were raising cotton in Texas in the 1850s. He disputed the conventional wisdom that white people were not capable of working in the sweltering cotton fields. For Olmsted, all that was needed was a good dose of northern capitalism to provide economies of scale to cotton production. Thus he bemoaned the fact that there were no joint-stock plantations in Mississippi as there were joint-stock cotton mills in Massachusetts.[17] Olmsted's analogy disregards the inherent risk

Although this photograph was taken in 1935, it is presumably similar to what would have been seen at harvest time in Southern cotton fields during the time of slavery (Library of Congress, Prints & Photographs Division, LC-USF3301–006217-M2).

factors and the uneven cash flow that made cotton farming unsuitable for corporations. Planters used land and slaves as collateral for loans.

Cotton and slavery were further connected because free whites were deemed more expendable than slaves for dangerous work. The monetary risk of losing slaves in the "malarial swamps" during levee[18] building work on the Mississippi River meant that "gangs of husky foreign ... particularly Irish [and] foreign laborers became a conspicuous feature of the lower Mississippi Valley, where they could be seen, winter and summer, struggling under the hard and grueling task of levee building." Labor contractors met immigrant ships in St. Louis, New Orleans, Cincinnati, and Cairo, Illinois, to recruit workers for levee construction. A planter, Walter Sillers, Sr., described the life of white construction workers in the cotton growing areas of Mississippi: "The levee along what is now Lake Beulah—then the Mississippi River—was built by Irish laborers under a Scotch contractor named Bain, before the War between the States. When paid off every Saturday night, the [Irish] workers invariably got drunk and caroused and fought and howled like Bedlam turned loose. Sunday morning found them badly bruised...."[19]

The South depended on cotton and cotton depended on slavery, but how well did they go together? Did they benefit the antebellum South? Some critics argued that slavery hurt rather than helped the economy of the South—hurt not just the blacks but the whites as well, not just non-slaveholders but also the slaveholders. It wasn't just that slavery was immoral; it was also an inefficient and wasteful economic system which degraded labor, led to misallocations of investment, stifled technological progress, inhibited industrialization, and thwarted urbanization.

When Daniel Webster, the antislavery Massachusetts senator, delivered his famous "Seventh-of March" speech on the Compromise of 1850, he observed that there had been a "general concurrence of sentiment" against slavery in America, but that a change had occurred: "This I suppose ... is owing to the rapid growth and sudden extension of the COTTON plantations of the South.... It was the COTTON interest that gave a new desire to promote slavery, to spread it and to use its labor." Cotton, Webster declared, had caused "the South to [become] connected more or less with the extension of slavery" in the West. He continued: "The age of cotton became the golden age of our southern brethren. It gratified their desire for improvement and accumulation at the same time that it excited it.... There soon came to be an eagerness for other territory, a new area ... for the cultivation of the cotton crop...." As for the territories of California and New Mexico, cotton could not be grown there, Webster said, so slavery would not sprout. Hence there was no need to ban the "peculiar institution":

I hold slavery to be excluded from these territories by a law even superior to that which admits and sanctions it in Texas.... I mean the law of nature, of physical geography.... Slavery cannot exist in California or New Mexico.... I mean slavery as we regard it; the slavery of the colored race as it exists in the Southern States. What is there in New Mexico that could possibly induce anybody to go there with slaves? ... And who expects to see a hundred black men cultivating tobacco, corn, cotton, rice or anything else on lands in New Mexico, made fertile only by irrigation? I look upon it, therefore as a fixed fact ... that both California and New Mexico are destined to be free, free by the arrangement of things ordained by the Power above us.[20]

In the mid-nineteenth century, the linkage between cotton and the extension of large-scale slavery was absolute. Outside of cotton, no other crop or industry provided a viable use of slavery. The union of cotton and slavery was never successfully challenged by other enterprises. Southern manufacturing and mining industries could not compete with cotton for slave labor. As has already been mentioned, the price for slaves moved with the price of cotton. As cotton prices rose—from 10 cents a pound in 1811 to thirty-four cents in 1817, and from 9 cents in 1830 to fifteen cents in 1838—it drove slave values higher. Slaves were more valuable in the cotton fields than elsewhere. An example of this was the attempt to use slave labor in the Tredegar Iron Works of Richmond, Virginia,[21] a company which had been chartered in 1837. In 1846, in order to cut costs, the director of the firm, Joseph R. Anderson, brought in some slaves. The employment terms provided that the slaves would have specific jobs that required ten hours of work each day. Leased from owners, the slaves could earn money based on overtime or piecework in excess of quotas. When the slaves began to work in skilled positions, the white workers went on strike to "prohibit the employment of colored people in the said Works." Anderson responded by hiring still more slaves. The number increased from 41 in 1847 to 117 in 1848. In 1850, one hundred of the 250 workers were slaves. On the eve of the Civil War in 1860, eighty of 800 workers were slaves.

The slave experience at Tredegar was not successful. The company's prices were never competitive with northern or English iron production because the combination of labor and raw material costs was too high. The continued use of slaves during the war could not prove the efficacy of this type of worker since there was no profit motive.

The South's slave-produced cotton dominated the American export market from 1803 onwards and was the backbone of its power and sense of nationhood. Cotton was unique—it maintained a clout that slave-produced sugar never commanded. In the 1790s, an estimated 400,000 Britons boycotted this sugar, but no boycott on American slave-produced cotton was possible because the cotton was too difficult to replace. The *Times* of London dramatically asserted that "the destiny of the world hangs on a thread—never did so much depend on a mere flock of down." That "flock of down" was cultivated by millions of black slaves. By 1860 the approximately four million slaves in the United States were estimated to be worth between 2 and 4 billion dollars. The value however, existed only on paper, since too many slaves being offered for sale would cause the price to plummet. In addition, planters could not sell their slaves unless they had an alternative labor source.

The abolitionists also became involved in the economics of slave-based cotton production. Initially, they based their crusades against slavery on moral grounds. Slavery was described as a "Hellish Practice'" and "the greatest Sin in the World, of the very Nature of Hell itself." In the 1820s, the abolitionists began to shift their arguments. While morality was still at the center of their objection to slavery, the new tactic was to attack it on economic grounds. Cassius Marcellus Clay, a cousin of Senator Henry Clay and also a Congregationalist congressman from Kentucky, began publishing an antislavery newspaper called the *True American,* an economic critique of slavery. His main arguments were that slavery was inefficient because it "impoverishes the soil," and because, in comparison with whites, slaves were "not so skilful, so energetic, and above all, have not the stimulus of self-interest: because three million slaves performed "only about one-half of the effective work of the same number of whites in the North"; because slaves not only "produce less than freemen" but also "consume more"; because slavery was "the source of indolence, and destructive of all industry"; and because slavery caused the "poor" to "despise labor" by "degrading" it while simultaneously turning the "mass of slaveholders" into "idlers."[22] Another point Clay made was that slavery retarded economic growth and development by restricting education, diverting capital into the purchase of slaves—where it became a "dead loss"—discouraging the development of "mechanical" skills, and retarding the growth of manufacturing.

Another abolitionist was the author Hinton Rowan Helper. His book *The Impending Crisis of the South*, published in 1857, was reviewed very favorably by the *New York Tribune*, a review which resulted in first-year sales of thirteen thousand copies. The Republican Party condensed the book and distributed a hundred thousand copies, which were used to bolster Lincoln's candidacy. As opposed to Clay, Helper attempted to use proof that cotton-based slavery retarded southern economic growth. He compared three pairs of states, one pair in the North and one in the South, and their growth over the period between 1790 and 1850: New York vs. Virginia, Massachusetts vs. North Carolina, and Pennsylvania vs. South Carolina. In each pair, Helper showed that the economies in the free states far surpassed those of the slave states in categories such as total wealth, manufacturing production, investment in railroads and canals, new inventions, and the value of agricultural production.

Helper attributed the poor performance of the South to economic inefficiency that was entirely due to slave labor in the cotton fields, which produced a very low rate of return for the planters on their capital. While his book was hailed by abolitionists as a "most compact and irresistible array of facts and arguments," he unfortunately offered no proof of his assertions and, additionally, his "facts" were for the most part incorrect or missing.

In 1852 the editor of the *New York Times* hired a New York farmer and traveler, Frederick Law Olmsted, to write a series of articles about slavery in the South based on first-hand observation. While not an abolitionist, his writings showed an overwhelmingly negative impression of slave-based agriculture in the South. His conclusion was that the peculiar institution kept the entire South, not just the slaves, in deep poverty. Included were the landless free farmers and those planters who had substantial amounts of land and slaves. In Olmsted's words, the "majority of those who sell the cotton crop" were "poorer than the majority of our day labourers at the North." Planters with as many as thirty-five slaves could still barely eke out a living, earning on average "hardly more than a private of the New York Metropolitan Police Force." To live "in a moderately comfortable way," a planter had to own at least fifty slaves. Thus slavery was a boon only for those at the very top of the southern economic pyramid—just the top 2 percent of slaveholders.[23]

Like Helper, Olmsted blamed the poor economic situation on the slaves who worked in the cotton fields. Their labor was simply very low in productivity, since it took twice as many slaves as free northern laborers to accomplish any given task. "Four Virginia slaves do not, when engaged in ordinary agricultural operations, accomplish as much, on an average, as one ordinary free farm labourer in New Jersey." Furthermore, this low productivity permeated every aspect of the economic life of the South. Because of this low standard, white workers were "driven to indolence, carelessness, indifference to the results of skill, heedlessness, inconsistency of purpose, improvidence, and extravagance." Thus southern white labor was even less efficient than slave labor.

It was only the advantage of climate that made the South, rather than the North, the leading producer of cotton. Far from being an advantage in cotton production, slave labor was a hindrance in this activity also. Free German laborers who were employed in some Texas cotton fields not only picked more cotton per hand than slaves but "the cotton picked by the free labour of the Germans was worth from one to two cents per pound more than that picked by slaves in the same township, by reason of its greater cleanliness." Olmsted concluded that slave plantations were really relatively inefficient even in cotton production. There was, he said:

> No physical obstacle in the way of our country's supplying ten bales of cotton where it now does one.... Given the South a people moderately close settled, moderately well informed, moderately ambitious and moderately industrious, somewhat approaching that of Ohio, for instance, and what a business it would have! Twenty double track railroads from the Gulf to the lakes, and twenty lines of ocean steamers, would not sufficiently meet its requirements. Who doubts, let him study the present business of Ohio, and ask upon what, in the natural resources of Ohio, or its position, could forty years ago, a prediction of its present wealth and business have been made, which would compare in value with the commercial resources and advantages of position possessed today by any one of the Western cotton states?[24]

What made the slave-based cotton production system work at all? To Olmsted, the answer was the internal slave trade, "which makes slaves valuable property, otherwise then for labor." For even if slave labor could not produce a profit in the cotton fields, it persisted because the increasing value of the stock of slaves made slaveholding a profitable venture.

The last nineteenth-century commentator on the effectiveness of slave-based cotton production was John Elliot Cairnes, a British economist and academic who had never seen the American South. The idea behind his writings was that England should not support the Confederacy during the American Civil War, since a southern victory would perpetuate slavery. In his book *The Slave Power*, Cairnes relied heavily on information from Olmsted's books to form his conclusions. Like Olmsted, Cairnes agreed that the problem was the low quality of slave labor which led to the destruction of fertile land. Slave labor, he argued, was so inept that the cotton growers were "obliged to employ their negroes exclusively in the production" of a single crop:

> Whatever crop may be best suited to the character of the soil and the nature of slave industry, whether cotton, tobacco, sugar, or rice, that crop is cultivated, and that alone. Rotation of crops is thus precluded by the conditions of the case. The soil is tasked again and again to yield the same product, and the inevitable result follows. After a short series of years its fertility is completely exhausted, the planter—"land killer" he is called in the picturesque nomenclature of the South—abandons the ground which he has rendered worthless, and passes on to seek in new soils for that fertility under which alone the agencies at his disposal can be profitably employed.[25]

For Cairnes, there had to be four conditions for slavery to be profitable: demand for a crop which could be produced on a large scale; crops that required extensive labor; unlimited excellent soil; and a profitable slave trade. As long as these conditions were met, slavery would indeed be profitable.

4. Slavery

While Clay, Helper, Olmsted, and Cairnes did not believe in the profitability of slave-based cotton production, another antebellum commentator, J.D.B. De Bow, editor of *De Bow's Review* and an ardent supporter of the South and slavery, did:

> Negro slavery, from natural laws, if not interfered with, must ultimately be confined to that region of country South, where, from heat of the climate and the nature of the cultivation, negro labor is more efficient, cheaper, and more to be relied on than white labor. Virginia is a slave state, yet natural causes have almost excluded slavery from the larger half of her territory. Why not, therefore give the whole subject up to the higher law of Nature to regulate?
>
> If negro slavery, from mistaken notions, be carried into a state or territory where slave labor is less efficient and profitable than white labor, natural causes will correct the mistake, as they have done in the northern states and in Alpine Virginia, by forcing it out again.[26]

Like Helper, De Bow had his own comparison between a northern and southern state, in this case Georgia and New York:

> The white population of Georgia is about one-sixth that of the state of New-York. Yet Georgia has nearly half the property. Hence a white person in Georgia is on an average nearly three times as rich as one in New-York. Even if slaves are excluded from the property of Georgia, she is wealthier in proportion to white population than New-York. And then the health of Georgia is vastly superior. Out of a total population of 908,711, the deaths in a single year were 9,099. In the single city of New-York with about half the population, they were about 18,000, or nearly double. Hence the average mortality of the city of New-York is four times as great as the state of Georgia.
>
> The taxation of Georgia, state and county is about half a million—that of New-York exceeds seven millions. Hence the taxation of Georgia, compared to that of New-York on the basis of population is less than one-fourth, on the white basis is less than one-half—on the property basis is less than one-sixth! Yet with this overwhelming evidence of the superior social, political, and financial condition of Georgia, she is excluded by New-York from a common territory as immoral and unthrifty and—submits![27]

During the nineteenth century, opinions on the subject of whether or not cotton-based slavery was a benefit to the South was colored by each holder's opinion of the efficacy of slavery itself. In the present day, the economic historians who are intensively examining the various manifestations of the antebellum South are no longer interested in either attacking or defending slavery. No one any longer denies the brutal, exploitative, and repugnant character of slavery in the United States or attempts to justify it as a "civilizing" process. Rather the present controversies center around such questions as the effect of slavery on the growing of cotton in the antebellum South. A major historian to comment on the benefits of slavery to the South was Douglass C. North in his work, *The Economic Growth of the United States, 1790–1860*. His thesis was that slave-based cotton production was not a benefit to the South:

> The South was a region characterized by production for the market of a number of agricultural staples in which slave labor was both the major capital investment and an important intermediate product. The nature of [primarily] cotton production (and of tobacco, rice, and sugar production), and the economic and social consequences of investment in this form of capital, affected not only the economic structure of the area, but molded the pattern of settlement and urbanization and the distribution of income as well. The consequence was that the expanding income from the marketing of these staples outside the region induced little growth within the South. Income received there had little multiplier effect, but flowed directly to the North and the West for imports of services, manufacturers, and foodstuffs.[28]

For the historians A.H. Conrad and John R. Meyers, it was only in the West that slave-based cotton growing was of value: "It was not simply that cotton production was the most efficient use of resources, throughout the period [before the Civil War] investment in new cotton lands in the West yielded a return upon capital high enough to attract funds from the old South, the Northeast, and Europe."[29]

Most of the controversy on this subject centers around the work of Robert William Fogel and Stanley L. Engerman, authors of *Time on the Cross: The Economics of American Negro Slavery*, and a second book on the subject by Robert Fogel, *Without Consent or Contract: The Rise and Fall of American Slavery*. Their findings are as follows:

1. Southern agriculture as a whole was about 35 percent more efficient than northern agriculture in 1860.
2. Both southern plantations using free labor and southern plantations using slave labor were more efficient than northern farms. Compared with each other, however, southern slave plantations were more efficient than southern free farms. Compared with northern farms, southern free farms were 9 percent more efficient, while slave plantations were 40 percent more efficient.
3. There were economies of scale in southern agriculture. This means that a single large plantation could produce more than a group of small plantations. In general, the larger the plantation, the greater the economies of scale.
4. Economies of scale were only achieved with slave labor. There were no large-scale southern plantations based on free wage earners. The larger the plantation, the larger the percentage of persons who were slaves.
5. There were significant differences in the relative efficiency of slave plan-

tations within the two major subregions of the South. On average, the plantations of the newer, or slave-buying, states were 29 percent more efficient than those of the older, slave-selling states. The slave plantations of the Old South exceeded the efficiency of the free northern farms by 19 percent, while slave plantations of the new southern states exceeded the average efficiency of free northern farms by 53 percent.

In order to attain these conclusions, the authors used the "geometric index of total factor productivity," which measured the relative efficiency of agriculture in the North compared to the South. Their conclusions indicate that the large southern slave-based cotton plantations were more efficient than northern farms because, on the average, they made better use of their resources. This was also true for the southern farms using free white labor. The main key to this efficiency was the size of the plantation; small farms either North or South could not make effective use of their total resources the way a large plantation could.

The next point has to do with soil depletion. The authors contend that there was little loss of soil quality in the slave exporting states (Virginia, North Carolina, and South Carolina). Cairnes and Olmsted differed. Their proof is that the value of farmland in these states increased between 1850 and 1860. Also, the slaves in the upper South were sold to the cotton-growing region of the South not because the soil in the upper South had given out but because of the demand for these slaves in the lower South.

The two main developments in the lower South that made these lands suitable for cotton production, which of course had become the main southern crop, were the use of the rivers by steamboat, which allowed planters to move further inland, and the use of better management techniques, which permitted the planters to introduce large-scale slave-based cotton plantations. These techniques included discussion of problems in agricultural journals, the organization of agricultural societies to bring about "best practices" in various aspects of farming, and, the most important, labor management. "The organization of slaves into highly disciplined, interdependent teams capable of maintaining a steady and intense rhythm of work—appears to be the crux of the superior efficiency of large scale operations on plantations, at least as far as field work is concerned."[30] The authors contend that Olmsted, in watching this operation at work, missed the significance of this teamwork, instead seeing it as the "stupid, plodding, machine-like manner in which they labour." As far as soil depletion in the lower South was concerned, because of the potential profit from cotton production great care was taken to maintain soil fertility, a point continually emphasized by southern agriculturalists and southern political leaders.

These efforts were basically successful based on the value of plantation land as well as on cotton yields. Also, as long as there was a continuous movement of slaves from the upper to the lower South and new lands to open, the system could continue indefinitely.

The authors also make the point that racism played a part in the minds of those who did not believe cotton-based slavery was successful. To them the plantations could not be profitable, since the slave workers were "incapable of all but the rudest forms of labour," "evasive," incapable of maintaining "a steady routine," "incorrigibly indolent," "wanting in versatility," and unsuited for any activity that required "the slightest care, forethought, or dexterity." Against these stereotypes, the authors found the following:

> Among large plantations without overseers, 61 per cent had only one adult male over the age of nineteen in the planter's family. In these cases the planter was the only adult male in his family who was in residence, or else the father was absent or dead and his only resident son was running the plantation. In any event there was no second male family member to take up the duties of the overseer. On 6 per cent of the large plantations there were two adults over nineteen, but the second of these persons was at least seventy years of age, and hence was probably too old to be actively involved in the business affairs of the plantation. Another 9 per cent of the plantations had no male at all over age nineteen in residence. Thus for 75 per cent of the plantations without overseers, there were no sons or other males who could have assumed the duties of the overseer. The conclusion indicated by these findings is startling: On a majority of these large plantations, the top nonownership management was black![31]

While Fogel and Engerman criticized historians such as Olmsted, Cairnes, Clay, and Helper, their work was in turn examined by contemporary historians. Some of these historians, even though they attacked slavery as an inefficient system, had to agree that slave-based cotton production could generate high profits and attendant growth rates under three conditions: fresh land, a steady supply of cheap labor, and a high level of demand on the world market. The economic indictment of slavery has focused on structural consequences. The origins of the prosperity of the slave economies lay primarily in the force of the world demand for certain staples. At the same time, these high levels of growth and profit disguised deep structural weaknesses that condemned slave societies to underdevelopment, eventual stagnation, and political disaster.[32] No slaveholding country or region became industrialized, and in most instances the abolition of slavery came about through blood and disorder. Examples are a revolution in Saint-Domingue and a civil war in the United States.

The final point is that Fogel and Engerman used farm revenue as their measure of output when comparing southern plantations to northern farms.

Two contemporary historians, Paul David and Peter Temin, take issue with the comparison because, since cotton could not be grown in the North due to the constraints of climate, the comparison must be between unlike products. The northern agricultural product was probably for domestic consumption, while cotton was the nation's chief export product. Therefore the apparent advantages of slavery were not based on any technical superiority, but merely on the fact that southern planters grew a valuable crop that yeoman farmers of the North could not produce.

5

The Impact of Tariffs

Virtually from its founding the United States has not followed a free trade policy. Tariffs were the principle source of federal revenue in the nineteenth century and protection of domestic industries was a significant factor as well from the first tariff act, in 1789, onward. One of the more interesting (and controversial, at least in the antebellum period) questions in American economic history as well as in international trade and development is what the effects of such a protective policy in fact were. It is well known that a country with monopoly powering international trade can improve its lot over the free trade equilibrium. Also, at some point by increasing its tariff it should be able to improve its terms of trade to increase its national welfare. The antebellum United States may well have had such power due to its position as the major world supplier of raw cotton. In the period between 1840 and 1860, the United States produced almost two-thirds of the world's cotton, while the United Kingdom, the major consumer of raw cotton, purchased 80 percent of its cotton imports from the United States.[1] This chapter will show the huge importance of cotton through an examination of the tariffs promulgated by the United States during the antebellum period.

The commercial and industrial rise of New England at the end of the 18th century was not an accident. It was a deliberate event in which the South at first willingly participated. This plan was instituted by Alexander Hamilton, and his goal was to increase the prosperity and independence of the whole nation. But the result, from the South's point of view, turned out rather differently. Southern New England was the first section of America to become overcrowded. At the end of the Revolution, it had too many families, not enough good farmland (the soil was too rocky), and too few jobs. To assuage the situation, the federal government set out to encourage commercial trades to the area, especially shipbuilding and shipping, along with manufacturing, which would take advantage of the area's waterpower. The raw material for northern factories, and the cargoes of northern merchantmen would come from the South. Washington's "Farewell Address" makes this economic trade-off the chief practical argument for a continued union of the sections: "The *North*, in an unrestrained intercourse with the South, protected by the equal Laws of a common government, finds in the productions of the latter, great additional resources of Maratime [*sic*] and commercial enterprise and precious materials of manufacturing industry. The *South* in the same Intercourse, benefiting by the Agency of the *North*, sees its agriculture grow and its commerce expand."

The American tariff history begins with Alexander Hamilton. The basis of his program to strengthen the "infant Government by increasing the number of ligaments between and the interests of Individuals" was the national bank conceived in the early 1780s " to engage the monied interest immediately in it by making them contribute the whole or part of the stock and giving them the whole or part of the profits." The bank would link "the interests of the state in an intimate connexion with those of the rich individuals belonging to it."[2]

This wealthy group consisted mainly of well-established merchants who had accumulated their fortunes trading within the British Empire during the colonial period and after the Revolution. A significant portion of this trade involved the exchange of British manufactured goods for the raw and semi-finished produce of the colonies. Hamilton approved of this trade not only because of the merchants' role in his financial stabilization program, but also because it provided the 80 percent of tariff revenues that provided funds to service the debt and operate the government. After the Whiskey Rebellion of 1792–1794 had shown the fierce opposition to internal taxes, the federal government learned to draw most of its revenue from taxes on foreign imports. To the extent that Americans paid taxes, they mostly paid them through tariffs. This consideration led Hamilton to a pro–British foreign policy and instilled in him a profound wariness of any action that might jeopardize the flow of English goods into America. He consistently opposed any trade discrimination and preferred "a strict national or commercial friendship with Great Britain." His economic program made such an Anglo-American alliance in "the best interests of this Country." He thus tied his political economy, his party, and the nation itself to the greatest manufacturing power in the world.[3]

While Hamilton's policies and projects related to manufacturing, he never sought to comprehend the manufacturers themselves. While favoring the wealthy class of merchants, he expected patriotism, coercion, or some profound sense of national interest to retain popular support for his programs. Because of this situation, the manufacturers appealed to Congress for assistance in protecting their industries. They assailed "foreign luxuries," particularly British manufactured goods, as draining American wealth and causing economic hardships and, they requested tariffs to protect American manufacturers.

The "tradesmen and manufacturers" of Boston asked for a tariff "intended to exclude such [manufactured] importations, and, ultimately, establish these several branches of manufacture among themselves."[4] These manufacturers were requesting in an extreme form what all the manufacturers wanted: a strong protective tariff. In Congress James Madison proposed protective tariffs specifically directed against England, but his proposals were defeated and what was in effect a revenue tariff was imposed with Hamilton's wholehearted approval.[5] Favoring a "moderate" tariff productive of revenue, Hamilton argued that when duties "are low, a nation can trade abroad on better terms— its imports and exports will be larger—the duties will be regularly paid, and arising on a greater quantity of commodities, will yield more in the aggregate, than when they are so high as to operate ... as a prohibition."[6] The need for revenue overrode the demand for protection of manufacturers.

The Hamilton Tariff of 1789 was the second statute ever enacted by the new United States government. As secretary of the treasury, Alexander Hamilton was anxious to establish the tariff as a regular source of revenue for the government. At the end of 1791, Hamilton was handed an opportunity to shape new tariff legislation after the defeat of American forces by Indians in the West. On March 8, 1792, Congress asked Treasury's advice on how to raise additional revenue in order to finance the increased expenditures for the protection of the western frontier.

Hamilton wasted no time in taking advantage of the House's request and sent his recommendations to Congress just ten days later. His report presented three ways to raise the needed funds: selling the government's stake in the Bank of the United States, borrowing the money, and raising taxes. Hamilton objected to the first, arguing that if the government should liquidate its bank shares, the money should go to reducing the public debt rather than financing additional expenditures. He also objected to additional borrowing when the national debt was so high; as he put it, "Nothing can more interest the nation credit and prosperity, than a constant and systematic attention to husband all the means previously possessed, for extinguishing the present debt, and to avoid, as much as possible, the incurring of any new debt."[7] While recognizing that "taxes are never welcome to a community," Hamilton recommended higher import duties. One advantage of the tariff was that "an increase of duties ... will serve to promote essentially the industry, the wealth, the strength, the independence, and the substantial prosperity of the country."[8]

While this tariff, according to Hamilton, would only be temporary, southern members of Congress began to defend their own interests during the debates of the tariff; Representative White from Virginia noted "when it is considered that many of the duties are designed to encourage the manufacturers of the United States, [and] thought that equal attention should be paid to the agricultural interest, an interest as important as any other." Representative Mercer of Maryland asked whether "the submission of a provision to defend the frontier should authorize a system for the encouragement of manufacturers.... Independent of the constitutional question of the right of Congress, why should we be compelled to consider the extensive range and delicate refinement of encouraging manufacturers by extensive duties operating as indirect bounties, under the pressure of providing for an Indian war? Representative Page of Virginia announced his intention of voting against the tariff, arguing that "it is not a bill for the protection of the frontiers, but for the encouragement of certain manufacturers.... It is a bill very different from what it ought to be."[9]

When the votes were cast, the tariff passed by a vote of 37 to 20. Thirteen of the 20 nay votes came from southern congressmen. According to Gerald Clarfield, the tariff passage did not have much political support and passed only by having been tied to increased military expenditures to protect the frontier: "Had circumstances been different, it is extremely doubtful that this tariff proposal would have stood much chance in Congress. By linking military appropriations to the impost, however, Hamilton managed to neutralize a good deal of the opposition."[10]

Another indication that Hamilton's priorities did not lie with the manufacturers, either, came later in 1792 when he was confronted with an increasing need for larger government revenues. He could have met the need by raising tariffs and partially fulfilling the manufacturers demand for protection. Instead his fear of antagonizing importers with higher duties led him to enforce the tax on domestically manufactured liquor and snuff; the slight increases in the tariff that he recommended were predicated on the declining cost of imports and therefore were of little protective value. Moreover, Hamilton noted that even this small tariff increase would "not be of very long continuance."[11] By the end of 1793, Hamilton's pro-importer stance was driving manufacturers into opposition to his party, the Federalists. This opposition crystallized in the Democratic Societies, which in the cities drew their largest membership from artisans and manufacturers. This growing dissent marked the emergence of an opposition coalition that later became the Republican Party.

Next, Hamilton again became involved in national defense. At this point, he might have seized the opportunity to aid domestic manufacturers through the dispensation of government defense contracts; instead, he turned to British importers. "It has been determined," he wrote Thomas Pinckney, "to import from Europe as expeditiously as may be the articles ... towards the construction of six frigates.... [T]he desire of dispatch principally has recommended an experiment to procure them from G Britain."[12] Although some of these imports may be explained by the lack of domestic production and credit needs, Hamilton overlooked the one American industry that could supply all the governments requirements: the cotton sailcloth manufacturers. "What sail Cloth shall we use for the Frigates," he asked Benjamin Lincoln and the other port collectors, "that of Domestic or that of Foreign Manufacture? National pride & interest plead for the former if the quality be really good. But is it really good?" Then he added, "Objections are made; that which is principally insisted upon is that it shrinks exceedingly." Lincoln quickly responded that American sailcloth was better than foreign and that there had been no problems for two years. This exchange is all the more puzzling since, in a draft of his *Report on Manufactures*, Hamilton had observed that Boston sailcloth "is asserted to be of a quality superior to any import."[13]

After he retired from office Hamilton's activities continued to be of dubious benefit to domestic manufacturers. He opposed Jefferson's decision to repeal internal taxes. He became involved in various land speculation schemes which were favored by the British because they diverted money from American manufacturing. The numerous efforts on Hamilton's part in and out of office to promote such schemes led one of his biographers, John C. Miller, to question "whether Hamilton did not actually do more during his lifetime for land speculation than for American manufacturers."[14]

Since imports were very substantial compared to domestic production at the beginning of the century, it could be argued that Hamilton's machinations were at least part of the cause. Most of the cotton textiles consumed in the United States before the embargo of 1808 were imported. This condition was short-lived. Domestic production began to rise rapidly soon after the embargo was instituted in December of that year and continued through the war years. Imports from India and China fell in 1809, but revived briefly during 1810 and 1811 when the embargo was relaxed. In the protected environment of the War of 1812, the modern cotton textile industry of New England grew by an order of magnitude from 1809 to 1815, spearheading America's industrialization in the early nineteenth century.

With peace, however, came disaster, as domestic production fell by two-thirds in 1816. Although most historians talk of drastic price reductions as British imports were sold at auction, the price of cotton cloth continued its downward trend without any break. The cause of the dramatic fall was production. The New England cotton mills produced only about one-third as many yards of fabric in 1816 as in 1815; production collapsed back to the level of 1811.[15] It is not hard to see Francis Lowell and the Boston Associates anticipating disaster and ruin.

This tremendous fall in production had several causes. According to Caroline Ware, "the combination of the post-war slump, the dumping of British goods on the market after the peace, and the collapse of the western currency sent numbers of the old producers to the wall. 'Half the spindles' in the vicinity of Providence and Fall River were said to be idle in 1816."[16] The banking and currency problems in the western United States cut sharply into the domestic demand for textiles and left many manufacturers with debts from unpaid shipments. The import surge that followed the peace in 1815 also exacerbated the situation. The value of British cotton fabric exported to the United States in 1815 was over $20 million, almost half the value of domestic production that year. British imports fell by half from 1815 to 1816 and stayed far below the 1815 level. The imports from India and China were not large enough to have caused the dramatic contraction in domestic production, but they showed the effect of peace by rising sharply in 1816. The dramatic (if short-lived) decline in U.S. production suggests that domestic producers might have been far more responsive to imports than they would be two or three decades later, but even this is a highly tentative conclusion. Willard Thorp described the year 1815 as one of "financial panic" and 1816 as a "depression."[17]

The temporary increase in duties passed at the onset of the War of 1812 was slated to end one year after the conclusion of the peace treaty. Consequently, early in 1816, Congress took up the question of establishing new duties. Reporting on the subject, the Committee on Commerce and Manufacturers explicitly noted the difficulties of cotton manufacturers and the numerous petitions that had been received from them advocating greater tariff protection. Citing the perilous condition of these manufacturers, the committee went on to note that passage of a protective tariff would put the manufacturers "again into operation with increased powers; but should it be withheld they will be prostrated.... A capital of near sixty millions of dollars will become inactive, the greater part of which will be a dead loss to the manufacturers."[18]

Textile manufacturers' efforts to influence tariff legislation extended beyond petitioning Congress for support. It is apparent from the records of subsequent debate in Congress that for the first time a number of manufacturers were present in Washington during the discussion of the tariff bill, and that members of Congress consulted with them to ascertain the effects of potential legislation.

The result of the tariff was that cotton imports from Asia fell, although they did not vanish. Instead, they fell back from their peak and did not share in the growth of demand as the United States did. Imports from Britain fell as well, never to rise to their value in 1815. Even in 1847, after the tariff had been reduced sharply, imports were only about half as large in value as they had been in 1815. Beginning in 1816, domestic production revived quickly and resumed its rapid expansion; by the early 1820s the volume of domestic production exceeded that imported for the first time:

> The Commercial boom made government protection of economic growth the central dynamic of American politics. Entrepreneurial elites needed the state to guarantee property; to enforce contracts; to provide judicial, financial, and transport infrastructures; to mobilize society's resources as investment capital; and to load the legal dice for enterprise in countless ways. Especially they strove for a powerful gentry led national state, through which developmental policies they dreamed of rivaling British wealth and might.[19]

According to Mark Bils, without the tariffs half the New England industrial sector would have gone bankrupt.[20] We can infer from this upswing in production that the American cotton industry may well have been protected by the Tariff of 1816. The tariff extended the protection afforded by both the embargo and the war enabling the industry to grow. It is possible that the industrial growth achieved during the years of conflict with Britain could have been erased by free trade after the end of hostilities. Because the Lowell factories moved quickly in gaining the tariff benefit, this eventuality was forestalled and general economic conditions improved thereafter.[21]

For most of the early nineteenth century, the U.S. tariff on imported cotton cloth was a combination of an ad valorem[22] rate and a minimum valuation. The Tariff of 1816, for example, generally regarded as the first "protective" tariff, consisted of a 20 percent ad valorem rate on the imported textile along with a 25-cent-per-yard minimum valuation. This duty severely burdened textile imports that were priced under 25 cents per yard and thus shifted the composition of imports towards higher grade, higher priced products. The minimum valuation may not have been binding on British products, however, because goods worth less than 25 cents per yard were not typical of British products at this time.[23] Since the minimum excluded coarser cloths, it could have been aimed at the Asian cloth while not affecting imports from Britain.

As one of the principal authors of the Tariff of 1816, this rate structure was probably a deliberate strategy by Francis Lowell. As explained by his colleague Nathan Appleton, the minimum was designed to protect the fledgling industry in New England without antagonizing southern cotton exporters to

England. Cotton growers in the South exported raw cotton to Britain, and they were opposed to any tariff that would restrict the sales of their British customers to the United States. They worried about both loss of sales and further losses due to possible British retaliation. Lowell's tariff design shows that the sectional conflict over the tariff that would loom large at mid-century was already present at the start of New England industrialization.

Historians, in examining this act, have been impressed by the ardent support given it by the South, especially in South Carolina, where two of the South's strongest political leaders, William Lowndes and John C. Calhoun, voted for the measure in the House of Representatives. The thesis invariably advanced to explain southern support of the Tariff of 1816 is that southerners hoped and expected that textile manufacturing would become as important in their section as it had in New England:

New England Cloth Production, 1805 to 1816 (thousands of dollars)[24]

Year	$
1805	978
1806	1,353
1807	1,738
1808	4,073
1809	6,418
1810	13,984
1811	15,251
1812	20,087
1813	31,514
1814	44,453
1815	47,160
1816	16,355

This theory hinges upon the actions of Lowndes and Calhoun to a great extent, since they are credited with having been the leaders of the drive to bring textile mills to the South, and it has been assumed that it was their influence which persuaded other congressmen below the Mason Dixon Line to vote for the tariff.

Actually both men revealed a definite hostility toward manufacturing in their voting. Lowndes favored the reduction of textile rates in speeches he made on the floor of Congress and supported these speeches with votes to *lower* high protective duties. It is clear from these actions that Lowndes had no strong desire to protect cotton and woolen manufacturers. John C. Calhoun, like Lowndes, is supposed to have supported the Tariff of 1816 because he wished to see manufacturing develop in South Carolina. However, not once did Calhoun ever state that he expected industry to develop in the state, or, for that matter, anywhere in the South. In his famous speech in support of the Tariff of 1816, Calhoun referred specifically to the fact that his support was not based on any local manufacturing interests and that he believed solely in agriculture as a means of livelihood for the South.[25] On still another occasion, Calhoun made the assertion that no mechanical enterprise would succeed in the Palmetto State.[26]

That the actions of Lowndes and Calhoun reflected the sentiments of others in their home state is shown by the words of Langdon Cheves, one of the most prominent South Carolinians, who remarked, "Manufacturing should be the last resort of industry in every country, for one forced as with us, they serve no interests but those of the capitalists who set them in motion and their immediate localities."[27] Like Lowndes and Calhoun, most of the other fourteen southern congressmen who voted for the Tariff of 1816 appear to have had something else in mind than a wish to bring manufacturing to their section of the country.

Another method of examining the thesis that southerners supported the Tariff of 1816 because they hoped that textile mills would develop there is to view the voting on this bill by states. If the thesis were valid, then the states profiting most by it would have given it the strongest support. In the South, Maryland was the state having the most cotton and woolen mills.[28] Yet every southern state except North Carolina cast a greater percentage of its congressional votes for the tariff than did Maryland.

If most southerners did not support the Tariff of 1816 through a desire to have manufacturing, why then did they vote for it? The true reasons may well have been given in the actual tariff debates. They were (1) the need of the nation to raise additional revenue and (2) the fear of a new war, making it essential that America protect what limited industry it had, most of which had to do with cotton. Both protectionists and free traders were in agreement that the country needed more revenue. The need became evident when, in December of 1815, secretary of the treasury Dallas presented his budget for the forthcoming year. It revealed that by the end of 1816 there would be a deficit of about three and one half million dollars. Dallas said that the only way this deficit could be overcome and the budget balanced was by having a tariff with high duties.[29] It was the contention of some southerners that a high tariff would hurt the nation's revenue receipts because it would either stop people from importing cotton goods entirely or else lead them to smuggle in the wanted goods duty free.[30] Most congressmen must have felt that taking some action on the revenue problem was preferable to doing nothing at all. Lowndes was an example of a southerner who felt this way. Though he had opposed most of the high duties written into the tariff bill, he rose to his feet on the final day of debate to declare that he would still vote for the bill because it would help the revenue and general interests of the United States.[31]

Possibly an even stronger consideration with southerners, because their emotions played a stronger part in it, was the patriotic desire to build up America's defenses and to stop British cotton goods from flooding the American market. It was clear from the speeches made in Parliament by Lord Brougham that this dumping of goods was done with malice aforethought. In connection with British cotton products to America, he was quoted in *Niles' Weekly Register* as saying it was "well worthwhile to incur a loss upon the first exportation in order, by the glut, TO STIFLE IN THE CRADLE THOSE RISING MANUFACTURERS IN THE UNITED STATES, which the war had forced into existence, *contrary to the natural course of things*."[32]

Only a year had elapsed since America had been at war with Great Britain. During the War of 1812, the South had been one of the strongest supporters of the administration. This support was based, in part, upon a deep hatred of Britain stemming from the many slights and injustices America had suffered at her hands. The South had entered the war determined to show Great Britain that America would take no more insults. Southern feeling against England was still strong in 1816, and few southerners remained unmoved by the appeal that they now save the domestic industries from British attempts to destroy them by flooding the American textile markets.

One of the strongest speeches in favor of a protective tariff was made by John C. Calhoun. The entire speech was based on the fear that America might shortly be involved in another war with her primary antagonist, Great Britain. After warning that war might break out at any time, Calhoun declared that the United States must not again be so poorly prepared to defend herself as she had been in 1812. This time the country must be ready. The surest way to be ready was to aid, by means of a tariff, those industries (especially cotton) which would make the nation self-sufficient.[33]

The argument that war was liable to break out again made a strong appeal to the national patriotism of the South. This and the knowledge that the country needed more revenue combined to persuade Southerners to back the Tariff of 1816. The attitude of the South at that time is probably best recalled in a speech made by Representative Eldred Simkins of South Carolina:

> To give some protection to those establishments which had greatly helped to save us in time of war, and without which no nation on earth can ever be truly independent or safe, as well as to raise revenue, the Congress of 1816 passed a law, imposing a tariff, or a system of duties, on the most of these foreign articles which could be made among ourselves, and the extravagant importations of

which were about to bring ruin on our manufactures! This was wise, it was patriotic, it was in fact the duty of the Representatives of the nation.[34]

Additionally, first, the tariff was understood to be a temporary expedient to deal with clear and present dangers. The duties would be lowered in three years, by which time the problems with England would likely have subsided. Second, the tariff would be applied only to cotton, woolen products, and iron; the bulk of imported goods that the South regularly bought from foreign countries would not be affected. Finally, economic prosperity prevailed in the agrarian South at this time, easing concerns about the financial burdens imposed by the tariff.

The Tariff of 1816 was unquestionably a financial success. By the end of 1816, the new duties had brought in approximately twenty-seven and one half million dollars; in 1817 the total was seventeen and one half million dollars. The last complete figures were those for the year 1818, which showed a revenue from customs of nearly twenty-two million dollars, turning a previous treasury deficit into a surplus.[35]

This surplus only lasted one year. In 1819, the nation suffered a major financial panic. The South, the leading buyer of imported goods in the United States, was badly hurt by the panic, which left them unable to purchase imports as they had before. Raising the tariff would have only aggravated the situation. Additionally, the Panic of 1819 aided manufacturing. The fall of prices it brought about made the cost of raw materials cheaper and therefore proved to aid the industrialists.[36] The fact that prices dropped was no sign that northern factory owners were suffering. Congressman Philip Barbour of Virginia pointed out that in 1816 cotton had sold for thirty cents a pound. Now it sold at not more than fifteen cents a pound. Therefore, he stated, "If in 1816, cotton cloth sold at thirty cents a yard, and now it sells at twenty cents, it is substantially just as good a sale."[37]

Cotton had now become such an important crop in the South that southerners could no longer give up their economic interests. In 1816 it was not a desire for manufacturing, but a combination of prosperity, patriotism, and promises that swayed southerners. None of these factors existed in 1819 to influence them.[38] Also in 1816, when Britain was dumping her goods on the American market, the South had gone along with the North in its time of need; and finally, there was no need to continue strengthening the national defense. In January 1820, the secretary of state, John Quincy Adams, informed the president that "in our foreign relations, we stood upon terms with England as favorable as can ever be expected."[39]

The tariff of 1824 was the first in which the interests of the North and

South truly came into conflict. By 1824, the nationalism that followed the War of 1812 was transforming into strong sectionalism. John C. Calhoun embodied the southern position, that the protective tariff was a device that favored the North at the expense of the South, which relied on foreign manufactured goods and open foreign markets for its cotton:

> We are told by those who pretend to understand our interest better than we do, that the excess of production and not the Tariff, is the evil which afflicts us....We would feel more disposed to respect the spirit in which the advice is offered, if those from whom it comes accompanied it with the weight of their example. They also, occasionally complain of low prices, but instead of diminishing the supply, as a remedy for the evil, demand an enlargement of the market, by the exclusion of all competition.[40]

The driver of the dissent between the North and South was the "Panic." As a convention assembled in New York put it, "Our commerce is greatly prostrated; our shipping has sunk in value ... real estate is depreciated ... [and] numbers of our merchants, manufacturers, and farmers, are reduced to bankruptcy."[41] A higher tariff, the members of the convention assured Congress, would set things right.

In response, agricultural societies sprang up in Virginia, South Carolina, and Alabama to counter the charge that a higher tariff would solve the nation's economic difficulties. An increase in the tariff, they complained, made British exported goods more expensive, allowing New England manufacturers to raise prices on Yankee-made boots, shoes, nails, shirting, and carpets. This was nothing but a "tax in fact, to be levied principally on the great body of agriculturalists, who constitute a large majority of the whole American people."[42] Back and forth flew pamphlets and countercharges about how best to rescue the nation from the depression. A Philadelphia committee referred to the pro tariff literature from northern cities as "masterpieces of eloquence." Critics in the Virginia towns of Fredericksburg, Petersburg, and Surry called the same writings "the undefined projects and extravagant claims of the manufacturing associations."[43]

And how did this tariff affect cotton? Was it possible for the tariff to increase demand for it? The duties on cotton manufacturers, especially the minimums on cloth, excluded goods made from foreign cotton and were of minor benefit to the planters. However, the South feared that England, exporting cotton goods to many countries, would cease to buy American cotton to the extent that America ceased to buy English manufactured products (of which cotton was only a part, albeit a major part) and turned to Brazil, Mexico, and India—America's cotton producing competitors.

Congressman George McDuffie of South Carolina turned the protectionists' arguments against them: England's policy was to secure foreign markets for her manufactured products, and she would therefore not follow the principle of "buying cheapest" if her export market in the United States was restricted.

The essential issue, therefore, was the sacrifice of the interests of the cotton growing South to those of northern manufacturing and western agriculture. The South was accused of being selfish, and Henry Clay went so far as to ask "whether the interests of the greater part should be made to bend to the condition of the servile part of our population? That would, in effect, make us slaves of slaves."[44] Nevertheless, northern and western congressmen, whose constituencies produced product largely for the domestic market and were thus mostly immune to the effects of a protective tariff, joined together to pass the tariff, beginning the antagonism between the northern states and the southern states, as the latter fought to protect its economic mainstay—its cotton business.

Once behind tariff walls, New England would manufacture most of the cotton textiles sold in the United States. Manchester, Lowell, Lawrence, and Waterbury would become a new source of American wealth. Before the 1819 panic, American food exports were more significant than cotton exports; by the 1920s cotton exports were two to three times as valuable. With the protective tariffs, the country had no need to trade everything with everyone. In the pre–Panic economy, sugar was the crucial intermediate market instrument; now American cotton replaced sugar at the center of the new economy. Cotton went to Britain and then around the world.[45]

The Tariff of 1828 was labeled the "Tariff of Abominations" by its southern detractors because of the effects it had on the antebellum economy. The major goal of the tariff, as was the case of its predecessors, was to protect northern industries from being driven out of business by low-priced imported goods. Also, as was the case with previous tariffs, the South would directly suffer economically because of it. They would have to pay higher prices on goods that the region did not produce. They would indirectly suffer because reducing the exportation of British goods to the United States made it difficult for the British to pay for the cotton they imported from the South.

Instead of merely agitating against the bill as they had in the past, Calhoun and other southerners crafted their own tariff bill heavily weighted with items needed by the North. They believed that the legislators from the New England states would then oppose the bill. The southerners would then switch their votes, join the northerners and kill the legislation, hopefully blaming it on the North:

5. *The Impact of Tariffs* 91

What the plan was, Calhoun explained very frankly nine years later, in a speech reviewing the events of 1828 and defending the course taken by himself and his southern fellow members. A high-tariff bill was to be laid before the House. It was to contain not only a high general range of duties, but duties especially high on those raw materials on which New England wanted the duties to be low. It was to satisfy the protective demands of the Western and Middle States, and at the same time to be obnoxious to the New England members. The Jackson men of all shades, the protectionists of the North and the free-traders from the South, were to unite in preventing any amendments; that bill and no other was to be voted on. When the final vote came, the southern men were to turn around and vote against their own measure. The New England men, and the Adams men in general, would be unable to swallow it, and would also vote against it. Combined, they would prevent its passage, even though the Jackson men in the North voted for it. The result expected was that no tariff bill at all would be passed during the session, which was the object of the southern wing of the opposition. On the other hand, the obloquy of defeating it would be cast on the Adams party, which was the object of the Jacksonians of the North. The tariff bill would be defeated, and yet the Jackson men would be able to parade as the true "friends."[46]

Unfortunately for the South, the plan did not work. While the majority of the New England congressmen joined a majority of the Southern congressmen in voting against the tariff, it passed due to its support in the mid–

Notice of a National Convention in 1844 supporting Henry Clay and the tariff (Library of Congress, Prints & Photographs Division, LC-USZ62-22269).

Atlantic, western, and southwestern states. Worse yet for the South, England, faced with a reduced market for their manufactured goods and pressured by British abolitionists, reduced theirs imports of cotton from the United States, which weakened the southern economy even more. The tariff forced the South to buy their manufactured goods from American manufacturers, mainly in the North, at a higher price, while the southern states also faced a reduced income from cotton sales.

Because of continuous opposition to the Tariff of 1828 on the part of the South, a new tariff was enacted in 1832; it was still a protectionist tariff, largely written by former President John Quincy Adams, now in the House of Representatives. While it reduced the duties on many imported goods, it proved to be a far cry from fulfilling the demands of the South. It was known as the Compromise Tariff of 1833, so called because it was adopted to gradually reduce rates until, by 1842, they would match the levels set in the Tariff of 1816.

The ten-year continuous rate reductions were almost concluded when in 1842 President John Tyler, in attempting to relieve the problems caused by the panic of 1837, cancelled the last of the scheduled reductions and signed a new and higher tariff in 1842. As usual, support for a high tariff came principally from New England, where manufacturing was concentrated, and resisted in the South, which benefited from cheap imports. The Whig Party in control of Congress argued that, first, if the South wanted strong markets for its cotton, it would be more likely to come from the needs of manufacturing workers in the North than in Britain, and, second, since the tariff supported the federal government (there was no income tax at this time), a low tariff would be insufficient to fund the national government or it would come from a flood of cheap imports that would bankrupt New England manufacturers and create a national depression.

In 1846, the incoming Polk administration replaced the Tariff of 1842 with the Walker Tariff. This was one of the lowest tariffs in American history and came into being because it was supported not only by the cotton South, but also by the West, hoping to increase the exports of its agricultural products to Europe, where there were food shortages due to the failure of the potato crop not only in Ireland but also in England and on the Continent. It is at this point that economic historians differ over the effect antebellum tariffs had on American cotton. One school, whose most prominent adherent is F.W. Taussig, holds that "the tariff of 1816 may be considered a judicious application of the principle of protection to young industries," in part because domestic producers became strong enough to survive without tariffs "almost certainly by 1832." By this time, Taussig concluded, "the cotton manufacture was in the main independent of protection, and not likely to be much affected, favorably or unfavorably, by changes in duties.[47] The contrasting opinion, held principally by Mark Bils and Harley C. Knick, looks at the costs of producing cotton textiles in America in the 1830s and 1840s. Bils concluded that even after two decades of protection the domestic industry "was still unable to stand on its own.... [A]s of 1833, removing protection would have eliminated the vast majority of value added[48] in the cotton textile industry.[49] Knick concurred and conjectured that removal of the tariff would have shrunk domestic output to about 10 percent of domestic consumption even as late as the 1850s.[50]

Another group, Douglas A. Irwin and Peter Temin, support Taussig's contentions, arguing that a tariff reduction lowered the relative price of imports, and that this reduction, while stimulating greater imports, had only a modest effect on domestic production, because when the cotton duties were cut in 1846, while imports surged, domestic production remained high. This apparent paradox is explained by Irwin and Temin by pointing out that domestically produced textiles and imported textiles were different products. As support for their premise, they quote Robert Zevin: "Imports from Britain and the products of New England mills tended to fall into quite distinct product classifications.... The imports were largely ginghams, woven in intricate patterns to which the power looms had yet been adopted. New England power looms were supplying plain weaves—sheeting, shirting, and, somewhat later, twills,—usually made of lower count yarns than the British cloths."[51] They therefore conclude that high tariffs were not an essential component of the survival and success of the antebellum domestic cotton industry, as opposed to the opinion of the South that the protective tariffs were detrimental to their section of the nation.

Another argument against protective tariffs comes from two southerners, Thomas Roderick Dew, the president of the College of William and Mary, and William Harper, chancellor of the state of South Carolina. Writing before the Civil War, they contended that, according to the friends of protection, under the "restrictive system" a planter would find a new and expanded market for his cotton, a home market that would eventually replace Britain's. However, Dew and Harper demonstrated that this expanded domestic market could never replace the foreign, and no American textile industry could ever receive the amount of cotton consumed across the Atlantic and provide a market for cotton goods as extensive as that of a foreign one: "If we examine into this increase of market, it will be found so inconsiderable, so inefficient in its operation, especially when set off again the gradual loss of market in Europe, which will, in all probability, ensue, that it is entirely unworthy of the vast efforts which have been made to establish it."

Argued the two southerners, "if all the cotton manufactured in the United States could be manufactured more cheaply abroad, and sold more cheaply here, after paying the costs of transportation and duties for revenue, then it is certain that the market for cotton is injured in consequence of forcing manufacturers by means of protecting duties," and therefore Dew and Harper concluded that the "protecting system affords no new or additional market, but only substitutes a more limited and inferior market, for a more extensive and better one."[52]

By the mid-nineteenth century, America had emerged as the second largest producer of textiles in the world after the British. The growth of this industry came as a result of a number of factors: the high level of protection initiated between 1808 and 1815 by the Embargo and Non-Intercourse Acts together with the War of 1812. Also, the return of peace did not put cotton production back to its original position because of the substantial investments made in manufacturing the product, together with the large number of manufacturers who became involved in the political sphere which led to the passage of tariff laws that provided protection to the industry.

6

The Effect on the Economy

Before 1817, the basic American export product was flour, which was sent to the Caribbean. New England ship captains purchased molasses from the region, with which to buy manufactured goods from Europe and slaves from Africa. Caribbean slaveholders and New England merchants were the chief beneficiaries of this trade.

As trade rivalries between Britain and its former colony crumbled, events in England allowed British merchant bankers in the Anglo-American trade to succeed in the cotton trade. Formerly, these bankers invested in mining in South America, but as rumors of revolutionary violence, export bans, and explosions in silver mines in Peru surged through the British financial press, an English banking crash followed during the years 1824–1825.

But a few years after the Latin American mining crash, as Anglo-American trade grew, British bankers began to look at *North* American borrowers. In the aftermath of 1825 credit problems, the Anglo-American merchant houses this time looked to gain profits not from mining but from cotton. English firms like Baring and Brown had been trading in cotton for years and were now joined by newcomers Morrison, Cryder & Co.; Lizardi & Co.; Timothy Wiggin & Co.; and Thomas Wilson & Co. These banks and some others were referred to as the seven houses.

Safety now having become the objective, American cotton became the investment of choice rather than mining speculation—first because cotton exports from America were constantly growing and second because the gap between the price of raw cotton at an American dock and the price of the same cotton delivered to an English dock was large enough that lending money to cotton shippers seemed a predictable business.

While business was good for the seven houses in the cotton trade, they faced a competitor in Philadelphia. The Second Bank of the United States had proved tremendously capable after the 1819 panic and had also helped

America escape any fallout from the 1824–1825 bank problems in England. Like the seven houses, the Philadelphia banker Nicholas Biddle could see the value of bankrolling the import-export cotton trade. "Our great object," Biddle wrote in 1827, "is business men and business paper.... [W]e are obliged to keep every dollar we can in a state of activity."[1] President Monroe, believing Biddle to be a financial genius, made him the government's representative to the Second Bank of the United States.

Also in 1827, modeling his behavior on English banking practices, Biddle created something he called a "bank draft," a financial instrument that bore the stamp of the U.S. government. These bank drafts did not bear interest like English bills. But by treating the bank drafts as equivalent to bank notes, Biddle provided a financial instrument that was free from fee, making it desirable as a medium of payment. New financial instruments like the bank draft facilitated the movement of cotton from the American South to the north of Britain, doubling the import-export trade with Britain during Andrew Jackson's presidency. Biddle's drafts became more important because, with Jackson's war with the Bank of the United States, they provided a uniform currency that made inland trade, export, and import possible.

The delivery of New Orleans cotton was at the heart of cotton-based credit, the source of British lending, the source of American borrowing. And so New Orleans stood at the epicenter of the 1834 monetary contraction. "We are," declared Senator William Hendricks of Indiana, "in the hands of the New Orleans market, as the clay is in the hands of the potter. Accounts from that quarter are discouraging at present, and bode worse for the future. Bankruptcies unparalleled in number and extent, are spoken of in New Orleans, and the means of receiving and paying for our produce is believed not to be in existence there."[2] Other produce prices were tied to cotton prices as during boom times cotton planters devoted every acre to cotton, buying most of their food and materials from the North and West rather than producing them on the plantation. Flour, bacon, and clothing prices depended on stability in the cotton market with its bills of exchange and its bank drafts.

While the cotton boom plummeted in 1837 after reaching a zenith in 1836, it had been steaming forward since. Each year two-thirds of the entire cotton crop went to Great Britain.[3] Exports, declared the South Carolina planter and Senator James Henry Hammond, depended on the South: "The strength of a nation depends in a great measure upon its wealth, and the wealth of a nation, like that of a man, is to be estimated by its surplus production." And in 1857 the South was the nation's strongman. Of the $279 million worth of exports for 1857, Hammond declared, nearly $158 million came from the southern states. Indeed, southern exports in 1857 outstripped the entire nation's exports for any year before 1856.

The power of cotton was such that the South avoided the problems of the 1857 panic and was immune to criticism from the North: "No sir, you dare not make war on cotton. No power on earth dares make war upon it. Cotton is king." This attitude can be seen in Hammond's opinion on the 1857 panic:

> When the abuse of credit had destroyed credit and annihilated confidence, when thousands of the strongest commercial houses in the world were coming down, and hundreds of millions of dollars of supposed property evaporating in thin air, when you came to a dead lock, and revolutions were threatened, what brought you up? Fortunately for you it was the commencement of the cotton season, and we have poured in upon you one million six hundred thousand bales of cotton just at the crisis to save you from destruction.[4]

Hammond also went further concerning the importance of cotton. In addition to predicting southern secession, he was one of the southerners who proposed to separate the nation to create an empire around the natural center of the cotton market: New Orleans, at the mouth of the Mississippi River. This new free-trade, riverine civilization based on cotton would dominate the world.

At the planter level, the cotton economy was controlled by factorage. If the slave was in thrall to the planter, the planter was in thrall to the banker, called the factor or commission merchant, who was a combination moneylender and buying-selling agent. These men owned no land, planted no cotton, limited their risks and grew rich. The factorage system was an imported product. British factors acted as bankers and agents for their colonial clients. Recalling them, a writer for *De Bow's Review* said, "The principals of the mercantile houses resided in Great Britain, and junior partners conducted the business in Virginia. Some of these concerns branched out, like polypi, to the villages and court houses and some of them, also like polypi, consumed the substance of all that came within their grasp."

How did the Virginia planter fare under the factorage? One student of the system concluded that "no civilized people has been so badly paid for their labor as the planters of Virginia during the entire colonial era and for long years afterward."[5] When commercial cotton production began in the United States, planters at first used existing marketing organizations that dealt in the older staples of rice and tobacco. Commission merchants for these commodities now bought cotton outright or consigned it to London and so became cotton-marketing specialists. They initially lived in the seaport cities of Charleston and Savannah, but moved to Mobile and New Orleans as these cities became large-scale marketing centers.

The planter shipped his cotton to the factor, who sold it for a commission of 2.5 percent. But since the cotton was in his possession and prices often fluctuated widely, he often abused his agency relation to the planter by becoming both a buyer and a seller. In 1858, *Farmer and Planter* spoke out about this practice: "Many cotton *Factors* are also cotton *Speculators*, having an interest directly opposed to the interests of the planters and interior shippers. It behooves the latter to scan with a suspicious eye singular and improbable statements of estimates of the supply of cotton put forth by the former."[6] Because the planter lived far from the city and transportation was slow and difficult, the factor, a city resident, performed many services for him. He purchased items needed for the plantation and the planter's household: cloth, groceries, wines, etc. The factor charged these purchases to the planter at higher than market prices and then added his commission of 2.5 percent. Along with this profitable service, the factor also benefited by charging the planter for monies laid out for such items as costs of transportation of cotton, storage, insurance, drayage, weighing, sampling, and repairing cotton bales.

The factor was, above all, the planter's banker. The plantation system was a credit-capitalist enterprise that was basically speculative. It depended to a large extent upon items that had to be purchased rather than produced, often even food for man and beast. The system's expansion, calling for more and more lands and slaves, frequently acquired at high prices, made more and more credit necessary, which in these circumstances came to be widely used and abused.

Banks did not usually extend this credit. The antebellum South was not rich in banks and the banks that were there were not rich. They were usually located, moreover, not in the interior where cotton was grown, but in the seaports where cotton was marketed. Also, they engaged primarily in commercial banking rather than in financing cotton growers, so they financed planters only indirectly through the factors. Below is a typical letter from one of the largest commercial banks, Alexander Brown & Sons of Baltimore, to Mr. Charles Lippitt, a factor in Savannah, Georgia:

> Dear Sir   27 Oct 1835
>
> Annexed is rect for 60 Bales Cotton which please ship to Messrs Thad Phelps & Co New York with all the dispatch possible charging them with expenses—As you receive cheese from N York please ship them [*sic*] by such boats as you think will make the most speed and please use your best exertions to give them every dispatch practicable—
>
> Yrs
>
> W.B.
>
> N.B. The remaining 239 Bales went on board yesterday and I presume will leave here to day or Tomorrow
>
> W.B.

6. The Effect on the Economy

It was the factors then, who did the financing, lessening their exposure in numerous ways. One method was the taking of what amounted to a lien on the crops. Generally they charged whatever the traffic would bear, with their interest rates running between 8 and 30 percent per year. It was natural then that the planters would seek legislation for "cheap money" and just as natural that the factors should oppose it. The factor who made large profits from cotton granted credit to the planter on the condition that he grow nothing but cotton. Thus the factorage system, aside from the burdens that it laid upon the planter, had a profound societal result. It bound the planter to one-crop agriculture and held him in a form of cotton slavery.

But factorage was not all guaranteed profits. It was the factor's business to watch the cotton market and move in the right direction at the right time. The amount he earned in commissions depended substantially on how good his judgment was. If it were poor the planter could, and often did, change to a factor in whom he had more confidence. No one can read the correspondence of a cotton factor without becoming deeply aware of the competition among factors for the business of planters. Visits to the plantations in the back country, circular letters, a constant stream of price and market information, plus the hope—sometimes not realized—that goods and money advanced on credit would induce the planter to consign the cotton crop to him rather than a business rival, attest to the reality of competition. And competition sharpened the factor's need to make wise business decisions. A lesser result was that factor-marketing hampered the growth of interior markets and led to the concentration of wealth, power, and population in only a few major cities in the South.

The burdens of factorage, the dislike of commercial banks for cotton financing, the rapid expansion of cotton culture often accompanied by the making of quick fortunes, together with the speculation that has often marked the cotton economy came to a head in the 1830s when new cotton areas were being overwhelmed by an influx of new planters. Some were bankrupts. Some had exhausted their lands in other areas. Some were younger sons who arrived with a few slaves to get rich quickly in a new area. Others were planters who stayed home but established new plantations to be run by overseers or relatives.

The principal instrument of financing in this instance was state banks. Although they took different forms, they all had the same intent; namely, to relieve distressed farmers, planters, and landowners. What all these banks shared in common was the notion that the state should promote the general welfare and economic growth in the cotton regions. State-owned banks were principally organized to minimize the transfer of property when economic conditions demanded wholesale liquidation. Such liquidation would have been inefficient and would have imposed unnecessary hardship on a large fraction of the population. To the extent that hastily chartered relief banks forestalled inefficient liquidation, they served their purpose. Twenty years later all of them scattered over much of the cotton South had gone broke, requiring taxpayer bailouts. However, they were successful in that they reinflated local economies and allowed for an orderly disposal of property.

The most spectacular example of this was the Union Bank of Mississippi. Chartered in January 1837 with a capital stock of $15.5 million, it unfortunately opened at the start of the disastrous depression of 1837 and made loans to cotton speculators. By 1840 it was broke. In 1842, by vote of the people, the bank's bonds were repudiated. Those who had bought them in good faith, relying on the pledge of the state of Mississippi, got nothing. State banks in other parts of the South went broke in much the same manner as the Union Bank. A contemporary diarist, W.H. Willis of North Carolina, wrote about this situation:

> Speculation, speculation, has been making poor men rich and rich men princes. Men of no capital in three years have become wealthy and those of some have grown to hundreds of thousands. But as great as all the resources of Miss. and as valuable her lands, yet there were limits to both and these limits have been passed, lost sight of and forgotten as things having no existence.
>
> A revulsion has taken place and Miss. is ruined. Her rich men are poor and her poor men beggars. Millions and millions have been speculated on and gambled away by banking, by luxuries, and too much prosperity, until of all the states in the Union, she has become much the worst.
>
> We have seen hard times in North Carolina, hard times in the East, hard times everywhere, but Miss. exceeds them all. Some of the finest lands ... may now be had for comparatively nothing. Those that once commanded from $20 to $50 an acre, may now be bought for $3 or $5 ... while many that have been sold at sheriff's sales for 50 cents were considered worth $15 to $20.... So great is the panic and so dreadful the distress that there are a great many farms prepared to receive crops and some of them planted and yet deserted, not a human being to be found upon them.[7]

Finally, there were the plantation or property banks which made loans and issued bank notes on the basis of capital secured by mortgages on real estate. In short, behind the factor's credit to the planter was southern bank credit as well as New York mercantile credit. In one way or another the banks were involved in almost every transaction arising from the marketing of the cotton crop, especially southern banks because they were overwhelmingly agricultural lenders, either directly to planters, or indirectly to those who supplied the planters, i.e., the factors. The niche the property banks filled was shaped in large part by the fact that the South ran a substantial foreign export surplus, while the North ran a deficit.

6. The Effect on the Economy

When early in the nineteenth century cotton became the nation's chief export, a cotton-based cycle began. Each year with the coming to market of cotton in southern ports in October, merchants shipping cotton drew bills of exchange (orders drawn on buyers by sellers to pay in the future) on the foreign and northern purchasers of the cotton. These bills of exchange were then sold to banks, and the funds thus obtained were used to pay the southern planters who grew the cotton. The planters, in turn, used these funds to pay the factors. If a factor made advances on the crop in the form of a draft, the planter could discount it at a bank. Also if the factor received a bill of exchange from an English merchant to whom he had sold cotton, that bill could also be discounted at a local bank.[8] Normally the bank then sent the bill to New York for sale because that city was the importing center of the country and therefore the largest market for foreign bills of exchange.

Another facet of the cotton economy having to do with banks was that of having the banks purchasing cotton directly from the planters for the purpose of speculation. A report on the Bank of the United States made in 1841 stated, "In the course of this investigation, the attention of this committee has been directed to certain accounts, which appear on the books as 'Advances on Merchandise' but which were, in fact, payments for Cotton, purchased by direction of the then President, Mr. Nicholas Biddle, and shipped to Europe on account of himself and others."[9] The magnitude of this operation can be seen from this article from the *Financial Register* estimating the cotton stocks held by banks:

> The agents of the United States Bank here, Humphreys and Biddle, have an immense stock on hand and are daily receiving more.... [T]he principal holders of cotton here at present are as follows:
>
> | | |
> |---|---|
> | Humphreys and Biddle, | about 125,000 bales |
> | Brown and Company | 120,000 bales |
> | Baring Brothers | 55,000 bales |
> | Dennison | 50,000 bales |
>
> The whole stock on hand ... so say it reaches 500,000 bales. The Browns are the principal sellers—the other houses holding on as much as possible. Hereafter the American trade in cotton will be controlled by the three B's; the Biddles, the Barings, and the Browns.[10]

The transactions continued during the years 1837, 1838, and 1839 and amounted to about nine million dollars. Unfortunately for the Biddles and for the bank, the last shipments were unprofitable, losing about $960,000. There is little mention of this practice after 1839, probably due to losses and the sobering effects of the panic of that year.

The dominant position of the factors and the banks in cotton marketing have tended to obscure the roles of two itinerant merchants, the peddler and the speculator, in bringing the South's principal crop to market. To be sure, they were not independent of the factors to whom these traveling merchants sold their cotton. For the planter, however, they provided another market for his crop, and a description of their business activities can be justified on that basis alone. An analysis of their business helps to describe a changing southern economy. The earliest of these itinerant buyers, the peddlers, were the product of a scattered and exceedingly shallow market, served by the most rudimentary transportation facilities. They were well-known figures among backcountry folk; often the peddler was one of the few visitors these people saw and the news he bore as well as his goods were usually welcomed.[11] The lack of currency which often plagued the largely subsistence planters with whom he dealt did not prevent sales. The peddler frequently bartered his merchandise for farm commodities he would later sell in town.[12]

Cotton was the principal commodity taken in trade. In exchange the peddler offered a variety of wares often difficult for the isolated country folk to obtain. An English visitor to the South, Robert Sutcliff, in 1805, was told of riverboats on the Ohio River "fitted up with counters, shelves, and drawers, in the same manner as are shops on land, and well stored with all kinds of goods." At each stop the local people would gather about the boat to make their purchases. Payment would be primarily in cotton, and if not cotton, then other produce from the plantation.[13] When such facilities were available, peddlers in the South conducted their business much like the country storekeepers. They often distributed their goods on credit and then took payment in cotton at harvest time. After the first decades of the nineteenth century, the general merchandise peddler who took cotton in return for his wares became a rarer figure, although he never completely disappeared.[14]

Far more significant than the peddlers in the marketing of cotton was another group of itinerant merchants—the speculators, although not at the level of the bankers but at the local level. While they might buy on order for others, they more frequently made purchases for their own account, purchases often financed by factors who either provided them with cash or guaranteed their notes in local banks. Whatever the speculators' methods, their aim was usually profit through speculation. An example of how this type of peddler operated is informative. In the fall of 1858, W.H. Sims of La Grange wrote to Stephen Heard—a factor whose company, Heard & Simpson, was based in Augusta—that he and another man had "formed a partnership in the Grocery & Cotton business." His description of intent plainly indicated that Sims was more interested in cotton than in groceries. He did not plan to simply trade store goods for cotton, rather he expected to buy and speculate in the article:

"We intend to buy right & when it looks right take hold liberally, & when it does not have presence enough to keep out." Sims' purchases in the La Grange area would be resold in a number of markets including Augusta, and Heard & Simpson might have the opportunity to profit by the transactions if they were willing to invest with him. Additionally, Sims informed the Augusta factor that he was "anxious to make arrangements to make shipments to Heard & Simpson for all or most of my Augusta shipments." The "arrangements" he required involved financial backing. Heard & Simpson were to authorize the local bank "to take bills drawn by Sims," so that "we will then have no difficulty in getting the money we want." The money, of course, would be used to buy cotton.

The evidence describing the activities of these itinerant speculators is limited. It is ample enough, however, to warrant an assessment of the part they played in the marketing of cotton in the antebellum period. By gathering up scattered crops and sending them to another market for sale, they helped to extend the factorage system far into the interior. In doing so they not only facilitated the marketing of small amounts of cotton, but also provided the large grower with the opportunity for an immediate sale; planters who did not want to pay the cost or take the risk of a shipment to a more distant market could easily sell at home for cash "on the barrel." The itinerant merchants were therefore an adjunct to the cotton factorage system. They were clearly dependent on the cotton factors who financed them and sold their purchases. Ironically, however, the factors, by extending this credit, helped to destroy their own hegemony over the cotton trade in the South.

New York had a special role in the cotton trade. Manufactured goods, whether domestic or foreign, were apt to be sent to southern coastal cities by way of New York merchants, and substantial quantities of cotton were sent from southern ports to New York for transshipment. Additionally, cotton sent directly from the South to Europe was likely to be sent in a vessel owned by a New Yorker and insured by a New York firm. As numerous New York mercantile houses had branches or partners in southern cities, all the arrangements for cotton shipments were often made by New Yorkers. As a consequence, New Yorkers became another body that gained profits from cotton, and also collected the freight charges, insurance premiums, commissions, and handling charges arising from their participation.

As an example of an individual operating within this system, the following is part of the activities of William Bostwick, a commission merchant in the cotton trade whose business records have become available. Bostwick was typical of a large group of New Englanders and New Yorkers who settled in southern coastal and inland cities to seek their fortune in the cotton trade. Like other Factors, Bostwick dealt in cotton on his own account as well as that of others. In one instance he had a cargo of cotton shipped to Liverpool for sale on his own account. Valued at $8,000, the shipment made in May 1838 netted him a loss of $909. His records indicate that he did better when he sold his cotton in domestic markets. But his main earnings appear to have come in the form of commissions charged on cotton sales for the accounts of planters and country storekeepers and from profits on merchandise sold them, interest on credit advances, and charges on such services as storing cotton, receiving and forwarding merchandise and accepting drafts.

Bostwick's records reveal his connections with New York merchants, a number of whom supplied him with an almost incredibly large number of articles that he in turn sold to planters and shopkeepers. He appears to have made frequent annual trips to New York, apparently in late summer and fall, to buy goods in person, sometimes at auction, but mainly from mercantile firms. He paid for the merchandise mainly in cash, but also received credit for periods ranging from 4 to 10 months. After returning to the South, he continued his purchases, buying additional goods via letters to New York and other cities. His purchases cover such items as sugar, tea, nails, shirting, and buttons from New York; whiskey from Baltimore and Philadelphia; barrels of mackerel from Boston; and cheese from New Haven, among many more items from fellow merchants in the South. An idea of the scale of his operations is provided by his records, which show purchases from June 16, 1830, to April 1, 1833—a period of less than 3 years—amounting to $170,348.59.[15]

Bostwick's principal agent was Thaddeus Phelps, a New York commission merchant who dealt mainly in cotton but also other products. Bostwick summarized their relationship in 1841: "In my case, every bale of cotton that I have shipped to your market in the last ten years has been consigned to you. Every order I have had executed has been by you. Every draft I have drawn, in short every transaction in your city during that period upon which I have paid a commission has been with your self." The occasion for these remarks was discontent with Phelps's increase in the interest rate on his account, for he was in a fairly constant state of debt to New York, just as the planters were to him. He drew notes steadily against Phelps for purchases, chiefly from New York, and informed him every month of those about to mature. The following is a typical letter:

> Above I hand you check for $500, which please place to my credit. You will pay my 4 notes as they come to maturity in March as at foot. You may send me by Savannah 1000 lbs. bar lead in boxes or casks—the bars must be small, say about 3/4 of a pound each—one pound will not do—James McCullugh, Tucker &

Carter and James Kelso are the men I buy it of. The last I bot was at 6 months. Our cotton market continues to advance.[16]

Another aspect of the effect of cotton on the economy was its spread not only through the South but also into the West. In 1790, cotton growing was largely confined to a few islands off the coasts of South Carolina and Georgia. The invention of the cotton gin permitted the cultivation of short-staple cotton to move into the back country of Georgia and from there to South Carolina. For more than a quarter of a century this was the principal cotton producing region of the nation, as late as 1821, more than half of the of the entire cotton crop of the United States was grown in these two states.

Even with this concentration, the cotton belt was moving, first North into North Carolina and Virginia and then west over the mountains into Tennessee. Following the War of 1812, cotton moved again, this time to the Southwest, starting with Alabama then Mississippi and Louisiana, and eventually into Arkansas and Texas. By the mid 1820s, South Carolina and Georgia had begun to lose their original dominant position; by the time of the Civil War they accounted for less than a quarter of the nation's cotton output. Mississippi and Alabama had become the leading states with Louisiana not far behind. As an example of the impact on the economies of these states, New Orleans, the central point for cotton shipping in the West, received 37,000 bales in 1816, increasing to 161,000 in 1822, and 428,000 in 1830, and finally 923,000 in 1840. Expressed in terms of changing proportions, the states and territories from Alabama and Tennessee westward increased their share of the nation's total output of cotton from one-sixteenth in 1811 to one-third in 1820, one-half before 1830, nearly two-thirds in 1840, and three-fourths in 1860.

The primary reason for this shift to other cotton growing areas was that continuous farming of the same crop on the same piece of land eventually wore the land out. This situation was the same that tobacco farmers had experienced; when the soil lost its necessary nutrients, yields fell. Compared to Europe where fertile land was more finite, in the American West it was abundant and so became an inexpensive cost of production; it was capital and labor that were scarce. As a result, it was cheaper to move to a new location than devote resources to improving the productivity of the existing plantation. Below is a description of the result of this type of farming:

> The native soil of Middle Georgia is a rich argillaceous loam resting on a firm clay foundation. In some of the richer counties, nearly all the lands have been cut down, and appropriated to tillage; a large maximum of which have been worn out, leaving a desolate picture for the traveller to behold. Decaying tenements, red, old, hills, stripped of their native growth and virgin soil, and washed into deep gullies, with, here and there patches of Bermuda grass and stunted pine

shrubs, struggling for subsistence on what was once one of the richest soils in America.[17]

Equal to the "push" that sent the cotton farmers West was the "pull" that also produced this movement. In this case it was the lure of profits, not only from farming but also from the sale of improved cotton lands to those who would come in the next wave of settlers. This call of the West was sounded in promoters' publications, in private letters, and in newspaper reports of fabulous financial successes by the new settlers. While the newspaper stories were initially exaggerated, the Southwest turned out to be the source of the greatest profits in agriculture which the American people had ever enjoyed—because of cotton. The huge amount of fertile soil was suited to the cultivation of cotton. The numerous navigable rivers, coupled with the fact that cotton, having a large value in a small weight, could bear the expense of land transportation to the rivers from a long distance over poor roads. Also, when comparing the plantations in the Old South with those in the New South, not only were production costs lower but, since the New South was closer to the West, the costs of foodstuffs was less because of transportation.

The new settlements in the Southwest (comprising at the time Alabama, Arkansas, Mississippi, and Louisiana) became available because of the successful Indian campaigns of Andrew Jackson which opened up the fertile lands of the western half of Alabama in 1814. By 1818, the greater part of Arkansas, including a portion of northern Louisiana, fell to the planters. And while the Indian tribes for some years longer prevented cotton planters from moving into western Georgia, eastern Alabama, and much of eastern Mississippi, eventually cotton overcame the indigenous occupants of the entire area. To give an idea of the value of these lands, the historian Stuart Bruchey quotes a traveler's description of this cotton growing region:

> The plantations within these limits are superb beyond description. Some of them resemble villages. The dwelling houses of the planters are not inferior to any in the United States, either with respect to size, architecture, or the manner in which they are furnished. The gardens and yards contiguous to them, are formed and decorated with much taste. The cotton warehouses are very large and the buildings for the slaves are well finished. The latter buildings are, in some cases, forty or fifty in number, and each of them will accommodate ten or twelve persons. The planters here derive immense profits from the cultivation of their estates. The yearly income from them is from 20,000 to 30,000 dollars.[18]

Unfortunately, these scenes were few and far between:

> [C]omparatively little of the money drawn for the cotton crop is spent in the Southern States. Many of the planters spend their incomes by traveling with their families in the Northern States or in Europe during the summer, and a large sum

6. The Effect on the Economy

is required to pay the hog-raiser in Ohio, the mule breeder in Kentucky and, above all, the northern capitalists, who have vast sums of money on mortgage over the estates. Dr. Cloud, the editor of the "Cotton Plant," assured me that after these items are paid out of the money received for the whole cotton crop of the South, there did not remain one-fourth part of it to be spent in the Southern States.[19]

Although by 1840 the main outlines of the "Cotton Kingdom" were filled in, except in Texas, the stream of new planters continued to pour into the newer regions not yet well settled. By 1836, planters began to move into Texas in large numbers. By the 1850s, regular steamship connection with New Orleans had been accomplished. From 1840 to the outbreak of the Civil War, and, particularly from 1840 to 1850, the "Texas fever" developed almost into a delirium. Newspapers throughout the South were full of accounts of the wonderful fertility of Texas land, the moderate climate, and the enormous fortunes made in planting cotton. Texas land companies were formed in various parts of the United States, and land speculation, facilitated by the loose land policy of the state, became the order of the day. Throughout the South thousands of planters caught the contagion, sold their plantations and moved to Texas. From 1850 to 1860, total cotton production increased from 58,072 to 431,463 bales. The newly opened areas in the Southwest followed the pattern of the Southeast in planting as much land as possible in cotton, resulting in a trading connection with the Old Northwest (Ohio, Indiana, Illinois, and Michigan) for their needed foodstuffs. Also as with the South, manufactured products for the Southwest were imported from the North. Cotton, because it could be grown only in the South, therefore brought into being an economy made up of three interdependent regions: East, West and South. It was also the only region that could produce the goods from the three areas: its cotton; foodstuffs, since each plantation devoted some land to products such as corn, garden vegetables, and oats; and household manufacturing.

The influence of the cotton culture upon the North was not confined to the agriculture of the Northwest. It affected every other northern interest as well. The prosperity which cotton brought to the whole southern and western population increased the inhabitants abilities to purchase manufactured products and thus provided eastern manufacturers with a rapidly expanding market. Because of this, the internal trade of the country became important, trade that opened new opportunities for the merchant, the banker, the ship owner, the insurance company—in short, the whole commercial class.

The effect of all these changes upon the economic condition of the country was almost revolutionary. It opened the eyes of the populace to the economic possibilities of their situation and turned their attention for the first time to the exploitation of their natural resources. They could gain more use from cotton, for example, than was ever possible with crops such as tobacco, rice, and sugar. The enterprise and the capital of the country found a new field for its operation in addition to the ocean and foreign commerce. One of the most striking features of this new period was the increase in speculative activity everywhere in American industry. This was largely the result of the enormous increase in land values.

The choice cotton lands of the Southwest suddenly became immensely valuable. And because of the needs of the new cotton growers, farm produce in the North and Northwest more than doubled in value; and the value of the land in those areas rose correspondingly. From New York State in the East to New Orleans in the West, new towns were springing up along the lines of trade, and old ones were growing with a rapidity that was new in American experience. Two quotes from an early 19th century historian, Guy S. Callender, illustrate the diversity of products from the sections of the nation. He first quoted "Russell," a foreign visitor, who said, "The bacon is almost entirely imported from the Northern states, as well as a considerable quantity of Indian Corn." "Christy," a southerner, emphasized the solidarity of western and southern commercial interests and commented in a like vein: "The West ... had its attention now [after 1815] turned to the South, as the most certain and convenient mart for the sale of its products—the planters affording to the farmers the markets they had in vain sought from the manufacturers."[20]

This interrelation between the sections of the nation was never placid. By the 1850s, emigration from the East westward began to fill the states of Iowa, Minnesota, Kansas, and Nebraska, increasing the demand for foodstuffs. This demand coupled with exports increased prices beyond what the cotton planter could afford to pay. Correspondingly, the demand for cotton was increasing, forcing the planters to increase production or possibly lose markets to other nations such as India. This increased production meant an increase in the number of slaves who had to be supplied with provisions. If the planters grew their own provisions, they would have been unable to produce cotton for export and forced to depend on the North.

As the planters produced more and more cotton, the product gained control of another entity, this time a city—New Orleans. With the increased production came increased credit. New Orleans was overflowing with money in these flush times and lent it regularly. The credit system was now universal among the cotton planters and New Orleans became not only the lender of money at high interest rates but the depot of western supplies. New Orleans advanced credit in large amounts to the planters throughout the vast area that had river traffic ending in the city. The whole agricultural country along the

6. *The Effect on the Economy* 109

Drying cotton at a cotton warehouse in Charleston, South Carolina, ca. 1879 (Library of Congress, Prints & Photographs Division, LC-DIG-ds–01186).

lower Mississippi and its bayous and streams became, in a manner, the commercial slaves of the New Orleans factors. The western products such as corn, hogs, bacon, pork, wheat, and flour shipped down the river never stopped at the plantations, but was sent directly to New Orleans and from there transshipped up the river over the same route it had just traversed. As an example of the city's financial strength, when the Panic of 1837 came, the banks lost $7,000,000 of their capital of $34,000,000 but recovered so quickly that within a few years they had secured an even tighter hold on the planters.

Because of this immense river traffic fueled by cotton, New Orleans became confident of its future to the point that it was predicted not only in American newspapers but also in the *British Quarterly Review* that it must ultimately become the most important commercial city in America, if not in the world. *De Bow's Review* declared that "no city of the world has ever advanced as a mart of commerce with such gigantic and rapid strides as New Orleans."[21] This was no idle boast. Between 1830 and 1840, no city of the United States kept pace with New Orleans. When the census was taken, it was fourth in population, exceeded only by New York, Philadelphia, and Baltimore, and also fourth in amount of commerce of the port cities of the world behind London, Liverpool, and New York. The importance of New Orleans continued even after cities in the West such as Pittsburg and Cincinnati became important manufacturing centers. There was still no trade between these cities and the plantations; the commerce still went through New Orleans and would until after the Civil War when the railroads would cut into the river traffic.

Cotton also had an impact on investment in human capital, which was conspicuously lower in the South than in the North or the West. While the slaveholding states in 1850 had slightly less than half of the white population of the northern states (6.1 million compared to 13.2 million), they had less than one-third as many public schools, one-fourth as many pupils, one-twentieth as many public libraries, and one-sixth as many volumes in those libraries. It should be noted, moreover, that Maryland, Delaware, Kentucky, and Missouri are all included in these figures as they were slaveholding states and all were far higher than the southern average. Had they been excluded, and the policy ratio adjusted accordingly, the poorer educational investment in the South would have been even more striking.[22] Clearly, the structure of the southern economy played a critical role in the South's policy toward education. The concentration on cotton production, and the very unequal distribution of income were important factors. Even more significant were the attitudes of the dominant planter class, who could see little return in educational investment. Expenditures to educate the large percentage of white southerners who were outside the plantation system was something they vigorously opposed.

During the period 1850–1860, the increase in cotton production was greater than the increase over the entire previous century. Moreover, the rate of increase in cotton production accelerated as the decade wore on. Between 1857 and 1860 alone, cotton production increased by 1,500,000 bales. This spectacular rise was more than had been achieved during the four decades stretching from Whitney's invention of the cotton gin to the close of the Jackson administration. Fortunately for the South, this increase in production did not cause a significant decrease in the price of cotton as the output of cotton cloth by the manufacturers also increased due to a decrease in the price of the cloth over time as a result of improvements in the factory system. There were, however, slight declines in the price of raw cotton over the long term because of a steady increase in cotton productivity. Beginning with the first plantings of cotton in America there have been improvements in the varieties of seeds, the introduction of the cotton gin, the reduction in transportation and other marketing costs, and the relocation of production to the more fertile lands of the New South.

The key to examining the economics of cotton production is not the absolute level of prices but the level of profits. The 1850s constituted a sustained boom in profits for cotton planters. It was an era that outstripped the

1830s. Nearly every year of the decade was one of above normal profit. What is more, profits remained high during the last four years of the decade, with prices averaging 15 percent higher than usual, which is why cotton production rose so dramatically. If the planters erred, it was not in expanding cotton production by too much. Quite the contrary—they were too conservative. So it was not only the demand for cotton that caused the price to rise, but also because the planters did not increase their output rapidly enough to return cotton prices to a normal level.[23]

To ascertain the total economic effect of cotton on the nation during the antebellum period, there must be an explanation of the fact that there was a 25 percent gap in the level of per capita income between the North and South. Did this mean that the South was poor and the North rich? The answer is that the incomes in the North were extraordinarily high because the South was rich itself during the antebellum period. If we treat the South as a separate nation, it would have stood as the fourth richest nation on earth in 1860, richer than any nation in Europe with the exception of England. Also, the South was not a "colonial dependency" because of its large purchases of manufactured goods from the North, which purchased large amounts of railroad equipment from England. While the economic state of the South, fueled by cotton, was real, it seems to be the reverse because of the actions of southerners who became impatient with what they thought was an insufficient active role by their state governments to promote internal improvements that would accelerate the southern rate of economic growth.

While the immigration of people and particularly capital into the United States played an important part in the nation's growth during the antebellum period, it was the growth of the cotton textile industry and the demand for cotton which was decisive. In 1815 the previous sources of expansion, the re-export and carrying trade and manufacturers, were declining as a result of peacetime competition. The West was still largely unintegrated into the national economy. The United States was left with only cotton as the major expansive force. The vicissitudes of the cotton trade—the speculative expansion of 1818, the radical decline in prices in the 1820s, the booms in the 1830s and 1850s—were the most important influences upon the varying rates of growth of the economy during the period. Cotton was strategic because it was the major independent variable in the interdependent structure of internal and external trade. The demands for western foodstuffs and northern services and manufacturers were basically dependent upon the income received from the cotton trade.[24]

The transporting of cotton will be covered more fully in another chapter, but transportation is part of the overall financial aspect of the crop and its trade. The very nature of the cotton trade made it an article of speculation. In 1825, the world's foremost cotton trader, Jeremiah Thompson, and his Liverpool associates, the house of Cropper, Benson & Company, became involved in that year's cotton boom. At the end of 1824, it was announced that the stock of cotton on hand in Liverpool was about one-third less than usual and consequently prices rose rapidly. Cropper, Benson and a few other Liverpool traders decided to gather all the American cotton that was available, thereby achieving a corner on the market and driving cotton prices still higher. When the news reached New York by packet boat a few weeks later, a similar boom resulted. Thompson dispatched a fast pilot boat to New Orleans with word to his agents to buy up as much cotton as possible. One of the coastal packets owned by John W. Russell beat the pilot boat however, which allowed him to make heavy advance profits by buying in the still normal market. By the middle of April, the market began to crack in Liverpool when a Scottish firm threw a small amount of cotton on the market at a reduced price. On top of that an unexpectedly large amount of Brazilian cotton arrived in Liverpool, further skewing the calculations of the speculators. Because of this, cotton prices tumbled in England but continued at an abnormally high level in New York, where American speculators were buying as much cotton as they could get from the South. When the next ocean packet arrived in May, cotton prices collapsed in New York also, but they were still high in New Orleans until the news reached the South in midsummer, by which time cotton prices had become prostrate everywhere, leaving a trail of failures in its wake. Afterwards, from time to time, other speculative attempts were made to corner the market—particularly the ambitious but unsuccessful scheme of Nicholas Biddle in the next decade—but none reached the magnitude of the 1825 boom.

By the mid 1850s, a change took place in the shipments of cotton by the speculators. Its principal feature was a sharp drop in the amount of cotton sent from the South to New York. They instead shipped it directly to Europe, while sending to New York only the bills of lading and samples and thereby saving the added charges of freight and handling. The first annual report of the Chamber of Commerce of the State of New York called attention to this trade in 1859:

> In discussing the cotton trade of New York, it must not be forgotten that the import of cotton from the Southern States has been materially diminished by the mode of selling cotton at this port by sample, while on its way from Southern ports to Europe—especially to Liverpool—or, as the phrase is, "in transit."
>
> This mode of conducting the more speculative portion of the cotton trade only began to be commonly resorted to four or five years ago, and has been constantly on the increase since. There has always been a class of adventurers who

wished to have the option of terminating their operations by a sale in New York. A few years ago, this class—a very important one in moving the cotton crop—ordered the cotton to be shipped to New York; but this necessarily involved double freights, insurances, and expenses on the cotton with only the small advantage of selling for home consumption. Now, however, the plan is to ship the cotton direct to Liverpool, from the Southern port, and to send the samples and bills of lading to New York, where it can be sold, if the adventurer is unwilling to take the risk of the Liverpool market.[25]

A different area to become involved in the cotton trade was the territory, and later the state, of Texas. In the early stages of its economic development, cotton marketing depended largely on credit from abroad and barter at home. The planters had come to Texas to obtain cheap and fertile soil for growing cotton as a money crop. Not far behind them came the merchants, the middlemen who were to play a vital role in this underdeveloped land. The bankers, however, did not come as raw land on a distant frontier did not interest them. Undaunted by their lack of money, the planters and merchants resorted to transactions based on the exchange of commodities rather than on money, the planter supplying the cotton while the merchant imported goods to be traded for the planter's cotton. Consequently, a barter-credit system prevailed for almost a generation. Clumsy at best, the system proved costly in a land on the fringes of civilization with long distances, uncertain transportation and inadequate communication.

The first area to be planted was East Texas, which was, and remained, an area of small planters and limited production. Beginning in the 1820s its merchants and farmers linked themselves with the cotton factors and commission agents in New Orleans. This situation continued until the Republic of Texas was established. Even though the planters and merchants now had their own government, its currency had an extremely low value and purchasing power so that barter was still a way of life. It now, however, had two mercantile houses, McKinney & Williams and R. and D.G. Mills, which provided some banking services. To the northern and European textile factories that used its cotton, Texas was still a foreign country, but as a republic it now had a new status.[26]

By 1838, the competition between the two merchant companies, McKinney and Mills, over buying the cotton was becoming extremely heated. When Mills found out that McKinney had arranged to have an English ship sail to Texas to pick up cotton, he attempted to discredit McKinney, who wrote to his partner Williams about the situation:

> Mills has made a devil of a splash about our Liverpool vessel and tells the planters it is all humbug and tries to discredit our money which was sent out [.] Damn him I will give him a dose that will sicken him in a day or two [;] I am going

down to hurry up the cotton & will be ready for the Ambassador [.] I am in fine spirits and will keep So in relation to our business....

Give yourself no uneasiness about the Barque. She Shall go off speedily and satisfied.[27]

When the *Ambassador* arrived, Williams wrote to the historian Anson Jones:

I have the pleasure to announce to you the safe arrival in Galveston harbor of the English barque Ambassador, and some pride in saying that this is the vessel which has sailed from Europe direct to Texas, and without doubt will be the first to convey a cargo from Texas to Great Britain, which I expect will form an item among the numerous crimes which I have committed, and the innumerable evils with which I have inflicted the country. It is probably well for a man to be notorious for something—and if not for good, why for evil. The Ambassador was towed into port on the 25th of February, by the steam packet Columbia. Gen. Houston, and all the *big* men of Galveston went out and escorted her in, and made quite a frolic of it.[28]

Bringing the *Ambassador* to Texas was a triumph for McKinney & Company. This was a shipment from the new nation's (Texas) cotton market directly to a manufacturing center of another nation (Liverpool, England) and bypassed the cotton mart of the third nation (New Orleans, United States) through which the cotton customarily passed. For the planters this move was profitable. They realized from 1 to 2 cents more a pound in Liverpool than they would have made in New Orleans, "besides getting clear of the multitudinous shaving charges of the New Orleans commission houses." The experience impressed strongly upon McKinney the need for a bank in Texas, particularly if the firm sold the English goods quickly and profitably and if he cornered the cotton market in his area of Texas.[29] Within a year the *Telegraph and Texas Register* was reporting that "five or six vessels were freighting in England for the port of Galveston."[30] Not only did the English sends ships but their merchants also sent traders. In 1845, however, when Texas joined the union, it lost status. Foreign representatives were no longer stationed in Texas. Few foreign vessels came to her ports to pick up cotton.

During the final years of the republic, transportation by steamboat, which had initially been successful, was now almost nonexistent. The *Telegraph* reported that so many steamboats had been wrecked that only one boat was plying Texas rivers. From the 1820s onward Texans had utilized the major rivers from the Red River to the Rio Grande to move themselves and their cotton, but periodic low water, sand bars, and rafts of logs and brush made transportation highly unreliable. Moving supplies and cotton on Texas roads, which became quagmires in wet weather, was simply too slow and expensive. Thus, as the cotton farmer advanced inland, the movement of crops and supplies, never an easy matter, became increasingly difficult. Railroads offered a solution, but not without huge financial difficulties.

Railroad promoters, faced with a difficult task and armed with arguments about the obvious importance of improved transportation in Texas, insisted that the state, which chartered the state's first railroad in 1850, should subsidize construction. Their efforts to gain public aid to construct railroads focused on obtaining land grants and using the federal government bonds acquired in the settlement of the New Mexico boundary as a basis for the loans. Even with this aid, railroad building was a slow process in antebellum Texas; however, by 1860 the state had approximately 400 miles of operating railroad, almost all of it radiating from Houston.

By the advent of the Civil War, Texas cotton joined the Southeast as suppliers of cotton to the industrial areas of the United States and foreign lands. Such expansion could not have occurred without the activities, the optimism and gambles, the profits and losses of the cotton merchants.[31] Also, the state's economy mirrored that of the Deep South. A majority of Texans lived as small nonslaveholding farmers, but plantation cotton produced the state's wealth and provided its economic leaders.

Naturally, all the various businessmen of the South watched the cotton market attentively, but there were other variables they also had to monitor. The antebellum era was one of wild economic mood swings. The booming 1830s, fueled by cheap land prices and rising cotton profits, were followed by the major depression of 1837, when cotton prices fell precipitously and continued downward through 1842. Money that had formerly flowed into the South to pay for cotton no longer compensated for southern debts to the North. Cotton merchants found themselves ensnared by a depreciating currency with which to repay their increasing indebtedness.

A well-to-do planter in Columbus, Georgia, wrote in 1841 that "the few who have any credit can only return it by not attempting to use it." His friends were, "in the fashionable language of the day ... 'used up' ... They may recover but for my life I can't see how." He learned that things were just as bad on the Alabama side of the river, where the people of Henry County formally asked the sheriff to resign because he had auctioned off farms to meet creditor demands. A year later a Marianna, Florida, man declared, "Certainly ... there never was such a time of suffering for the want of money as now exists."[32] Those businessmen who weathered this great depression faced a new set of conditions in the last fifteen years of the antebellum period. The late 1840s and 1850s were again a time of phenomenal growth in which cotton prices rebounded and continued to rise. Only the brief panic of 1857 disturbed the South's prosperity in this last decade before the Civil War.

Juxtaposed against this fluctuating national economy was an equally volatile media of exchange. By modern standards, the monetary conditions of the nation during the antebellum period were deplorable, and because of them, normal business transactions were complicated and cumbersome. In the absence of a uniform currency provided by the federal government, every local economy had a distinctive currency which originated from scores of businessmen who held disparate assets—and consciences. Nevertheless, southern antebellum businessmen adapted to the particular monetary problems they encountered and, given the challenges they faced, were remarkably successful.[33]

7

Mills in the North

In 1800, Fall River, Massachusetts, was a village of less than one hundred inhabitants; by 1845 it had become a factory town of about 9,000 persons, with its mills employing 2,000 workers. This change was part of the larger shift in which commerce was being replaced by manufacturing as the dominant interest in New England. After the War of 1812, the maritime and commercial interests recovered slowly from the virtual stagnation of the carrying trade during the preceding five years. Although the tonnage of vessels owned in Massachusetts doubled between 1810 and 1850, this expansion was overshadowed by the rise of the cotton industry. In 1810, Albert Gallatin, then secretary of the treasury, reported that the cotton mills of the country, mostly concentrated in New England, contained 80,000 spindles and represented a capital investment of $4,800,000.[1] By 1840, there were 1,700,000 spindles in New England alone, representing a capital investment of $34,931,000, of which $17,414,000 was in Massachusetts.[2] With this expansion came a change in the position of the New England congressional delegation, from a free trade position in 1824 to one of protection in 1828.

This shifting from commerce to industry was accompanied by changes in the area's economic activity. Many of the coastal centers noted for their maritime activity declined in relative and absolute importance, while towns, and later cities, mushroomed beside the waterfalls of New England streams. This geographic relocation by no means severed the connection between the two economies. To industry, commerce contributed three basic elements: capital, entrepreneurial ability, and the mechanical skills of the inventors and artisans.

The first successful beginnings of the cotton industry occurred during a period of prosperity and rapid expansion in New England textile manufacturing. Between 1812 and 1814, sixty-two mills were built in New England, of which thirty-four were in Massachusetts. In the fall of 1814, however, there occurred financial problems in several of the major commercial centers followed by the flood of imported textiles after the peace of 1815. Most of the small spinning mills in southern New England were forced to close, many of them permanently. Expansion was greatly reduced: eleven mills were built in 1815 and only fourteen during the next four years.[3]

This was also a period of marked technical and organizational change in the infant industry and survival of a given plant was in large measure predicated upon successful adaptation to these changes. The development of the power loom was the key to these new trends. The success of the Boston Company started at Waltham in 1814 demonstrated the feasibility of this improvement and presaged the emergence of a "new form" which was to characterize the industry in the succeeding periods of expansion. Weaving techniques had caught up with spinning, and power spinning and power weaving could now be carried out in the same plant. This made possible the economies of large-scale production, which called for larger plants, more capital, and increased specialization in production and marketing. Joint stock companies became the prevailing type of organization and the production of textile machinery started to develop as a separate industry.

Locational as well as organizational changes occurred. Now for the first time, use could be made of the larger waterpower sites in New England, which provided the power necessary for the operation of the larger quantities of machinery and for large monetary investments. While expansion continued in the older centers of southern New England, the major growth during the next thirty years took place along the larger streams to the north. The Lowell works emerged as an example of this "new form" mill. The contributions necessary to turn a waterpower site into a factory town follow:

Technical Skill: The varied activities of commerce, boat building, operation of grist and sawmills and even agriculture provided a local training ground where several of the leading first generation cotton manufacturers received their early experience. Technical skill and familiarity with cotton machinery was even more necessary for success than general business experience and ability because this was the period of rapid technological growth. Although outside technicians were needed increasingly as the size and numbers of the cotton mills expanded, local men were more important during the industry's first three decades.

Labor Supply: Fall River is an example of this requirement. While, as previously stated, the population of the town increased from

100 persons in 1800 to 9,000 by 1840, the original population actually *decreased*. At first the mill's labor force was American: "in 1826 of the 612 total workers in Fall River, only 38 were foreigners, 28 of whom were employed in a printing company."[4] By 1842, however, Fall River citizens, in a petition to the legislature, complained that domestic labor could not compete with new cheap foreign labor with its low standard of living.[5] These immigrants were probably from England and Ireland and they marked the beginning of several waves of immigrants which flooded into Fall River during the rest of the century.

Capital: In the South, the necessary funds needed for the erection of a cotton mill basically came from the planter class. In the North, during the antebellum period, the situation was far more fluid. Capital for mill construction was supplied by a wide range of lenders: commercial banks, savings banks, trust companies, insurance companies, private individuals, and business concerns (including cotton mercantile firms and manufacturing companies), which gave the area a huge advantage over the small number of cotton mill financiers in the South.

Ordinarily most textile credit was obtained from institutional sources in Boston; however, when it became difficult to obtain funds in that city; the mill owners did not hesitate to turn to other areas and to noninstitutional sources. Since the Massachusetts market operated under the terms of a 6 percent usury law[6] (a law that appears to have been fairly well observed, at least by the major intuitional lenders, until the mid 1850s) and since during most of the period the rate charged by unregulated lenders appears to have been very close to or in excess of 6 percent, the cotton mills frequently found it advantageous to tap the New York money market, where less stringent interest limitations existed. Also in Massachusetts, the greatest suppliers of long-term credit were the institutional lenders—particularly the savings banks and the trust companies—and these institutions were prohibited by law from lending to persons or corporations outside the commonwealth.

The most interesting group of lenders to the cotton mills were the cotton mercantile houses.[7] While these companies supplied a significant portion of the mills' credit in good and lean times, their greatest lending activity was concentrated most heavily in periods when the mills experienced difficulty in borrowing elsewhere. The willingness of the mercantile houses to supply the mills' needs is not overly surprising. The houses' profits depended upon a continuous supply of cotton products. Moreover, the interest charged was at times in excess of the legal limit. As an example, although by 1857 the usury law was ignored by many lenders, some banks (particularly in Boston) still chose to obey. Thus as credit began to tighten in response to the deteriorating business conditions during that year, these banks, unable to increase their interest charges, began to reduce the maturities of their loans, and in several cases, to cease making loans altogether. To fill the gap, the mills turned to the mercantile houses for additional money.

The six cotton mills that were erected in Fall River completely changed the demographics of the area. This industrial development provided the necessary incentive and funds to overcome the transportation difficulties that had interfered with Fall River's earlier growth, which now included new roads, bridges, and a turnpike. Not only did these changes benefit the town in general, it also connected it with the harbor, which was improved with new wharves and piers and thus allowed raw cotton to reach the mills and the finished products to leave them quickly and efficiently. Additionally, with this increase in traffic and the establishment of regular freighter service to Providence and New York, Fall River became the leading port in the area, to which the customs house was moved in 1834 and where the railroad from Boston terminated in 1846.

The importance of New York City has been covered as part of the "cotton triangle." The following is how New England and especially Fall River fit into this orbit. Since 1815, New York had been the chief center for the distribution of imported cotton products, and, as the years passed, buyers from interior points began to find it inconvenient to make the additional journey to Boston to purchase the product of the New England mills.[8] As late as 1850, however, New York was distinctly of secondary importance as a market for domestic goods with only four large jobbing houses in the cotton trade. After 1850 the great increase in demand for domestic textiles was accompanied by a spectacular rise in the importance of New York as a selling market. By 1860, there were at least thirty jobbing houses of national importance in New York in addition to the branch offices which New England manufactures and merchants had found it expedient to establish there.[9]

Under these circumstances a location convenient to New York became an additional consideration for the textile manufacturer. By means of a cargo ship, textiles leaving the cotton mills at Fall River in the late afternoon could be delivered the next morning to lower Manhattan, near the textile merchandising and garment districts. Only a few mills could equal the speed, ease, and cheapness with witch Fall River cotton products could be delivered to New York. This did not escape the notice of the *New York Tribune*, which commented: "The fact that [Fall River] has direct water communication with New

York and that it is the terminus of a large steamboat line is of much advantage in furnishing ample facilities for shipment."[10] The following advertisement for the sale of the Troy Cotton Mill, which was experiencing temporary financial difficulties in 1827, gives an idea of the commercial advantages of Fall River after its development:

> To those who wish to engage in manufacturing, this establishment holds out peculiar inducements. It is situated on one of the most lasting streams in New England. The reservoir by which it is supplied contains an area of about four thousand acres. The surrounding country abounds in such kinds of laborers as are wanted in the manufacturing business. And its nearness to the waters of Narraganset Bay, gives it many advantages over more inland establishments.[11]

The first thirty years of Fall River's industrial history are an example of the transition that cotton caused in the New England economy. Influenced by a unique combination of geographic conditions, the new economy evolved within the orbit of the old. Aided by these conditions, the local capitalists and technicians were able to take the initiative in developing the waterpower sites that were available. By 1845, these entrepreneurs had developed a factory town for cotton manufacturing.

While Fall River made an important imprint on the production of cotton in the United States, the character of textile manufacturing in the nation was formed by Francis Cabot Lowell, although he never lived to see it. His group, the Boston Associates, not only established the textile industry in New England, but also set the pattern of industrialization for others in the country to follow. The pattern was that of a large plant containing the total process of manufacturing from raw cotton to finished product. It succeeded because of the combination of large capitalization, professional management, production of cheap goods in quantity, and protection by government tariffs. These were not all of Lowell's design but reflected his genius.

While Fall River depended on the local community and immigrants for its workers, the Boston Associates had determined as a matter of policy to avoid creating another industrial slum like Manchester, England. There probably was some altruism in this decision, but, on a more practical level, the decisive factor was to create a loyal and sufficient work force. In order to accomplish this the Boston Associates hoped to attract the daughters of New England farmers to work in their mills. In order to attract the women, and even more to allay the fears of their parents, the associates planned and built handsome, substantial, and clean brick boardinghouses where the operatives could be housed in relative comfort and with moral safety. These boardinghouses were to be the trademark of this new type of industry and were copied by all the subsequent textile communities.

On March 1, 1826, Lowell was formally incorporated as a town with a population of twenty-five hundred. The profits from the production of cotton had created the Lowell Experiment, which grew and developed so rapidly that much of the early careful planning was trampled underfoot by boomtown economy and psychology. As an example, by 1845, the Merrimack Company, another of the Boston Associates' companies, ran 5 cotton mills and 155 boardinghouses for its workers.

As in all the new industrial cities, the Lowell companies paid low wages. In relation to what women could earn in the early nineteenth century, the mill girls did fairly well, certainly better than their counterparts in the English textile factories; but on an absolute scale, the wages were low. In the early years the Lowell companies paid unskilled labor between $1.50 and $2 per week above the fee for room and board, which averaged between $1.25 and $1.50 and was deducted from the wages. Also, the hours were long, even for young workers.

Despite the low wages, the workers were frugal. The mill girls entered the workforce for specific reasons: to accumulate a dowry, to put a brother through school, or to pay off a family mortgage. Whatever the reason, cotton was the basis of their income. In response to the workers' desire to save, as early as 1827 the Hamilton Company began holding their savings, issuing bank books, and paying interest. The company had no state charter for this activity, which was of questionable legality. In the South, the banks were investors in and suppliers of credit for cotton selling activity. In New England, they were needed to supply a form of investment for, the workers and so in 1829, the Lowell Institution for Savings accepted its first deposit. The companies' and Lowell's leading citizens who sat on its board had created a bank that had supplied the mill girl's needs and also created one of the city's most durable institutions.

In the 1840s, the cotton market decline that disrupted the rest of the nation also caused problems in the New England mills. The decline affected the mill girls in a way that would later come to haunt the mill owners: the advent of unions. In order to avoid paying lower dividends on the company's stock, the mill owners began to exploit the labor force. Wages were cut about 10 percent for the skilled weavers and up to 20 percent for the unskilled. The companies also tried to increase profit margins by speeding up the machinery and by increasing the number of machines each worker tended. Perhaps the most demoralizing of the mill's innovations was the hated premium system, which granted bonuses to overseers who succeeded in getting more work out of the operatives than was expected. Because it changed the whole relationship between the girls and the overseers from one of general informality and congeniality to one of rivalry and antagonism, this system probably contributed more than any single factor to the demise of the mill girls as a labor force.

For years, the existence of the famous mill girls had aided the mills in selling their cotton products, justifying their profits, and improving their own social image. As one author asked rhetorically, "If a Lucy Larcom[12] read Milton and translated Schiller after a long day in front of the machines, did it not follow that a Nathan Appleton was a sage, a man of honor, and a public benefactor?"[13] Under the premium system, overseers became tyrannical and hard driving and the girls resentful and suspicious. Such conditions, combined with a growing influx of Irish workers fleeing famine conditions in Ireland in the 1840s and 1850s and the failure of the mill workers in Massachusetts to win passage of a ten-hour bill in the legislature, effectively closed one of the brightest chapters in the early history of cotton manufacturing in the United States. The strained relationship with the labor force might have been avoided had the mill owners been more farsighted. However, despite such problems, by 1856 Lowell had become a city and the mills now had 400,000 spindles and 12,000 looms that consumed 36 million pounds of cotton per year.

The fortunes that cotton had brought to New England and to the factory owners in Lowell did not extend to the city and its inhabitants. Twenty years after its founding Lowell began to change. Some areas of the city were congested and the slums were spreading. Company management began to be challenged on the one hand by dissident stockholders complaining of mismanagement and lower dividends, and on the other by less submissive workers, who had begun to rise up against constantly increasing pressures to increase production combined with lower wage scales. Even the rooms in the corporation's boardinghouses had become more crowded in the 1840s than they had been in the 1820s and 1830s. It was small compensation that the women spent less time in these rooms because they worked more hours in the factory. By 1841, the workday was fifteen minutes longer than it had been in 1829. Lowell, which had been a model of working conditions for other parts of the world, now suffered in comparison.

Lacking a heritage of wealth or tradition and depending on the success of manufacturing products from cotton for its very existence, Lowell could not admit to failures, setbacks, or faults. In many respects, the successes were real and worthy of acclaim. Economically the mills were a success. Any city would have been proud of Francis Cabot Lowell and his partner, Nathan Appleton, who first realized the possibilities of using cotton to create the modern corporation for large-scale manufacture. The early Lowell entrepreneurs were truly men of ingenuity and ability. They deserved much credit and they were not reluctant to take it. In a letter to the Middlesex Mechanics Association, Appleton wrote:

> I certainly look back with satisfaction upon the part which I have had in leading to this result [the successful establishment of the cotton mills in Lowell]. I do not say this with any reference to pecuniary interest. I could not say it, did I not conscientiously believe that the introduction of cotton manufacture has added greatly to the mass of human happiness in those immediately concerned in it, as well to the aggregate wealth and prosperity of the whole country. I could not say it, did I perceive in the system any tendency toward a relaxation of the moral purity which has ever been a characteristic of our beloved New England. My mind was early turned to a consideration of this question. I could never perceive any just ground for the opinion which formerly prevailed extensively, that occupation in manufactories was less favorable to morals than other manual labor. This opinion has, I believe, universally given way before the light of our experience. It is the elevation of all labor above the right to a mere subsistence, which gives it character and standing in society, and constitutes the elementary difference between American and European labor. That this elevated position may be strengthened and perpetuated by our institutions, is my ardent wish.[14]

During the decades preceding the Civil War, "King Cotton" dominated the thinking as well as the economy of the city of Lowell. The Boston Associates and their successors, the manufacturers of Lowell, had many personal contacts with the South: business dealings, cotton buying trips, and visits by southerners to Boston and by Bostonians to the South. One such trip was the lengthy goodwill tour by Amos. A. Lawrence in 1836 and 1837. The relationship was profitable and both the Yankee "Lords of the Loom" and the slave holding "Lords of the Lash" hoped to continue it.[15]

The same attitude prevailed among the lesser figures in the cotton textile industry in Lowell. It was felt by overseer and loom operator alike that the city's continued prosperity depended on the continuance of the friendly and cooperative relationship with the southern cotton growers. If for any reason the flow of raw cotton into Lowell stopped, the mills would be forced to close, and all would be out of work. This attitude was startlingly demonstrated in the fall of 1843 when George Thompson, the social reformer who was responsible for the abolition of slavery in the British West Indies, came to Lowell on a speaking tour. Thompson was to deliver three lectures on successive days: "Slavery and the Bible," "History of San Domingo," and "History and Results of West India Emancipation." During the second lecture, three rocks were thrown through the window of the hall, narrowly missing Thompson. The next morning the southern sympathizers send Thompson an anonymous letter advising him to leave town, and placards appeared throughout the city:

Citizens of Lowell, arise! Look well to your interests! Will you suffer a question to be discussed in Lowell which will endanger the safety of the Union?—a question which we have not, by our constitution, any right to meddle with. Fellow-citizens, shall Lowell be the first place to suffer an Englishman to disturb the peace and harmony of our country? ... If you are freeborn sons of America, meet, one and all, at the Town Hall, THIS EVENING, at half-past seven o'clock, and convince your Southern brethren that we will not interfere with their rights.[16]

It is perhaps surprising that the workmen of Lowell should have agreed so completely with their employers and that they should have reacted so violently to Thompson's speeches; but the reasons were probably not only some pressure from the mills about their jobs, but also support of the manufacturers' position from the local newspapers.

Lowell also attracted politicians. In 1834, Colonel (and congressman) David Crockett of Tennessee attended a banquet in Lowell. Although the trip was mainly for political reasons, the congressman claimed that he had heard so much about Lowell that he wanted to see "the power of machinery." He also wanted to see "how it was that these northerners could buy our cotton,

Cotton mills in Lowell, Massachusetts, around the turn of the century (Library of Congress, Prints & Photographs Division, LC-USZ62-90893).

and carry it home, manufacture it, bring it back, and sell it for half nothing, and in the mean time, be well to live, and make money besides."[17] Another politician, Thomas Hart Benton, Democratic senator from Missouri, visited Lowell during a New England tour. The main theme of his speech was that the preservation of the union was of utmost importance and that disunion would be a disadvantage for both sections. The speech was well received in Lowell because of its dependence on its cotton manufacturing industry.

There were also remarks by a southerner who was appreciative of Lowell, albeit in an amusing way. In 1845, William T. Thompson, planter, editor of the *Savannah Morning News*, defender of slavery, and, later, advocate of secession of the Confederacy, visited the mill. Under the pseudonym of "Major Jones," Thompson published his impressions of the mill girls of Lowell in "Major Jones' Sketch of Travel (1843–1848)":

> They cum swarmin out of the factories like bees out of a hive, and spreadin in every direction, filled the streets so that nothin else was to be seen but platoons of sun-bonnets with long capes hangin down over the shoulders of the factory galls. Thousands upon thousands of 'em was passin along the streets, all lookin happy and cheerful and neat and clean and butiful as if they was boarding school misses just from ther books. It was indeed a interesting sight, and a gratifying one to a person who had always thought that the opparatives as they call 'em in the Nothern factories was the most miserable kind of people in the world.[18]

But it was not all happy and cheerful for the mill girls at work, according to Stephen Yafa in *Big Cotton*:

> Within the mills themselves, however, time slowed to a deadening crawl; fine hairs of cotton lint circulated through the hot air and mingled with particles of machine oil that gave off an acrid, burnt scent and seemed to coat walls, posts, and beams on every floor with a thin sheen. To maintain a high level of humidity, managers often nailed windows closed. During summer months temperatures soared. In balance, cotton's welfare mattered more than the workers'. Airborne lint hairs, one mill girl noted, fell as thickly "as snow falls in winter." They sometimes piled up on workers' clothing and hair; inhaled for more than twelve hours a day in the absence of fresh air, the lint caused frequent lung diseases that were difficult to diagnose and impossible to treat effectively.... Then there was the work itself—sufficiently tedious to numb the mind, rarely challenging enough to stimulate it. In these mills, all the brains were built into the machines, more technically advanced than in any other industry in America. No matter how bright you were, you were paid to tend the machines, like the nannies of idiot savants who lacked all personal skills.[19]

How did the women cope with the situation? To many, the answer was religion. In April 1829, mill girls from three textile mills in Taunton, Massachusetts, abandoned their looms to protest a reduction in wages. Bedecked in their colorful working attire—black silk dresses, red shawls, and green calashes, the women marched into a local public hall. Their leader was Salome Lincoln, a twenty-two-year-old mill girl who had been working in the mill for eight years. Lincoln was also a lay preacher in the Freewill Baptist Church, a denomination whose theology held out the possibility of salvation for all and whose clergy would play a role, disproportionate to their numbers, in subsequent labor protests in New England.

What we know of women's involvement in reform areas during the early nineteenth century basically concerned middle and upper middle class women and their work in such pursuits as temperance, abolitionism, and rights for themselves. Here, however, was Protestant involvement in the lives of working-class women. These women, because of their occupation of working in the production of cotton, comprised much of the early factory workforce in America. Two literary magazines, the *Lowell Offering*, written by and for female textile operatives, and the radical *Voice of Industry* form the basis of the mill girls' ideas, religious beliefs, and understanding of their oppression. An outcome of this involvement in their situation was the formation of the Lowell Female Labor Reform Association (LFLRA), whose activities were regularly reported in the labor press.

To understand these women, we must look at their confrontation with the factory. They left family and friends in their country homes for a strange new world created by cotton, which put them into company-sponsored boardinghouses and behind textile machines. What they left behind—"the green hills and fertile vales ... where the pure air of heaven, gave life and animation to the whole being"—became at once a touch and a refuge for them, a standard by which they judged their present circumstances and a sanctuary to which they retreated, literally as well as figuratively, when these circumstances seemed too harsh to bear.[20] For these young women, most of them in their late teens or early twenties, going to work in a cotton mill was a wrenching experience.

The source of the mill girl's intellectual, moral, and spiritual energies was Scripture. As it was in their childhood, so it was in their new lives as mill workers. When *Factory Girls' Album and Operatives' Advocate* appeared in February 1846, the lead article was entitled "The Bible." It is a thing always to be had," the author wrote, "always within call, and ever at hand, and very portable."[21] The cotton mills prohibited reading at work. Lucy Larcom recalled that some of her sister operatives believed that Scripture was exempt from that ban. Lucy herself tore pages from her Bible and carried them with her to work. It was common, she claimed, for a mill operative to "have a page or two of the Bible beside her there, committing verses to memory while her hands went on with their mechanical occupation." The overseer would confiscate these materials whenever he found them. According to Larcom, the overseer's desk was full of Bibles.[22]

One instance where the Lords of the Loom and the operatives agreed was on the issue of church participation. This was because in many cotton mills, workers were required "to be constant in attendance upon public worship." Although the editor of the *Lowell Offering* insisted that this regulation was not always "strictly enforced," it was generally a technical condition of both employment in the mill and residence in the company boardinghouse.[23] The mill owners no doubt conceived the rule as part of their broader design: to create (and control) a morally upright community of factory operatives, thus countering popular fears and prejudices and ensuring a steady supply of labor. But as Hannah Josephson observed in her study of the mill girls, strict rules governing morality and Sabbath observance reflected "the standards of behavior of young women all over New England at this time." Thus the mill's recruiting agents traveling in the countryside would carry a copy of the mill's regulations to assure parents that their daughter's virtue would be protected in the factory town. The textile corporations were not inaugurating anything new, Josephson pointed out; rather they were bowing to the mores of the era.[24]

Sarah Bagley, the most prominent female labor leader of the 1840s, pointed out some of the problems involved in the church-going mill community. "Can it be reasonably supposed," she asked, "that those who are called to their task every morning at half past five, and kept until seven at night, will have sufficient energy to be constant in their attendance at church on the Sabbath?"[25] But the most common complaint had a particularly female cast. Mill girls could not emulate contemporary fashions. "Our Agents and the aristocratic class to which they belong," Bagley observed, "have ordained fashions in dress and equipage, which the operative is unable to follow, and they must at any rate *ape them*, or they will be wanting in self-respect." As for those who went to meeting in their "plain country dress" because they could find neither the time nor the money to keep their "wardrobe in church-going order," Bagley said they "are almost stared out of countenance."[26]

Organized Protestant denominations at this time generally supported the women in their discontent with working conditions in the cotton mills, especially Calvinist and Freewill Baptist. But other denominations were involved. During the 1836 "turn-out"[27] in Lowell, a local Methodist minister dispensed certificates of dismissal, in essence membership transfers, to some sixty or seventy female strikers in his church who chose to leave town rather than return to work.[28] When factory girls in Amesbury, Massachusetts, "turned-out" over an increased work load, they met in the local Baptist vestry to choose officers and to pass resolutions.[29]

It should come as no surprise that the mill girls in antebellum New England became involved in religion to foster their labor aims. As female Americans, they had been taught to protect the moral virtue of the republic; as Christian Americans, they had been taught that they had a special responsibility to save themselves and humanity.[30] As an example, "Juliana" roused her sisters with messianic imagery drawn from the Old Testament: "Let the thought that we are engaged in a good work nerve us on to duty. The battle is not to the strong, nor the race to the swift—but to the righteousness of the cause. In the strength of Elijah's God, the God of Right, let us march boldly on to the conquest. Let us take no rest until the shout shall rend the earth and heavens—'Goliath is fallen!'"[31] God's presence loomed large in their rhetoric. Ending nearly all their letters, announcements, and speeches with appeals for divine favor, the mill girls sometimes referred to the deity as the "Omnipotent power" or the "All-seeing eye." In this circumvention of earthly authority, they no doubt found an antidote for their sense of powerlessness, not only as workers, but also as female workers.

Their religious beliefs also provided these operatives with powerful ammunition against their employers. In her "Advice to Mill Owners," in which she advocated allowing operatives to leave work for "an hour or two, or a day even," a factory girl in Exeter, New Hampshire, chose to address her employers as churchgoing Christians. "The man who is unkind to his female help," she announced, "cannot be a Christian, if he is a church member, a deacon, or even the carrier round of the contribution box."[32] At all times be wary of the "Lords of the Loom," Sara Bagley reminded her sisters, because of what awaited them should they fail to maintain their vigilance. While she and the defenders of the factory system agreed that, as she put it, "the standard of virtue in Lowell, is far above that of any other city of its size in the Union," she was hardly sanguine about the moral climate of "life among the spindles." Temptation abounded, Bagley believed, and Satan was its merchant: "Never, never, in the name of heaven, permit Lowell to boast her 'nymphs of the pave.' At the dance, upon the street, at the social gathering, in the church, or by your own fireside shrink as from the abyss of infamy, from the steady gaze or stealthy touch of the fiend in human form, who for a paltry job would rob you of bliss in your life, and destroy a lone girl's happiness, away from friends and home."[33] Basically, these women were simultaneously traditionalists, calling for a return to the principles and values of a gentler age, and radicals who sought to root out the sin and vice they believed attended capitalist industrialization.[34]

What was the condition of wage earners in the early textile mills of New England? Were they a symbol or a victim of the "Machine Age?" Nathan Appleton of the Boston Associates reported that a wage earner who saved his earnings could accumulate in one year "a very considerable capital," so that he could quickly become an investor and employer.[35] John Aiken, an agent of the Lawrence Manufacturing Company, developed the same thesis. "In the United States," said Aiken, "almost every free laborer has begun to be a capitalist as soon as he has begun to labor.... Among our native population, laborers for hire do not exist as a class. Young people of both sexes often begin life in this way; but without an intention of following it permanently. Their object is to gain a capital, with which to establish themselves in business on their own account. And this purpose is carried out in the vast majority of cases."[36] Abraham Lincoln, campaigning in Connecticut in 1860, appealed forcefully to this self-help ideology.[37] But already in the 1830s, voices were raised against the conditions in the New England cotton mills. Seth Luther,[38] warned that "our rights are not only *endangered*, but some of them already wrested from us by the powerful and inhuman grasp of monopolized wealth.... A spirit of monopoly exists in this country, as well as in Europe, which is sapping and mining the VERY FOUNDATIONS of our free institutions."[39]

There were also clashes about the wages and savings of the antebellum cotton mill girls. By the 1840s, journals in New England were saying that significant numbers of women mill workers had been reduced to the level of destitution. These women, finding themselves "obliged to dress poorly or run into debt," allegedly began to supplement their factory earnings by resorting to a less honorable trade.[40] "Few of them marry," said the *Boston Quarterly Review*; "fewer still return to their native places with reputation unimpaired." As opposed to the *Review*'s opinion, a Boston piano manufacturing company claimed that it had sold eight pianos at prices ranging from $250 to $350 to Lowell mill girls during a six-month period.

Other features of the situation of the cotton mill workers remains in doubt. Protests and petitions were offered against the long hours of labor in the mills, which averaged about 12 hours per day over the course of a year. But on the other hand, in some cases the mill workers did not want a reduction in hours that would have made a reduction in pay.[41] A physician reported in 1849 that poor ventilation in the mills was very destructive of the health of the operatives, but an investigating committee of the Massachusetts legislature concluded that working conditions in the mills were good.[42]

So there were a variety of views concerning the antebellum production of cotton in New England. Wages were high enough that some mill women saved thousands of dollars, but wages were so low that hundreds of mill women were forced into prostitution. Working conditions were very good, except that factories were overheated, stuffy, and lit by noxious and inadequate lamps. Everybody in New England had an equal chance to succeed, but there was monopoly, an aristocracy of wealth, and a high degree of class stratification. Some mill women could not escape from the mills, but there was no permanent factory population. The hours of labor were intolerably long, but not so long as in other occupations which were more tedious and exhausting. The boardinghouses for operatives were disgracefully congested and uncomfortable, but they more comfortable than the typical living quarters of the time.[43]

Probably every one of these assertions is true regarding some cotton mills or some operatives; none of them is true regarding all cotton mills or all operatives. The problem basically has to do with the ability of the newspapers of the day to report accurately and in an unbiased manner. In 1910, the historian and writer Helen L. Sumner wrote of the cotton mill situation:

> [I]n many instances statement of facts are directly contradictory. So far as material exists, great care has been exercised to present both sides in all manner of controversy, as closely as possible in the original words, and always with the authority cited. The reader must take into consideration the character of the material and the relative value of the sources of information, just as he would in reading similar material of recent publication."[44]

In order to best ascertain the mill conditions in antebellum New England, in addition to local sources and historians there are also business records, and public documents.

In 1852, the mill at Holyoke added a second production facility. As output rose, the company quickly ran into a shortage of labor. Also, since this mill was producing a finer grade of cotton, it could not use local inexperienced workers. The solution was to import skilled women weavers from Glasgow. The women emigrated to Holyoke because the pay was better than they received in Scotland. The mill advanced the women money to make the trip and to resettle in Holyoke. According to company records, 56 of the 67 women hired paid off their debt to the company through earnings four months after their arrival; the remaining seven did not pay their debts at all.

While it is true that these women had no dependents and they had a skill when the arrived in America as well as jobs with a firm that badly needed persons with that skill, they proved that a mill girl could save money. The fact that the mill girls were single was a major factor. A working-class family in the 1850s typically "spent at least half its income for food, probably at least a fourth for shelter, and most of the rest for clothing. Certainly less than 10 per cent remained for all other goods and services."[45] According to the cotton mills records, the ratio of savings for the 56 Scots women was at least 25 percent, and in several cases more than 50 percent.[46] The structure of wages and prices at this time were such that, whereas single persons could save large portions of their incomes, those with dependents were hard driven to subsist.

The next consideration is the cotton mills' ability to acquire operators. In this effort there were no problems, especially with importing Scots women. The flow of labor from Scotland to Holyoke resulted from four factors. First, the wages at Holyoke were higher than those in Scotland; second, the strong demand for labor in Holyoke; third, the relatively degraded status of textile workers in Scotland; and finally, the low cost of transatlantic passage, as the ships carrying cotton to Europe brought back human cargoes.

The reason that the mills continually needed operators is not that they were expanding, but because of the extremely high rate of labor turnover. The company could get workers; it just could not keep them. In view of the high possible ratio of savings to income, this was a remarkable fact. The problem was the Panic of 1857, which led to an economic downturn. The company, in order to exist, had to cut expenses. Instead of laying off its employees, the company, while loath to institute layoffs, cut back on employee hours. The mill moved from six days a week to three days in November 1857 and a four-day schedule in April of 1858. Because of these cutbacks, employees left for better positions. On March 11, 1858, Jones Davis, in charge of the Lyman Mills at Holyoke, wrote to George W. Lyman, the company treasurer: "Most of the best work people have left the place and others are following every day.... It will cost a large sum of money to supply the Lyman Mills with a new set of work people, particularly the No. Two Mill."[47]

Even after the depression, the turnover continued. Generally however, the immigrant operators stayed with the cotton mill for at least a year, not knowing another means of support. After that time, as their personal relationships and general knowledge expanded, they moved on to better jobs elsewhere, or they married and left the labor force entirely, as seems probable in the majority of cases. Labor turnover at Holyoke may also have been exceptionally high for noneconomic reasons. Living conditions in the town were far from ideal, at least by modern standards.[48] Housing was not only scarce, but also unattractive, and rents were relatively high. Holyoke had few trees and much dust. The town was unsanitary, so that serious epidemics occurred. A woman at the Fall River mill wrote back to the hiring agent at Holyoke: "i received your letter and thenks you for your kind offer to us i think i might have likt your work very well but i am shure that i would not like the place."[49]

Cotton mills in other locations were beset by the same problems which haunted Holyoke. In the year 1853, the two Pepperell mills at Biddeford, Maine, hired 866 people, "more than the average number at work in the mills."[50] Since Pepperell was not expanding at the time, its rate of turnover was more than 100 percent per year. In view of the short tenure of most employees, the Holyoke mills required every new employee to stipulate "that whenever it shall be my intention to quit their service, [I shall] give the Agent or Overseer under whose charge I serve, Two Weeks Notice of my said intention, before leaving. And leaving their employ without said notice shall be a forfeiture and release of all arrearages of wages then unpaid."[51]

Provisions like this did not stabilize the labor force. Employees who were brought to the United States from Europe flowed in a stream though American cotton mills. In 1858, as an example, a Holyoke recruiting agent in Glasgow wrote to the mill that she was "very sorry to hear that the girls had turned out so bad," some of them having fled from the ship in New York instead of journeying to the cotton mill.[52] Also in 1858, in contrast to 1857, some immigrants who actually went to Holyoke were sending letters of complaint to Scotland, to the point were the Glasgow agent wrote again to the mill that "some of the girls sent home word that you had taken a heavy persentage of their wages, so I had double work in finding others for the end of the month."[53] Under these conditions, Holyoke began to recruit in other countries in Europe.

This high degree of labor mobility was a source of great pride in New England, especially during the early days of Lowell. Elisha Bartlett, the first mayor of Lowell and a physician, indignantly denied charges that "there is accumulating here, a permanent factory population, degraded in character, deteriorated and worn out in body, living in a slavish and entire dependence in the mills, and *unable to get away with advantage*! All this is gravely asserted and argued, but a purer piece of fiction was never gendered in the brain of a lunatic. *There is no such class here.*"[54]

But this high rate of labor turnover created serious problems for the early cotton manufacturers. It was not only the fact that recruiting activities in Europe was expensive and troublesome, but also that at this point in the nation's history most Americans lived and worked on farms. Additionally, the strong demand for labor in America resulted in high wages relative to Europe. If American cotton manufacturers were to meet foreign competition, they had to substitute machinery for labor so as to increase output per man-hour. But, since two-thirds of their labor force consisted of transient employees, they could not use methods which required much skill from the average production worker.

To make the best use of the good that cotton could provide, the mills depended on a small group of managerial and technical employees. The task of these experts was to devise methods of production which would lower costs while utilizing a labor force composed of "a succession of learners."[55] This rapid pace of technological advance in the United States was simply a continuation of the inventive spirit that had epitomized the earlier growth of machinery beginning before the Revolution. An automatic stop motion (or cutoff) for drawing frames was invented in America and promptly introduced throughout the domestic cotton production industry. It was not used in England, where the operatives were believed to be more skilled by the mill owners. The substitution of the power loom for the hand loom and of the throstle for the spinning mule proceeded much more rapidly in the United States than in England, "and the consequence is that female labour here takes the place of male labour employed in England."[56] Nathan Appleton also boasted of American inventiveness when he declared, "It was the Americans who first introduced the manufacture of heavy goods by the application of the least amount of labor to the greatest quantity of raw materials, thus producing a description of goods cheaper to the consumer than any heretofore existing."[57]

The era of the mill girls lasted about twenty years; when the new mill was erected in Holyoke, Massachusetts, in 1850, the local farmers' daughters were ceasing to apply for mill jobs.[58] Operatives were not wanting however. Of the several hundred persons first employed, about one-third came from the general area. But from the very beginning, the number of Irish immigrants nearly equaled all of the American workers, and they were not in the same proficiency category as the Scots operatives. As had been the case in other areas, "King Cotton" ruled over the mill, the town, and the inhabitants. The cotton barons built the boardinghouses and paid taxes, but the town was responsible for everything else.

As an example of "everything else" is that the influx of foreigners, mostly extremely poor, created complications. Ill fortune or indolence soon produced a large number who became a public charge. The cholera epidemic of 1849 left some persons dependent on charity, and accidents increased the number to the point that if the commonwealth of Massachusetts had not intervened to support these persons Holyoke might have been bankrupt before it was ten years old. And then was no financial help from the cotton mill.

The school committee also had a difficult problem. The number of foreign children whose parents could not or would not send them to school suggested the need of a campaign of parental education. One-fourth of all the children in the town between the ages of five and fifteen failed to attend school at all in 1850–1851, and many others attended only part of the school year. The owners of the cotton mill promised to cooperate in enforcing the school laws so that every child employed in a factory should have at least eleven weeks of schooling in the course of a year. But the school committee, having seen the attitude of the Lords of Cotton towards other non-mill problems was not convinced:

> The system of *primary schools* is fraught with interests which should thrill the breast of every American citizen. The children now in a course of common school education in our country, are hereafter to guide the destinies of a great

and growing nation! More, they are to exert a mighty influence upon the destinies of every nation on our globe! With what unspeakable importance, then is their moral and intellectual training stamped? *Our free institutions cannot be sustained by ignorant or vicious men, as the history of all republics proves.* "Ignorance is the mother of vice." It is only by *educating the masses, even all the people, that we can hope to perpetuate our republican form of government.*[59]

    Holyoke was the typical cotton company town. Nonresident stockholders had invested money in it for the purpose of deriving a profit, and more and more the townspeople began to express the feeling that the town's interests were being sacrificed to the financial welfare of the company. As an example, the cotton mill owners believed that the town would continue to grow, and as such, they could make more money using their land in the community for real estate speculation than as dwellings for their operatives. As a consequence, in 1855 there were only 514 houses to accommodate 778 families. Yet the cotton mill owners prided themselves on the wholesome living conditions in their town. They offered free vaccinations to all employees "who have not had the kinepox." Water from the reservoir was piped to all the boardinghouses. Additionally, in 1857, a "bathing tub" was placed in the "W.C." of the office "for the use of overseers and others connected with the works under circumstances which should be creditable to the company." All mill employees who had no families in the area were expected to live in the boardinghouses, where "respectable keepers," were to keep track of their boarders' conduct, "the doors to be closed at ten o'clock in the evening" and inmates not to be allowed "to collect on the front steps or sidewalk in front of their tenement."[60]

    Working conditions in the mills had not become any easier as more mills were built. Accidents were frequent, and the risk of fire was great in the crowded rooms where lint filled the air and oil lamps at first and gas later supplied the illumination and sperm oil lubricated the machinery.[61]

    Wages were little more than enough to live on. Women's wages in the Holyoke mill averaged about $3 per week, without board, compared to $1.50 to $2 twenty years earlier at the Lowell mill. In both cases board averaged $1.50 per week. The operatives were paid usually every month, although it could be as long as six weeks between pay periods. The hours were as long as the wages were small. In winter, lack of daylight cut down the day's work, but in summer even children worked nearly seventy hours a week. A law passed in 1842 forbade children under the age of twelve from working more than ten hours in any one day, but that was at least occasionally evaded in Holyoke in the early 1850s through either inadvertence or intention. The mills probably simply ignored the law because of the complications involved in having one group of operators working a full shift while another, the children, worked less.

Beginning in the 1830s and becoming far stronger in the 1840s and 1850s were the divisions not only between the Lords of the Loom and the operatives, but also between the operatives themselves. Gone were the local single women who constituted the famous mill girls. Now there were foreigners—Irish, Scots, and English, in the main, later joined by some Germans and Swiss—who all had their own cultures, religions, and languages. The operatives also began to organize to protect themselves.

This sense of unity began among the mill girls at Lowell. It started when one of their number wished to be absent for half a day; two or three others would tend an extra loom or frame apiece so that the absent one might not lose her pay. This unity allowed the mill girls to fight the Lords of the Loom in 1834, when the cotton market had entered a downturn. As a result of this drop in production, the mill owners decided to pass on their declining profits to their mill workers by imposing a 15 percent to 20 percent wage cut. The mill women again banded together, claiming "Union is Power." The mill owners retaliated by firing the women who held meetings to organize protests. After the firings, the mill girls took to the streets in protest and struck against the mills. Unfortunately for the women, because of the overproduction of textiles which had caused the slowdown in the market, the mill owners were not affected by the strike and consequently did not need the operatives. Although the strike did not turn out in favor of the women, it laid the foundation for further actions against the mill owners.

There was another strike against the mill in Lowell in 1836. But in the main, after the era of the mill girls the short tenure of most employees helps to explain the industrial relations of antebellum New England. Strikes occurred but they commonly sputtered out without achieving their ends. No formal trade unions were formed before the Civil War, and formalized collective bargaining lay several decades in the future.

8
Mills in the South

The principal reason for the beginnings of cotton manufacturing in the South was not a pursuit of profit as it was in the North, but rather one of opposition to the policies of the federal government. In 1829, a group of entrepreneurs broke ground to construct a cotton factory in Athens, Georgia. The local newspaper editor informed his readers that this was the beginning of a southern counteroffensive in the protracted struggle against the protective tariffs of Henry Clay's "American System." The report of the start of Athens' first factory also suggested that this experiment in industrial style manufacture constituted a revolution in social organization, that reorganizing the basis of production was as inherently social as it was political and economic.[1]

Even before the factory was built and before the 1828 "Tariff of Abominations," southerners publicly debated whether, and how, they should introduce cotton manufacturing to the South. Baltimore's *American Farmer* specifically invited a discussion of the topic of southern industrial manufacturing. It suggested that a peculiarly southern mode of industrialization using slave labor could make the South independent of its oppressors. After making this call for a thorough investigation of this model of industrial manufacturers, the *American Farmer* ran a lengthy series of articles over the next year which other southern newspapers often reprinted or commented upon. Foremost of these articles was the Fisher Report.[2]

In 1828, newspapers throughout the South excerpted the Fisher Report, a document produced by a committee of the North Carolina legislature charged with investigating the viability of southern industrial manufacturing. The committee calculated that a factory erected in the South could profit more than one of similar size in New England because of reduced transportation costs due to the close proximity of the cotton; there would also be reduced labor costs from the proposed use of slaves. Not only would southern production cost less, it would also prove more efficient than northern production since an enslaved workforce could neither strike nor quit. Fisher predicted a victory for southern industry in what appeared to be an economic war between the sections of the country. He concluded: "Let the manufacturing system but take root among us, and it will soon flourish like a vigorous plant in its native soil.... Nature has made us far more independent [of the North] than they are of us. They can manufacture our raw materials, but they cannot produce it.... We anticipate the time, when the manufactured articles of the South will be shipped to the North, and sold in their markets cheaper than their own fabrics."[3]

Also in January of 1828, the Athens newspaper, the *Athenian*, declared that southern people possessed sufficient capital and business sense, and it called for the immediate establishment of southern cotton factories to gain the desired economic independence from "Northern Harpies." As the *American Farmer* had done, the *Athenian* editor, O.P. Shaw, explained how the South could out-produce northern competitors. Raw material cost less in the South, and energy sources abounded. The South featured a superior topography for manufacturers as well, since, unlike New England, snow would not prevent the use of waterpower in the winter. Similarly, underutilized southern forests could provide the fuel for steam-engine power. Clearly southern supporters of industrialization believed they could undersell northern manufacturers, if only they tried. To convince southern cynics, a number of papers published financial calculations of what was at stake.[4]

The *Athenian* also reported on the downside of manufacturing. Factory work, the newspaper stated, upset traditional gender roles. Women seemed to cease acting like women when they worked in factories. The paper also worried about the morality of female workers. One article excerpted in the Athens paper claimed "the women become men in the female costume." Not only did they lose their "domestic" virtue, but worse still, as wage earners women exhibited an independence not expected in a patriarchal society like the American South.[5]

The benefits of cotton manufacturing, however, were strong in other parts of the South. Hoping to stimulate interest in its manufacture, southern industrialists proclaimed the good that cotton mills offered planters. The *Tuscumbia North Alabamian*, for example, argued in 1841 that a cotton mill kept the money at home, and, by increasing the local demand for cotton while drawing off capital and labor for cotton cultivation, helped raise cotton prices.[6] The *Montgomery Independent* spoke for most of the black belt reformers in its declaration that local manufacturing of cotton was the only "safe and effective remedy" against the oppressions of the Northern tariffs.[7]

Industrial crusaders also credited local cotton mills with the ability to secure the institution of slavery from northern antislavery attacks. Pro-industrialists reasoned that an industrialized South, no longer dependent upon the North for its goods and services, might strike at the North's pocketbook. Southern manufacturing promised double relief from antislavery abuse, not only insuring southern economic liberation but also forcing northern manufacturers, who wished to buy southern cotton and prevent the rise of rival factories in the South, to drive the antislavery groups from the South. The *Mobile Daily Register* captured the spirit in its editorial: "Let us not stop [investing in manufactures] till we have effected a thorough emancipation from the trammels of those who, while drawing millions from our pockets, are impertinently interfering with our most delicate social relations, and waging a relentless war upon our dearest rights."[8]

The most comprehensive statement of the South's pro-industrial position appeared in an 1846 speech by Henry W. Collier, chief justice of the Alabama supreme court and later governor of that state. Addressing a manufacturers convention in Tuscaloosa, Judge Collier declared that it was now time "to inquire for whom we have been growing the article [cotton], and who has received the profits of our labor." Always eager to purchase more slaves and to plant more cotton, Alabama planters who refused to diversify their labor contributed little to the state's wealth while depreciating the price of cotton through overproduction. Worse, continued Collier, "we nurture and employ our slaves for those who feel no sympathy with us." Alabama received only one-fifth of the profits from her cotton, yielding the remainder to English and northern manufacturers and financiers. Collier added, "Thus you see, that we are foregoing large profits which result from slave labor, and allowing others to realize them, who are denouncing us with all bitterness, as slave breeders and relentless taskmasters."

Establishing cotton mills in Alabama promised to be an easy and remunerative experience, Collier believed. Alabama possessed numerous natural advantages for manufacturing including the proximity of raw material, a mild climate which conserved fuel and housing expenses, and an abundant supply of cheap labor, slave and free. In regards to labor, manufacturers had the special mission of providing employment for "the thousands who, without any visible employment, live as an incubus upon the bosom of society." From his own observation at a Cincinnati factory, Collier allayed southern fears that manufacturing necessarily corrupted morals or health: "My firm conviction is, that labor in a cotton factory, under the improved state of machinery and building, is as little prejudicial to health as any other indoor employment.... There is nothing in tending a loom, to harden a lady's hand; and in a well ventilated and properly heated house ... there is nothing to cause the rouge upon the cheek to fade, although the skin may become bleached by remaining so much in the shade."

Rather than corrupt the health and morale of the workers, Collier said, employment in cotton mills might reclaim the South's indigent white population and rear children "to habits of industry." Finally, he believed that cotton manufacturing would provide the impulse for agricultural reform and improvement in the mechanical arts, promote "neatness, comfort and elegance" on the farm, elevate public morals, increase the flow of wealth into the state, and diffuse knowledge "in proportion as we can induce the idle and profligate to labor."[9]

There was also the idea that cotton manufacture was not beneficial, which led Alabama representative Augustin Clayton to expound on this theme on the floor of the United States Congress. He stated that he would rather live in the South with the anxieties of a possible slave rebellion than with endemic class rebellions that accompanied the industrial societies of England and New England. He declared that England's government was "obliged to keep a standing force to overawe the turbulence of the manufacturing operatives" in order to protect property and order.[10] Clayton also argued that not only did factory-based manufacturing inherently inflame class differences, but it also enslaved its operatives. When one person owed her livelihood to another, as an employee of a cotton factory, the working person lost the liberty to act independently. Understanding slavery as the opposite of liberty, Clayton explained: " A slave is a slave; the color of the skin does not relieve oppression; and depend upon it, white slaves are as dangerous as black ones, and all experience hath shown they are quite as ungovernable."[11]

Finally, when the factory was built in Athens in 1829, the *Athenian* printed this seemingly contradictory message: "A sense of safety and a feeling of independence, combined doubtless, with an expectation of profit, have urged gentlemen to an understanding, against which their political convictions are most understandably at war." While their opposition was probably to the tariff and the American System, rather than factory-based manufacturing, to gain economic independence they would manufacture and earn a profit while doing so.[12]

By 1835 there were only three new cotton factories in North Georgia. The problem, first, was the initial investment. A buyer could purchase a modest plantation for about the same price as purchasing partial ownership of a factory, in the range of $5,000 to $10,000. But most southerners continued investing in the known perils of commercial agriculture; few southerners risked the unknown challenges of industrial investment.[13] There were also the known hazards; fire posed a constant threat to cotton factory investments, and water-powered factories faced flooding problems, as well as water damage from severe rains. Finally, there were the risks incurred when a cotton mill ownership dissolved due to the death of a partner. To solve this problem, southern mill owners formed corporations. One could not control fire, flooding, and other acts of God, but human transactions could be made less perilous.[14]

Industrialization served to develop the community, not just to enrich a few investors. Town boosterism played a major role in the economic expectations of the early southern cotton industrialists. These investors, in order to serve the community, provided work for the indigent and manufactured goods for consumers, and to promote a degree of political independence for all, they sought to limit competition among themselves. Their view was that excessive competition from oversupply destroyed investment capital needed to advance the economic development of the community and destroyed shared financial resources used to build factories, construct the railroad, and to finance banking and credit schemes.

The results of this lessening of competition were high profits and an excellent return on investment, which caused southerners like Congressman Clayton to expect the repeal of the tariff. Nathan Appleton of the Boston Associates contended that Clayton "only went to show ... how much advantage the South might engage in manufacturing, if they were so disposed. If anything like such profits should be made in the North, they would be instantly brought down by competition."[15] Also in the debate on the tariff, the *New York Journal of Commerce* concluded that the tariff produced the desired effect; it encouraged manufacturing where none previously existed.[16] Meanwhile, the southern press used the same data to discuss the perceived cupidity of northern industrialists, as in an *Athenian* editorial that claimed the local factory's profits would aid in defeating the tariff. The writer reasoned that when northerners discovered southerners "share in the profits as well as the burdens, the system will not find such zealous supporters."[17] The high profits did affect the state of Georgia, where, within ten years of the founding of the first factory in Athens, there were fourteen more cotton factories.

The southern cotton manufacturing market strategy reveals an interesting means of producing product and keeping the goodwill of the planter class, who opposed the tariffs. First, the southern cotton mills were of small size compared with the northern "monopolists," which were characterized by large-scale New England mills. Second, the southern cotton mills tended to increase southern liberty by decreasing the region's economic dependence. And third, these mills priced their products to the planter class at a price under that of the northern mills.

The beginnings of the establishment of southern mills was different than that of the North in that there was not a progression from home manufacturing. Instead, southerners imported managers who built ready-to-operate factories for them and trained the workers. Also, since this was the case, the southern cotton mill owners did not need to steal industrial secrets, like the early New England industrialists had done from England from the 1790s through the 1820s.

The initial idea for workers in the southern mills was to use slave labor basically because slaves lacked mobility. They could not strike for better wages or better working conditions or leave when they had saved sufficient money to head west and buy a farm. While in some cases industrial slave labor continued into the Civil War, the largest detriment to using slave labor was its cost. Most mills paid the same for both slave and free white labor, usually seven dollars per month (the payment for slaves was in the form of rent). Additionally, however, the factory had to provide food and lodging for the slave, so slaves ultimately proved to be the most expensive form of labor. An additional problem was that, especially when cotton prices were high, masters chose to maximize their profits by keeping as many slaves as possible working in the cotton fields rather than risk damage to their valuable property in the potentially dangerous environment of a cotton factory for only marginal profits.

The free white workers also proved to be a problem because they had no industrial background. They had never seen a frame, a loom, or a spreader. Continuous hours of close attention to machinery contrasted with the simplicity of agriculture. They were not accustomed to coordination of effort or to receiving more than basic directions. The old economic controls of master and servant were relaxed; now the brains of management had to be joined to the dexterity of operatives. Further, the owners of factories and the workers in them had not been partners before as the South's labor system had made them economic enemies. Those not offering to be purchased and not able to purchase others were left out of the scheme of things. The plantation slaves pushed the poor white workers out of economic participation. Had the poor whites possessed the means, most of them might have emigrated and left no great gap behind them. Remaining of necessity, they made places for themselves on the fringe of society and in most cases were just tolerated. The simple problem for cotton manufacturing was that cotton was king and interest in other activities like manufacturing was minor.[18]

It's not that the industrial reformers did not try to find factory employment for southern indigent whites in the cotton mills. In 1848 the *Montgomery Tri-Weekly Flag & Advertiser* asserted that Alabama had 50,000 idle poor whites for employment.[19] The *Montgomery Alabama Journal* suggested that manufacturers should utilize Alabama's "large population born on the soil who have not capital to engage in agriculture, who do not wish to emigrate, and who wish employment."[20] Pro-industrialists also pointed out that wage earning poor whites increased the local demand for mechanical services and farm products. One newspaper conceded that if employed in local textile factories, "a large class of our population who are non producers now, will contribute largely to the aggregate wealth of the community."[21]

The problem was that before indigenous white labor could be successful, the manufacturers had to offer a means of uplifting them. The *Mobile Herald & Tribune* did this by assailing the evils of northern factory labor and then warning the southern industrialists not to repeat the moral and physical abasement of white operatives which characterized the northern industrial experience. The editors were especially concerned about female operatives, laboring "in the crowded, heated apartments—only the hand and the eye at work (there is no time for thought at a spindle or a loom). These girls cannot possibly be prepared for the duties of life, and in proportion as women degenerate posterity will suffer."[22]

Still another group that had an opinion on the question of the southern economy and cotton mills were those in favor of slavery and an agricultural economy. They believed that the South could not survive the introduction of cotton manufacturing cities similar to those in the North or in England. In addition to the criticism that cities were unhealthy and nourished the vices of prostitution, alcoholism, and gambling, the cities were also nests for antisocial conspiracies of every caste and color, advocating the heresies of socialism, Fourierism, or worst of all, abolitionism. A delegate to the Nashville convention of 1850 declared that the consequence of northern industrialization and urbanization was labor's "growing and monstrous disregard of all the usually recognized securities of society. Mobs, riots, murders, mark the daily events in their progress."[23] During the 1850s a whole anti-industrial literature emerged among proslavery novelists, who fashioned tales in which young factory girls relinquished their virtue for a loaf of bread and all factory operatives slept in cellars, breathed fetid air, and knew only despair. Defenders of slavery repeatedly employed images of squalor and moral decay in their polemics, exhorting southerners to prevent such pauperism in their own states.[24]

The South did, however, have an individual by the name of Daniel Pratt, who believed he could erect successful cotton mills in the South which would rival those in the North. After first building one successful mill, he began his campaign of industrialization using poor whites by addressing the prejudice against manual labor that was widespread in the South. Pratt said of this, "I am aware that it is thought degrading by many to be seen following the plow, or the jack-plane, saw, trowel, hammer, or any other mechanical tool in their hands." But he regarded such values as myopic and harmful to southern economic growth. His idea was to build a cotton factory and manufacturing village "for the purpose of dignifying labor in the South, and to give the laboring class an opportunity of not only making an independent living, but to train up workmen who could give dignity to labor." With good pay and proper attention to morals, Pratt was confident that his village of Prattville would attract enough poor whites to begin his experiment. Through religion and education, Pratt hoped to introduce his employees to the positive New England virtues of sobriety, thrift, and hard work, which might earn for each operative "a neat substantial dwelling, the front yard adorned with shrubbery and flowers, a good vegetable garden, a pleasant wife, and cheerful children."[25]

In his reform program, Pratt was careful to endorse manufacturing villages rather than industrial cities. Villages, he maintained, were healthier and more amenable to social control than cities. With a small homogeneous population, villages were secure from crime and social "isms" which disrupted northern urban life. Pratt believed that his villages, which would be placed near the cotton fields, would complement the cotton and slave system. The location of such villages was important to the success of Pratt's social and economic experiment. Manufacturing, said Pratt, required "concentration and capital to make manufacturing profitable, and that capital and machinery will concentrate where the greatest facilities are found." Numerous small villages located from ten to twenty miles apart along the rivers used for the mills seemed for Pratt "far preferable to the same amount of capital concentrated in one place." He continued: "With many small manufacturing villages, we might expect better health, better society, and as changes seem necessary for some persons, they could go from village to village, without inconvenience to themselves or their employers ... and we would not fear epidemics in this piney woods range."[26]

Pratt's biggest problem was money. First, he wanted the planters to invest because "it will enrich them [the planters], and induce them to settle permanently." With a fixed agricultural population providing markets and capital, the mills could grow. Next, because of the potential benefits that cotton manufacturing would give the state, the state in turn should remove special taxes on industrial property. In 1849, two years after he opened his factory, Pratt was continuing to look for state aid to industry; this time the problem was the banks. Pratt complained that Alabama had an unimaginative banking policy that restricted credit to agricultural investments, retarded industrial development and drove wealthy Alabamian's out of the state to areas "where they can make it more to their interest to invest their capital." If Alabama's cotton

8. Mills in the South

Mill Number One of the Prattville Manufacturing Co. in Prattville, Autauga County, Alabama (Library of Congress, Prints & Photographs Division, HAER ALA, 1-PRAVI,5—5).

mills hoped to keep pace with their competition, the state must reevaluate its attitude towards banks.

Another problem was the lack of banking facilities in the state, which caused manufacturers to sell their goods in New York rather than locally. The manufacturer who sold his products in the South was frequently "obliged to sell his goods on a six months' credit and wait until his paper matures before he can realize anything from it."[27] By marketing their products in New York, manufacturers received cash or a twelve months' credit for northern goods. Also, New York merchants possessed the banking facilities to immediately discount their notes on goods sold. Pratt's take on the situation was that "we should not be dependent on the New York merchants, but sell all our goods here and save the freight, insurance, and commission, and our citizens who held stock in our banks would reap the profits of the discount, instead of the New Yorkers."[28]

Pratt's mill, however, did not suffer from a lack of funding, but rather had the same problem that early mills in the North encountered—finding skilled workers. In 1848, he journeyed to New York and hired a superintendent, a master weaver, and a competent machinist. With his management problems under control, Pratt looked to his mill workers. Employees at Prattville were largely local poor whites with little or no education. While he preferred to hire families, he also took on single girls and children to work in the cotton factory. The worker's remuneration was approximately the same as that at Lowell. In 1847 the average wage for cotton mill operatives at Prattville was $8 per month, and De Bow reported that at that wage "there is no difficulty in getting operatives ... and Negroes have not been employed from the abundance of other labor." In 1850, at least 73 adult women and 63 men worked full time at the cotton factory, women receiving an average monthly wage of $9 and men $16. Pratt furnished his operatives with cottages for a small rent, and the workers were expected to "obtain their provisions at local shops and neighboring farms." Each of the 65 worker cottages available in 1850 was "neatly painted and of a uniform size" and set against the hills amid trees and shrubs so as not to disturb the invigorating pastoral environment of Prattville.[29]

Pratt went further than the Lowell manufacturers, offering his operatives a company day care center and school. He also petitioned the state legislature to establish a mechanic's school, but he was turned down. More important than technical skill was the workers' religious instruction, which stressed the virtues of hard work and temperance. Shadrach Mims, Prattville's answer to Lowell's Lucy Larcom, as an employee of Prattville and a writer praised Pratt for the "good done to operatives and their families, both in a pecuniary way and in the improvement of mind, manners, and morals." The cotton mill employees who "were of the very poorest class ... withal ignorant people from obscure parts of the country ... having never enjoyed any religious privileges," largely benefited from Pratt's religious programs. Although several of the "drunken and abandoned" fathers kept up their old habits and some of the children were "far from being as good as they might be," most children, after the initial distaste for religion wore off, experienced in Mims' eyes an "agreeable change."[30]

Another village of this type was established in Graniteville, South Carolina, by William Gregg. This village, larger than Prattville, covered about 150 acres, contained two Gothic churches, an academy, a hotel and stores, and about 100 cottages belonging to the company and occupied by operatives. In referring to his community, Gregg stressed its fatherly rather than its business aspects:

> We may really regard ourselves as the pioneers in developing the real character of the poor people in South Carolina. Graniteville is truly the home of the poor widow and helpless children, or for a family brought to ruin by a drunken, worthless father. Here they meet with protection, are educated free of charge,

and brought to habits of industry under the care of intelligent men. The population of Graniteville is made up mainly from the poor of Edgefield, Barnwell, and Lexington districts. From extreme poverty and want they have become a thrifty, happy and contented people. When they were first brought together the seventy-nine out of a hundred grown girls who could neither read nor write were a by-word around the country; that reproach has long since been removed.[31]

As in New England and villages like Prattville and Graniteville, since the moral and mental culture of the operatives received a great deal of attention, the use of alcohol was not permitted. Also, young people, particularly males, were not allowed to remain in the villages in idleness, and good moral character was necessary to continue residence.

Not everyone agreed that Gregg produced such laudable results. A contributor to the *Edgefield Advertiser* professed deep dismay at the long hours that Graniteville operatives were "doomed to toil." The Edgefield factory seemed too willing to copy the type of labor practiced in the northern factories. The critic lamented the sight of "so many poor, puny looking children ... there confined and breathing a polluted atmosphere for thirteen hours a day." How would such poor, ignorant creatures ever be able to "take an honorable position in society?" Better for Graniteville to follow the northern example of recently enacted ten-hour laws than to sacrifice the sons and daughters of South Carolina "at the shrine of wealth and ambition." A former employee of the Graniteville weaving department likewise saw benefits in the ten-hour law. "There is no class of people as much opposed by labor as the operatives in Cotton Factories," he declared. A ten-hour law in South Carolina would save "the poor female and orphan children" of Graniteville from being sentenced to toil "thirteen hours per day from year to year."

Others leery of Gregg's industrial revolution cast a wider net. In a letter to James Henry Hammond frequently cited by historians as de facto evidence of widespread anti-industrial sentiment in the Old South, Charleston banker Christopher Memminger expressed broader misgivings over Gregg's model of white wage labor in the South:

> I find an opinion gaining ground that slaves ought to be excluded from mechanical pursuits, and everything but agriculture, so as to have their places filled with whites; and ere long we will have a formidable party on this subject. The planters do not perceive how it affects their interests, and very frequently chime in with this cry. I think of our friend Gregg of Graniteville, with those who are agog about manufactures, without knowing it, are lending aid to this party, which is in truth, the only party from which danger to our Institutions is to be apprehended among us. Drive out negro mechanics and all sorts of operatives from our Cities, and who must take their place. The same men who make the cry in Northern Cities against the tyranny of Capital—and there as here would drive all before

them all who interfere with them—and would soon rise hue and cry against the Negro, and be hot Abolitionists—and every one of these men would have a vote. In our Cities, we see the operation of these elements—and if the eyes of the planting community are opened, the dangers may be averted. Fill Barnwell with some hundred Lowellers, and how do you think they will vote at elections?[32]

By a wide margin, observers approved of what they saw at Graniteville and the factory quickly became a source of immense pride for the area. Also, by diluting the possibility of class conflict among whites and striking a blow at the sway held by northern industrial interests, Gregg and Pratt seemed to strengthen, not threaten, the conservative regime of cotton and slavery. They pulled off the impressive task of making large-scale manufacturing palatable to southern spokesmen. While denying that wage labor should replace slavery, they nevertheless gained a qualified acceptance of wage labor in the agrarian landscape.

While cotton, as a product to be manufactured, was the key necessity to the erection of these mills, there were limitations. Few urban centers were available as sites for the establishment of cotton mills where a labor supply could be obtained. By necessity therefore the manufacturers in the South, as in the North, established their mills where waterpower was available and built villages around them for the housing and accommodations of their employees. In opposition to their pronouncements, the cotton mill village was thus established as a social and economic necessity and not as a paternalistic intention on the part of the manufacturers. The success of some mills in his state led an optimistic editor in North Carolina in 1838 to point out the advantages of abundant and cheap water supply, nearness to raw material and willing labor:

> We may venture the opinion that in two years, North Carolina will not only supply her demand for her own consumption with the coarser cotton fabrics, but will also send them out for sale into the markets of the world. On the whole the manufacturers of the northern states need not much longer count North Carolina as one of their markets, they may regard her as a competitor, and one, who, from the great advantages she possesses, will soon become very formidable.[33]

It would be naive to attribute the kind of paternalistic factory village development which occurred in the South through the use of cotton to Daniel Pratt or William Gregg alone. However, in many respects the South's demographic, economic, and social climate in the 1840s allowed for this type of industrialization. Idled white laborers were indeed abundant, cheap and eager for work, and the prospects of long-term unemployment and disaffection among large numbers of non-slaveholding whites could be a problem for the planter class. For Prattville and other communities like it, instruction, hard work and religion reinforced the work ethic and enabled the cotton mill owner to reduce the independent but indigent whites to factory operatives.

The cotton planters, however, held sway over the South, and when any threat to agriculture appeared, they were quick to note and object to it, as when the following pro-industrial editorial was printed in the *Montgomery Tri-Weekly Flag & Advertiser*: "We should like to see our city, a manufacturing city. We should like to see it the focus of a large industrial population. We should like to see the air above our city filled with the sound of labor. We like to hear the anvil and the hammer, the saw and the plane, the rattling of machinery, and the rumbling of the steam engine, for all these things speak of life and animation, of busy industry and thriving prosperity."[34] Local planters, aghast at such heresy, quickly informed the editors that massive industrialization was unacceptable. Agriculture, not manufacturing, was the true source of all wealth—material and spiritual. Some degree of industrialization was acceptable only so long as it served the interests of agriculture. The planter refused to be "Yankeeized," fearing that the acquisitive materialism of manufacturing was out of step with the social and racial harmony of the slave system.[35]

The power of the cotton growing planters was so strong that the press backed off and not only recanted but became supporters of the planter's position, speaking now of the positives of manufacturing only as it supported agriculture. As an example, when a newspaper in the area learned that some local entrepreneurs were contemplating constructing a cotton mill, the editors remarked that 200 idle farmers and agricultural laborers might now find jobs, and that the factory, with its payroll and purchase of farms products, would stimulate the area's agriculture.[36]

The advantages and disadvantages of cotton manufacturing were debated throughout the South. Men like John Randolph[37] and Landon Cleves[38] were opposed to cotton mills, whereas John C. Calhoun contended, "It is better for us that our cotton go out in yarn and goods than in the raw state." A newspaper in Athens, Georgia, attempting to walk a fine line between those in favor and those against mills, wrote concerning the establishment of a mill in the area:

> A sense of safety and a feeling of independence combined, doubtless, with an expectation of profit have urged gentlemen to an undertaking against which their political connections are at war. And we are authorized to state that these sentiments have by no means undergone a change; that their project is certainly not to give countenance to a system which they have always denounced but it is to be regarded as a measure unquestionably defensive.[39]

The small size of the Southern cotton manufacturing sector was due to planters investing little capital in the production of the product. If these men had participated, the southern economy might have had a large, viable, and diverse industrial base. Only 6 percent of the wealthy slaveholders (those owning twenty or more slaves) invested any capital in cotton manufacturing[40] and, unlike the North, this one class held the lion's share of investment capital. Many of the leading industrialists in the South owned plantation-sized farms; but as opposed to the planters, who put agriculture first, for these men manufacturing dominated their interests. The leading industrialists were not planters primarily.

Yet, of course, the crucial question is what can explain the lack of manufacturing in the South? One explanation, with the implication that it did not cost the South, is that agricultural specialization was the South's comparative advantage. While capital for investment in manufacturing was reduced by investment in land and slaves, the profitability of these investments meant that there was no direct reduction in investible funds in the South. Any reduction would come about from any of several possible indirect effects. There are a number of arguments concerning the causes of an inefficient specialization in agriculture and a too-small southern manufacturing sector. One hypothesis is the lack of internal markets in the South, resulting in a large quantity of imports from abroad or from the northern states. The failure of the southern market size is attributed both to the extreme inequalities of the southern income distribution and to the low density of the southern population. If the market size was small, southern investors were acting reasonably in not investing in manufacturing. It was the failure of demand which, in this argument, made manufacturing unprofitable. It has been pointed out that the small optimum size of most cotton manufacturing establishments and the magnitude of southern manufacturing imports makes a hypothesis somewhat doubtful. Thus any absence of manufacturing would best be explained as a supply-side phenomenon, either as the outcome of the class interests of the planters in maintaining power over the rest of white society, or else to their interests in precluding urban uses of slave labor as a form of control over their property.[41]

In the summer of 1842, several young gentlemen of Barnwell, South Carolina, formed the Demosthenian Debating Society. The society gave members an opportunity to hone their proficiency in debate and oratory, skills essential to one's standing in proper South Carolina society. The questions discussed at their meetings covered a spectrum of topics from the virtues of novel reading to the susceptibility of females to mental improvement. But at their gathering on June 23, 1843, the members debated what they considered a somewhat weightier question: "Is Agriculture or Manufacturers of more benefit to Society?" A spirited rhetorical contest quickly ensued. The debate was so fervent that the sides deadlocked, with neither side able to claim victory or admit defeat. Unable to select a winner, the membership proposed "that the President decide the question." After giving careful consideration to the merits of each side, the society minutes recorded that "the President decided in favor of agriculture."[42]

In hindsight, the outcome of the debate seemed predictable. A victory by "Agriculture" over "Manufacturers" was hardly shocking in a debating club composed of the sons of planters in the antebellum South. But the spirit and tenacity of the contest suggests that the victory was hardly a forgone conclusion. The relationship of manufacturing (preponderantly cotton), both foreign and domestic, to southern agriculture remained a topic of frequent discussion throughout the South before the Civil War. As an example, the subject became particularly volatile in the nullification era when the leading politicians in South Carolina seldom passed up an opportunity to rail against the malignant influence of northern manufacturing interests in the national government. Even after the tariff problems had passed, the subject of manufacturing remained prevalent, as the agricultural depression of the 1840s prompted calls for industrial development in order to strengthen the southern economy. The problem remained, though. Slaveholders maintained deep suspicions towards industrial societies, particularly the ones that existed in New England and Great Britain; but at the same time they decried the lack of an industrial sector that left the South as an economic and political vassal of the North. The planters wanted manufacturing without a manufacturing society.[43]

9

The International Situation

Until approximately 1780 the cotton imported into Great Britain came almost entirely from the Mediterranean, chiefly from Smyrna. Occasional parcels were imported from the West Indies, but nothing of consequence. In the article "Cotton" in *Postlethwyt's Dictionary of Commerce* published in 1766, there is no mention of America as a source of cotton supply. Small shipments of cotton were made from Charleston in 1748 and 1757, but they were probably of West Indian origin. In 1784, a little over a year after the independence of the American colonies was acknowledged by England, eight bags of cotton were imported in an American vessel from the United States into Liverpool. As the greater part of the cotton hitherto imported from the colonies had consisted of West Indian product, the British custom house officials believed that the eight bags of cotton were also of West Indian origin and as such could not be legally imported in the vessel of a *foreign* country under the existing Navigation Laws. The cotton was therefore detained until it could be proven that it was produced within the United States and imported on a British ship.

It may seem odd that so little cotton was sent to Great Britain. The cause was undoubtedly the limited market which the American cotton grower was sure to find for his produce. As important as the American domestic manufacturing was for supplying the home trade with articles of clothing, this domestic manufacturing was discouraged and even forbidden to the colonists. Therefore, with only a slowly expanding domestic market for his product, the cotton grower was not encouraged to raise a greater amount of product. In the closing years of the first half of the eighteenth century, the Swiss and German colonists in Georgia did raise some cotton, which they manufactured into cloth and sold. But the report of their operation caused the trustees of the colony in England to send a letter to the president of the colony in America, in which it was stated that "as to manufacturing the produce they [the colonists] raise, they must expect no encouragement from the trustees, for setting up manufactures which may interfere with those in England might occasion complaints here." The letter further advises the colonists to turn their attention to "the produce of silk, which they will receive immediate payment for."[1] In the face of such opposition the domestic manufacturers of cotton goods did not make much headway until the Revolutionary War cut off manufactured products from England and compelled the colonists to supply themselves with clothing.[2]

As far as foreign markets were concerned, trade with the Continent by the colonies had been prohibited by the Navigation Acts of the seventeenth and eighteenth centuries, and although it went on in spite of the legal restrictions, the risk which it underwent and the stationary character of the cotton industry of the Continental countries offered little encouragement to American planters to produce cotton for these markets.

Even if the American colonies had been able to supply Great Britain with raw cotton, it would have been of little use. The spinning and weaving of cotton had been carried on there since the late sixteenth and early seventeenth centuries, but American manufacturers were unable to produce the soft muslins and "painted calicos" that since 1631 had been imported into England from India and were so popular with the "fine ladies," including the queen herself.[3] Although the demand for this class of goods formed the basis for later developments in the British cotton industry, every effort to fabricate all-cotton products in England before the introduction of machinery proved futile. As this was the case, the cotton industry made slow progress and the probability of finding a growing market in Great Britain was therefore not great.

The second cause which retarded cotton cultivation in America was the difficulty in cleaning the seed and other impurities from the raw cotton since the British manufacturers could not make use of the cotton until it was cleaned. It would not be until 1893 that Eli Whitney solved this problem.

The third obstacle which lay in the way of an early cultivation of cotton in the English colonies was the profits which accrued to the prerevolutionary Americans from growing other crops. In Virginia, as an example, the production of tobacco was nearly as old as the colony itself and despite the efforts of the mother country to divert the energies of the inhabitants to the raising of other commodities,[4] the tobacco trade was so lucrative that it was easily the main crop grown in Virginia. The average annual export of tobacco from all the colonies from 1699 to 1708 was 28,868,666 pounds, and from 1744 to 1766, 40,000,000 pounds; three-fourths of the prerevolutionary production of this staple was raised in Virginia.[5] Prior "to the American Revolution, it [tobacco] constituted in value between a quarter and one-third of all of the exports of the American colonies, now the United States."[6] In South Carolina

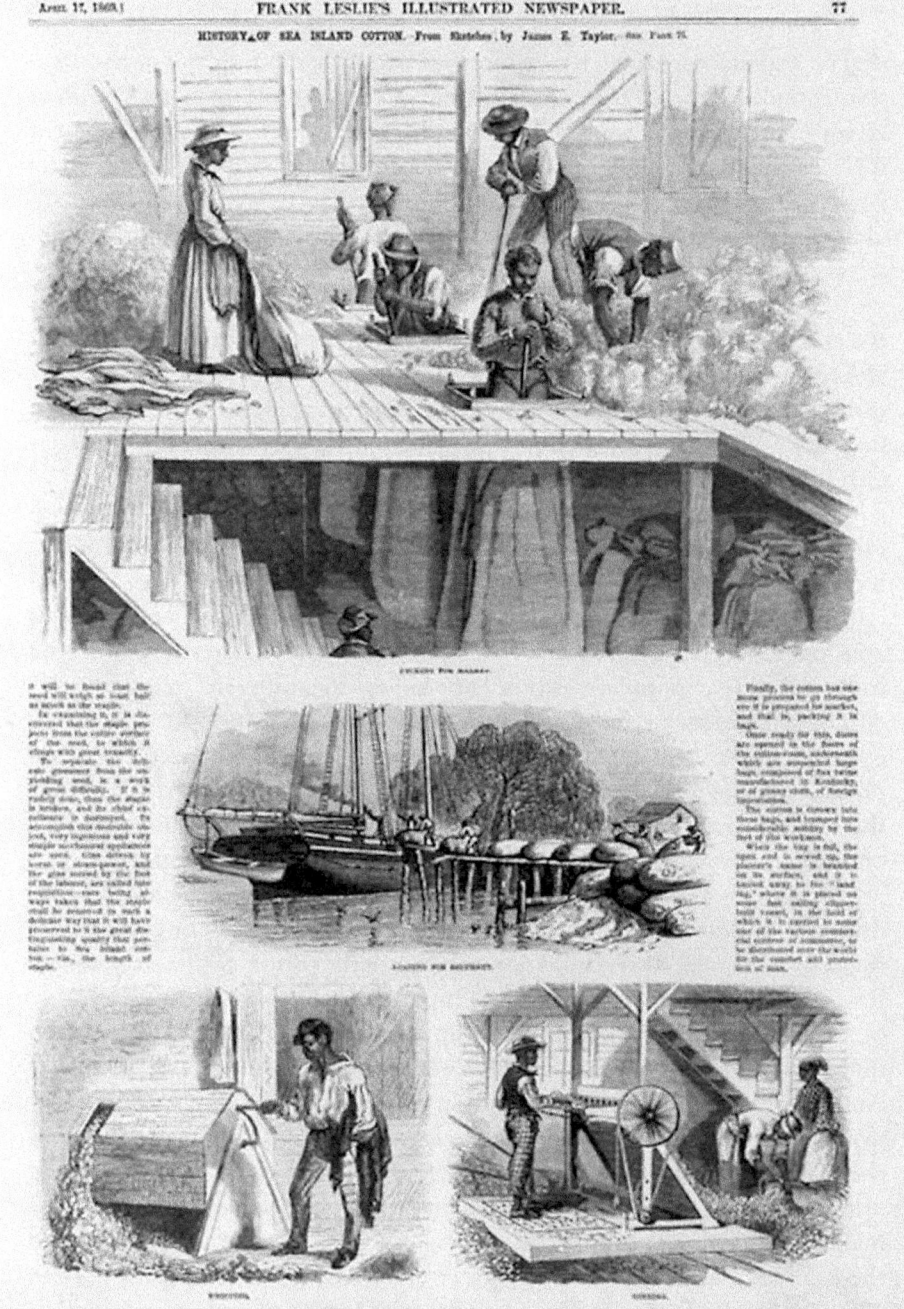

A depiction of the history of Sea Island cotton as published in *Harper's Weekly* on April 17, 1869 (Library of Congress, Prints & Photographs Division, LC-USZ62–116579).

and Georgia, the main crops grown were rice and indigo. Both of these products had such a steady demand that in these colonies there was little reason to move to a product such as cotton.

The final reason for the dearth of cotton production in the colonies was that of the original thirteen colonies, only two, South Carolina and Georgia, had become great cotton producing regions. It was not until after the Revolution that the cotton growing areas of these states became fully populated. As far as South Carolina was concerned, the most valuable of all cottons, the sea island variety, was not introduced into the United States until after the Revolution.

The importation of cotton into Great Britain had in 1784 risen to a high of 28,700 bales from a low of 13,000 bales in 1781. Importation received a great impetus in 1785 when Arkwright's patents, which had been stolen by outsiders (see the chapter on machinery), now became public property, expanding the number of mills. Imports of raw cotton reached 46,000 bales in that year, with increases in quantities in subsequent years. The problem with the increased imports was that the prices of raw cotton also rose due to the fact that England had only two suppliers—the West Indies and Brazil. The British mills therefore urged the East India Company to promote the importation of cotton from the territories in India under their jurisdiction. The company, looking for additional business, sampled the mills with Indian cotton, which unfortunately was of such poor quality it could only be sold at extremely low prices. "It is evident, therefore," says a letter of the Hon. Court, dated May 20, 1792, "notwithstanding the flattering allurements held out by the British manufacturers, that the article will by no means answer."[7]

The answer to the problem turned out to be from an unexpected source. In 1784 doubts were raised as to whether so large a quantity as eight small bags of cotton could have been raised in the Carolinas. In 1792, the probability of the American South becoming a large cotton producing area was considered so remote that John Jay, in the treaty he negotiated with Great Britain, gave his consent to an article which stipulated that no cotton should be exported from America, the object being not to exclude American cotton but to ensure to British shipowners the carriage of West India cotton to Europe.

The changes in the United States which would bring about the reliance on cotton as the country's primary export crop came about because of the problems the nation began to have with the agricultural products it had always relied on. The southern colonies suffered most from the devastations of the Revolutionary War, for, in addition to the natural poverty of the South, it had never been free from the presence of the enemy; and guerrilla warfare rendered almost impossible the raising of crops. Prosperous towns in Georgia such as

Sunbury and Frederica had been destroyed and New Ebeneezer with its flourishing silk industry had ceased to exist.[8] The rice cultivation which had been carried on along the coasts of the Carolinas and Georgia had greatly declined, owing to the fact that so many of the slaves had been killed or carried off during the war. The crop of 1783 was less than one-half the average annual production at the beginning of the war. Indigo, which before the war had been such a profitable crop, was so no longer, owing to the loss of a market. During the war, the East Indies had made large shipments of this commodity to England as it could be produced there cheaper than in America, so Great Britain no longer had an interest in buying from her former colony. The loss of this staple to America became permanent.

Even the sales of the colonies' major agricultural product, tobacco, was declining. The cause in this case had nothing to do with the war, but rather poor farming methods. The crop had been planted and replanted on the same land without rotation and without the application of fertilizer. The result was that the tobacco farms were quickly becoming exhausted. Jefferson, writing in his "Notes on the State of Virginia," in 1781, said that the culture of tobacco "was fast declining at the commencement of this war," and that "it must continue to decline on the return of peace." Among the "valuable substitutes when the cultivation of tobacco shall be discontinued," there will be, he adds, "cotton in the eastern part of the state, and hemp and flax in the western."[9] Although the production of tobacco did not show an immediate decline after the war, it was only because of its being grown in new areas, principally North Carolina, Kentucky, and especially Georgia, where it became the staple crop for a few years following the Revolution.[10] After the war, immigrants from the North and from Europe began to settle in the southern states and began raising wheat and corn. Although the wheat crop was basically successful, it did not do as well as it did in the North because of a blight called rust, and the corn crop was mainly used to feed livestock.

The biggest change concerning cotton at this time took place in Great Britain with the marketing and use of raw cotton. The first of these was the rise of a commercial class whose business was supplying the spinners and weavers with product and finding markets for the finished product. Close on the heels of this new class of industry came the great inventions in the textile industry: the spinning jenny, the water frame, the self-acting mule, and the power loom, in connection with the establishment of the factory system. Because of the new increases in production, the next step in the process was a large-scale producer of raw cotton.

The contribution of the United States to the process took place in 1786 with the introduction of long-staple cotton into the country. The advantages of this type of cotton over the short-staple, or upland, variety are found in the length and strength of its fibers and in its silky character, which render it capable of being spun into long threads. Also, it was more easily prepared for market than other cottons, for its seeds could be separated from fiber with little trouble using a roller gin. As valuable as this variety of cotton is, it soon attained its maximum cultivation, since it could be grown only on the sea islands in Georgia and a narrow strip of the adjoining mainland running from about Charleston, South Carolina, to the mouth of the St. John's River in Florida.

The answer was to have a type of cotton that could be grown in almost all areas of the South. The short-stapled variety fit that parameter and also had a strong fiber and the "wool" was much whiter in appearance than that of any other variety of cotton. The downside was that the green seeds of this cotton were very difficult to detach from the wool in what was now known as "upland cotton." The southern planters believed that if this cotton could be cleaned, it would prove to be superior to all other kinds as a marketable commodity. Various attempts had already been made to solve this problem. In India and other Asiatic countries, there had been in use for centuries a small hand mill called a *churka* to clean cotton. This machine, which had been introduced into America, was successful in cleaning the long-stapled cotton; however, it was found to be of no value in cleaning the upland, or short-stapled, cotton. The solution to the problem, as is well known, was furnished by Eli Whitney in 1793.

Whitney is an example of the type of person covered in the chapter dealing with the American inventive spirit. At the time he began work on his invention he confessed "that he had never seen either cotton or cotton seed in his life."[11] He was instead an individual with an ability for close observation, quick perception, and the application of an idea. While Whitney did not fully reap the rewards from his invention, his countrymen, especially the southern planters, did not fail to profit by it. The last obstacle to the cultivation of American export cotton had been removed, causing the spread of upland cotton throughout the South. Before this the British had complained about the dirty condition of American cotton on the market. But after the invention of Whitney's gin, cotton from the United States steadily became the product of choice.

In 1793, cotton exports from the United States were about half a million pounds; seven years later the export of raw cotton from the United States to Great Britain amounted to sixteen million pounds. This sudden development of the cotton producing powers of America was due to the economical results of Eli Whitney's cotton gin and caused great consternation among the West

Indian importers. The British commission merchants, Messrs. Ewart, Rutson and Co., said in a circular dated November 2, 1801:

> The quantity [of cotton] produced in Georgia and Carolina and on the banks of the Mississippi, in favourable seasons, will, in point of weight, exceed all the West Indian islands put together, and will have a serious tendency to depress the value of our own West India cotton. The consumption of New Orleans and inferior Georgia is become very general, and already precludes the sale of middling and inferior West India at the proportionate price we have formerly been accustomed to.[12]

Cotton had almost entirely monopolized the southern planters. Cotton displaced indigo as an export crop and checked for some years the expansion of rice growing. The southern farmers who had been meeting with some success in the growing of wheat now abandoned it for cotton, and the recently erected gristmills were left standing idle. Corn which in 1792 had been exported from South Carolina to the extent of nearly one hundred thousand bushels soon had to be imported for domestic use.[13] Tobacco, hemp, flax, barley and silk had all been exported from the South but were abandoned in favor of "King Cotton." In his *History of South Carolina*, David Ramsey said of the impact of cotton production, "It has trebled the price of land suitable to its growth, and when the crop succeeds and the market is favorable, the annual income of those who plant it is double to what it was before the introduction of cotton."[14] In 1802, the importation of American cotton exceeded that of the West Indies, and on March 1 of that year Messrs. Ewart, Rutson and Co. spoke of this increasing growth as "almost exceeding belief."[15]

After the Napoleonic wars and the War of 1812, there began an expanding industrialization of England and the rest of Europe accompanied by a gradual relaxation of restrictions on trade. The principal restriction was that of a tariff on imported cotton imposed during the eighteenth century for the purpose of impeding cotton manufacturing at the request of woolen and linen producers.[16] The other reason for the tariff was the British need for revenue because of the war with France during the closing years of the eighteenth century. While the immigration of people and capital into the United States played an important part in its growth in the thirty years after 1815, it was the expansion of the cotton textile industry and the demand for cotton both internationally and domestically which was decisive, In 1815, the previous sources of expansion—the reexport and carrying trade and manufacturers—were declining as a result of peacetime competition, and the American West was only a small part of the national economy. The United States was left with cotton as the only major export product. And this product was subject to the vagaries of the market, the speculative expansion of 1818, the radical decline in prices in the 1820s, and the boom in the 1830s, all of which were extremely important influences on the rate of growth of the American economy.

Cotton dominated the export trade. It constituted 39 percent of the nation's exports from 1816 to 1820, and increased to 63 percent of total export values from 1836 to 1840. Thereafter it dropped somewhat, but the high level continued and were over half the value of total exports for the remaining years before the Civil War. Great Britain alone took over half of the nation's exports, with France taking an additional 12 to 17 percent. The expansion of the cotton trade also had an impact on American shipping, which was now confined to the nation's import and export trade and engaged less in trade between foreign countries.

By 1846, the cotton of the American South had come to play an important and at times decisive part in Anglo-American relations. Cotton was to most people, both at home and abroad, chiefly the product of slave labor in the southern states, while wheat and agricultural produce in general from the North and West was a product of free labor. In the minds of many people, slave grown cotton from the southern states also had a certain stigma attached to it in England[17] because it had long enjoyed comparatively free access to the British market, where it held a commanding position, while "free grown" agricultural products, especially wheat, had been excluded from these markets to what was believed to be an injurious degree by the corn laws.[18]

With respect to supplies of raw cotton for her manufacturing centers, Great Britain was definitely and vitally dependent upon the United States and had been since about 1823.[19] In 1828, three members of Parliament, William Huskisson, John Gladstone, and William Meyers, who were also representatives of the British merchant shipping interest in the East India trade, looking to protect their interests against American competition seized upon the enactment of the American "Tariff of Abominations" in that year as an occasion to urge a retaliation in the duties on raw cotton produced in foreign countries.[20] Huskisson rose in the House of Commons on July 18, 1828, and delivered an unusual speech in which he plainly intimated that Great Britain might, in consequence of the American tariff, find supplies of raw cotton as well as markets for her manufactured goods elsewhere. A year later he declared that his purpose had been "to alarm the Southern States," where nullification of the tariff laws had already been threatened.[21]

Huskisson's speech may have had unintended consequences. American newspaper editors in favor of protective tariffs seized upon Huskisson's address, which was widely circulated in the American press as evidence of an inherent British hostility and for maintaining a tariff to keep British manufactured goods out of the country. The American people, the editors declared, were fully aware of the high degree of British dependency upon them for raw cotton supplies and "expect her [Great Britain] to be a very quiet friend of ours for the next three or four centuries."[22] The remarks of the *City Gazette* of Charleston, South Carolina, were even more pointed: "This celebrated speech is the boldest experiment upon the credulity and fears of the American people ever attempted.... He thought to frighten us.... Now either she is or she is not able to do without our Cotton and Rice.... Our course is plain. Raise less Cotton, buy less supplies, and by protecting our own manufactures prepare a home market."[23] Such observations naturally produced reverberations in the British press, newspaper, and periodicals. The net result was that now the citizens of both countries were aware of a situation which has continued to be important in the history of Anglo-American relations, not merely in the diplomacy of the American Civil War but from the 1820s to the present day.

How far southern politicians and statesmen acted after 1828 on the knowledge that Great Britain was seriously and even vitally dependent upon their constituents for supplies of raw cotton remains in large part to be shown. But it seems that northerners, keenly aware of the potency of the weapon in the hands of southerners and afraid of the possible consequences of its use, presumed too much and allowed their fears and suspicions to stand in the place of realities.[24] Northern antislavery leaders soon alleged that southern slaveholders were in control of the federal government and conducting the business of the State Department in commercial negotiations in their own interests and grossly neglecting the agricultural interests of the free labor sections of the North and the West.[25]

During the 1830s, the British cotton industry, which was rapidly expanding and keeping pace with the extension of the cotton culture in the United States, suffered from high prices whenever the American cotton crop fell short of expectations. During the period from 1838 to 1839, the problem was greatly aggravated when Nicholas Biddle, together with a group of investors, attempted with some success to corner the cotton market and to charge exorbitant prices. The result in Great Britain was a return to the situation in 1822 when the East Indian traders and the cotton manufacturers allied with the English antislavery movement to promote cotton growing by free labor in India. To support this effort, a British India Society was organized on June 1, 1839, with George Thompson[26] as secretary; the society was allied with British cotton manufacturing interests.

By 1839, the crisis caused by Biddle and his associates had passed and by 1841 good growing seasons and the westward expansion of cotton growing in the United States throughout the South into Texas restored abundant supplies at low prices and made possible another expansion of the British cotton industry through the erection of many new mills in the north of England. Because everyone involved in the cotton business on both sides of the Atlantic was making money, the trade promptly forgot Biddle's speculation and the precariousness of its position with reference to an adequate supply of raw cotton in the event of a shortage of product in America and became indifferent to the work of the British India Society. Thompson's flaming speeches were dismissed as so much antislavery rhetoric.

By 1846, however, the situation had reversed itself. The cotton cloth markets, especially those in India, had become saturated with goods pouring in at declining prices. Two consecutive short crops in the United States, those of 1845 and 1846, had produced first an exhaustion of surplus stocks of raw cotton on hand and next a sudden realization in the autumn of 1846 that the speculative rise in prices, evident in September, would continue to the point of stopping purchases for consumption by the mills. A corresponding rise in the price of cotton cloth was impossible. Orders would cease to come in, and manufacturers would refuse to build up stocks of expensive goods due to the high prices they would have to pay for the dwindling supplies of raw cotton.[27] By late 1846, the question of the British raw cotton supply was once again thrown into the political sphere, along with antislavery, the latter being used by the British cotton interests to promote its own ends.

The rapid development of the production of American cotton enabled the manufacturing industry of Great Britain to make much more progress than would otherwise have been possible. But so large an amount of capital and labor being dependent upon a single source of supply for the raw material necessary to keep the mills running and the operatives employed soon began to be regarded as a problem that needed to be addressed. So long as the stocks of cotton accumulated and the prices declined, there was no cause for alarm; but the moment the stocks dwindled and prices climbed the question of cotton supply came to the fore, generally in the shape of grumbling at the government for not having an alternate source of supply.

The *London Economist*, a free-trade journal three years old at this time, had acquired great authority and standing in the commercial community. Its editorials on the subject of cotton and the supply situation in 1846 came down on the side of encouraging cotton growing in India. The journal therefore supported John Bright[28] as leader of the Anti-Corn Law League to champion it in Parliament. In a speech on May 6, 1847, Bright moved for a select committee to inquire into the progress of the cultivation of cotton in India, declaring:

> That what potatoes are to Ireland, cotton is to Lancashire.... If we could conceive the raw material of the cotton manufacture greatly to fail, we should see calamities overspread this country to equal if not exceed that which has overtaken the

population of Ireland.... We ought not to forget that the whole of the cotton grown in America is produced by slave labor.... Whether it comes to an end by peaceable means or otherwise, there will, in all probably, be an interruption to the production of cotton; and the calamity which must in consequence fall on a part of the American Union, will be felt throughout the manufacturing district of this country.[29]

From the viewpoint of the British government there was such a difference between the cotton growers of the United States and those of India that even under the most favorable circumstances there would not be enough cotton cultivated in India to ensure Britain's supply of the product if there was no production from America. But Bright's motion could not be resisted. The *Economist* declared on May 8, 1846, that the failure of the cotton crop in America was a terrible misfortune. Thousands of operatives were out of employment, on account of the high price of cotton, "at a moment when their labour, or, in other words, its produce, is most required for the food they consume." The select committee Bright required was appointed, and along with it another to inquire into the causes of the commercial distress. This Parliamentary committee examined a large number of witnesses who looked into the situation in India, finding that the problems were uncertain land tenure, high taxes, bad roads, careless cultivation, and vagaries of the climate, which all had a hand in retarding the growth of cotton production in India. However, all of these problems could be alleviated with an infusion of British capital and enterprise as well as the English mills guaranteeing to purchase all of the cotton raised regardless of the quality.

The investigations and the published reports of the parliamentary committees were of great interest to southerners like J.D.B. DeBow, who exploited the material in his *Review*. Another short crop of cotton in the southern states (the last of three successive years) carried the cotton crisis of Great Britain over into the fall of 1849. The testimony of A.H. Wylie to Parliament on the British cotton stock in 1849 included the following:

> We are just in this Position, that with the Stock we now have, and with our Prospect of Supply, we shall be entirely dependent upon the United States for even a Sufficiency of Cotton for the ensuing year; and if Goods should become in Demand and Trade revive it is possible that we may not have the cotton to meet the Demand, and in that a deficient Supply of Cotton would limit the business to be done.[30]

An unusually large cotton crop in the southern states in 1849 gave some relief from the shortages and high prices. Demand rose in the consumer market, the depression ended and the unemployed returned to work; but the British cotton trade had learned a lesson not to be dependent upon one source of cotton. As a result, Parliament was petitioned in 1850 that measures be taken to promote the cultivation of cotton in India.

The business recovery beginning in 1848 in Great Britain was accompanied by diverse demands. First was for the importation of cotton from the United States, and second was for the abolition of slavery, while the American South, seeing fresh evidence of British dependence on its plantations for supplies of raw cotton, had developed a sense of independence which was destined to grown until it was cut short by the South's defeat in the American Civil War.

From 1850 to 1860, the average annual price of American cotton remained, comparatively speaking, steady. Some of the years had considerable price fluctuations, owing to the fact that estimates of speculators and the mills failed to conform to the actual conditions of the crops when they were harvested. Interestingly, ten years earlier a Professor M'Cay of the University of Georgia warned the speculators, planters, and mill owners about the fact that production was outrunning consumption. "There is nothing in the history of the cotton trade," he said, "nothing in the present state of the demand and supply; nothing in the present and future state of the stocks on hand, to justify an advance over the prices of 1842; and all attempts of speculators to force prices can only recoil on themselves.[31] The importance of M'Cay's argument, which he supported with statistics, does not seem to have been appreciated by the planters, because the crops grown over the next three years were the largest ever grown up to that time. While the situation had not changed during the 1850s, the decade was favorable to the planters and the mills. Production increased at a more regular pace than in any previous decade, and the consumption of American and European mills also maintained an almost uniform rate of increase.

By the end of the antebellum period, cotton had become the center of the world's most important manufacturing industry. Taking into consideration the number of people employed, value of output, and profitability, the cotton empire was without equal. Whole regions, such as the mill towns of the American North and South, Alsace, Saxony, the suburbs of Moscow, and Lancashire where large-scale production had begun, had come to depend on a predictable supply of cheap cotton. In England alone it was estimated that the livelihood of between one-fifth and one-fourth of the population was based on the industry; one-tenth of all British capital was invested in it; and close to one-half of all exports consisted of cotton yarn and cloth.[32]

The American cotton industry brought great wealth to European manufacturers and merchants, and bleak employment to hundreds of thousands of cotton mill workers. It also vaulted the United States onto the center stage of the world economy.³³ After Eli Whitney invented the cotton gin in 1793, American cotton moved in ever greater quantities to the factories of Europe. The American South, with enslaved labor and vast tracts of land, some of it recently emptied by government actions against the indigenous Indians, replaced early raw cotton suppliers from Brazil, the West Indies, and India.³⁴ By the late 1850s, the United States accounted for 77 percent of the 800 million pounds of cotton consumed in great Britain, 90 percent of the 192 million pounds used in France, 60 percent of the 115 million pounds spun in the German Zollverein, and as much as 92 percent of the 102 million pounds manufactured in Russia.³⁵ When the British economist J.T. Danson looked at the cotton situation in the United States and Great Britain in 1856, he concluded that:

> In 1787, we received no part of our annual supply from the United States. In 1824–5-6 we received thence *sixty-four* per cent of all we imported; and in 1853–4-5 this proportion had risen to *seventy-seven* per cent. Whence it may be fairly inferred that the United States possesses advantages, in the culture and exportation of this article, which place them, in this respect, far a-head of all their competitors....
>
> There is not, and never has been, any considerable source of supply for cotton, which is not obviously and exclusively maintained by slave-labour....
>
> The cotton of India does not hold a high rank in the European market, in point of quality. And the price at which it can be imported does not admit of its being brought into active competition in Europe with cotton of similar quality from the slave-holding countries of the west....
>
> That for the last fifty years, Great Britain, seeking her supply of cotton all over the earth, with a preference, during the greater part of that period, for the produce of free labour, has yet received, during the whole of that period, and continues to receive, all the cotton she imports of the better qualities, and by far the greater part of all she imports, in bulk as well as in value, from countries in which it is grown by slave-labour....
>
> In the ten years, 1801–10, the whole quantity of cotton wool imported into the United Kingdom was 592,000,000 lbs. In the same ten years we imported from the United States 263,000,000 lbs., or *forty per cent of the whole.*
>
> In the ten years, 1811–20, our commerce with the United States was, for two years, stopped by war. We imported 1,004 millions of pounds; and obtained 449 millions, or nearly half of it, from the United States.
>
> In 1821–30 the total importation was 2,008 millions; and the United States' share of it was *seventy-one per cent*.
>
> In 1831–40 we imported, in all, 3,873 millions of pounds, and took *seventy-nine per cent* of it from the United States
>
> In 1840–50 the whole quantity imported was 6,335 millions of pounds; and from the United States 4,985 millions or seventy-eight per cent.
>
> And in the five years 1851–55, when we imported 4,361 millions of pounds, we obtained 3,424 millions, or *seventy-eight per cent* of it from the United States.

During a great part of this period we gave a decided preference to the produce of free-labour.

Danson's conclusion, keeping in mind his stressing the idea of England's obtaining raw cotton not produced by slave labor follows:

> I. *That in the present state of the commercial relations of the two countries, the cotton-planters of the United States are interested to the extent of about two-thirds of their exportable produce, in the maintenance of the cotton-manufacture of the United Kingdom;—and*
>
> II. *That, reciprocally, the cotton-manufacturers of the United Kingdom, and through them, the entire population of the kingdom, are interested, to the extent of four-fifths of the raw material of that manufacture, in the existing arrangements for maintaining the cotton-culture of the United States.*
>
> On the important bearing of these two conclusions, assuming them to be sound, upon any proceedings for modifying the existing system of slave-labour in the United States, I cannot but deem it superfluous to say one word.[36]

Even before Great Britain abolished slavery, there was the beginning of, and effort to, abstain from slave grown products throughout the empire. Initially, this effort was thought to be particularly suited to female antislavery societies and by the late 1820s many of these organizations were active.[37] These societies concentrated their efforts on a boycott of West Indian rum and sugar. But with the rapid growth of the British textile industry, based on raw cotton imports from America, the question of Britain's role in maintaining and extending American slavery began to become an issue.

The backbone of this effort was the British Quakers, who, while not entirely supporting American abolitionist activity, did join in an effort of sustaining antislavery sentiment in England through the use of the free labor movement. At its height in the early 1850s, the movement never succeeded in importing more than a few hundred bales of free labor cotton for manufacture into textiles, at a time when British imports from the American slave states amounted to between one and two million bales per year.[38] The free labor movement was motivated by a moral principal but its supporters were also overly optimistic concerning what could be accomplished in economic terms. Reformers remained adamant that cotton manufacturers were generally uninterested in the moral aspects of their industry or their dependence on American cotton until the mid 1850s.[39]

Supporters of free labor faced additional problems. In the normal course of business there was no differentiation between slave produced cotton and that produced by non-slave labor. Therefore, the movement required that cotton should be inspected at all stages of its production and marketing, making it a more complex and expensive operation. Additionally, throughout the movement's history unscrupulous retailers tried to sell cotton goods they claimed were made from free grown produce but which had not been manufactured under the strict controls the free labor movement tried to establish. The movement's supply of free labor cotton, principally from the United States, was also erratic and did not always include a wide enough range of long- and short-staple cottons to produce all types of textiles which the movement wanted. This resulted in shortages or the manufacture of goods from unsuitable raw materials.[40]

The free labor movement did not succeed in attaining its ends because they were not practical and because the movement relied heavily upon men and women who were also active in a wide range of other social reforms. But it was a facet of the cotton trade between England and the United States. In a sense the free labor movement's end did occur before the American Civil War because of the fear of a "cotton famine."

In 1857, there was a slight rise in the price of raw cotton because of a short crop in the United States, which produced the usual feeling of alarm among the English mill owners. As a consequence, the mills banded together and formed an organization called the "Cotton Supply Association of Great Britain." The association believed that "it had a duty to inquire whether an increased supply of cotton can be obtained from other countries, so as to lessen the dependence of Great Britain upon the United States." Their object was to "engage in gathering and distributing information respecting the capacity of various districts, and furnishing the best seed, tools, and other implements, wherever they are likely to be advantageously employed."[41] The association planned to obtain government aid to build up the Indian transportation facilities, but the plans were frustrated by a more serious problem—the outbreak of the Indian Mutiny in 1857.

The establishment of the Cotton Supply Association turned out to be fortuitous for the British mills. A "cotton famine" had long been the specter that had haunted them. Their fears were not based on an armed conflict in the United States, but on their doubts that the southern states could supply the ever increasing raw cotton needs of the Manchester mills. There was also the ongoing British problem that the production of cotton was dependent upon slavery, and since this was the case there was no hope of having a successful cultivation of cotton by free labor. But—realizing that the cotton consumption of their mills was growing at a more rapid pace than the slave population of the South—Britain became alarmed that, while they wished the abolition of slavery in the United States, their economy depended to a large degree upon the product of slavery.

This dependence can be seen by looking at the British cotton situation on the eve of the American Civil War. England had 2,650 cotton factories in 1860 containing over thirty million spindles and three hundred fifty thousand looms operated by four hundred forty thousand persons. Ninety percent of these workers were adults, and 56 percent were female. In 1860 alone over one billion pounds of cotton were consumed, producing for export two hundred and eighty million yards of cotton cloth and nearly two hundred million pounds of twist and yarn.[42] Of the supplies of cotton for this gigantic industry, 77 percent came from the United States, 16 percent from the East Indies, and the remainder mainly from Egypt, Brazil, and the West Indies. Contained in these figures was the situation in the English counties of Lancashire, Cheshire, and Derbyshire, where 2,195 of the 2,650 factories and three hundred sixty thousand of the workers[43] were located. This vast population in a small area was dependent for its daily bread upon the fortunes of the cotton industry.

Although the probability of secession and armed conflict between the North and the South had been recognized for some time in Europe and America, the cotton industry on both sides of the Atlantic was unprepared for a long war. As far as cotton stocks were concerned, there had been a production spurt in England in 1860 and an increase in imports from areas other than the United States due to the efforts of the "Cotton Supply Association of Great Britain," which caused an overproduction of cotton products. At the end of 1860, the cotton stocks in England stood at 594,505 bales, the highest it had ever been. To this total was added an additional 1,650,000 bales sent by American planters from the 1860 crop because of the threat of war. The stock of cotton goods on hand was so large that the first sign of distress appeared in October 1861 when many British mills began to operate on a part-time basis. This was due to the overstocked condition of the market rather than a lack of raw cotton, yet the British mills were not prepared to dispense with American raw cotton. The reason was that without American cotton, even if cotton supplies of other countries were doubled, the mills would only have enough cotton for one year.

Both the North and the South believed that the war would be of short duration. When this turned out not to be the case, and with the blockade of the southern ports, cotton exports to England fell drastically. By early 1862, cotton imports from the United States fell by 96 percent, and British mills began shutting down for a few days each week, or entirely. Tens of thousands of operatives soon found themselves out of work. By early 1863, a quarter of the inhabitants of Lancashire, more than 500,000 individuals, received some form of public assistance. Workers, demanding relief, rioted in the streets of several British cotton towns, underscoring the explosive social consequences of the cotton famine. Similar crises erupted on the European continent, as posters went up in the textile towns of Alsace proclaiming "du pain ou la mort" (bread or death).⁴⁴

While the loss of the raw cotton was having a disastrous effect in Europe, in the Confederate states it was looked upon as an opportunity. This was, first, because the South believed that the European governments would give it recognition since they shared a common interest, that of being opposed to the encroaching tendencies and commercial policies of the North. The second reason had a more substantial basis and is best described by the phrase "King Cotton" diplomacy. Here the belief was that since "King Cotton" occupied a commanding position in the world, the overwhelming majority of southerners took it for granted that Europe's dependence on American cotton would lead to recognition of their independence. When Europe hesitated, the Confederate government attempted to force speedy recognition by withholding cotton. In the meantime, the Davis administration directed defensive war operations to impress upon the North and the world that the Confederacy possessed the capacity to govern itself. According to this school of thought, independence and peace would follow recognition. The third idea was that the Confederacy should accept Europe's friendly cooperation if it was offered, but the best course of action was to vigorously prosecute the war. This militant school of thought reasoned that meaningful recognition would follow victory.

A few of these ideas had at least some factual foundation. On December 15, 1860, the future chairman of the Confederate Committee on Foreign Affairs, Robert Barnwell Rhett, visited Robert Bunch, the British consul at Charleston. He left this interview with the distinct impression that Great Britain could be persuaded to recognize the independence of the Confederacy, if it were offered attractive inducements.⁴⁵ The *Toronto Leader* on January 24, 1861, announced "in the most positive terms that it is the intention of the English Government to acknowledge the independence of the Southern Confederacy as soon as it is formed."⁴⁶ By the middle of April, Consul Bunch informed Governor Francis W. Pickens of South Carolina that Lord John Russell had advised him that a northern blockade of the Confederate ports "would immediately lead to the recognition of the Independence of the South by Great Britain."⁴⁷ The French minister to the United States, Count Edouard Henri Mercier, also intimated to his close friend, Senator John Slidell that prompt French recognition would be forthcoming. Significantly, Mercier had recommended such an action to the Quai d'Orsay on March 21, 1861.⁴⁸ When the supposed recognition did not come, the wife of Senator James Chesnut of South Carolina expressed Dixie's apprehension in this prayerful fashion: "The Lord help us, since England and France won't—or don't."⁴⁹

The strongest ties between Europe and the South were provided by cotton. The phrase that "Cotton is King" was more than a boastful slogan to southerners of the 1850s. Statistics confirmed that four million Englishmen and one million Frenchmen depended for their livelihood on southern cotton. British textile manufacturers, politicians, and newspapers had encouraged the South to believe that their government would, if necessary, use its fleet to remove any obstacle in the way of the uninterrupted flow of cotton from America. Southerners accepted it as gospel truth that by shutting Britain off from their supply of cotton, they could "create a revolution in Great Britain." To prevent a social upheaval, they assumed, Britain would without delay recognize the independence of the Confederacy, a matter of vital importance to the newly proclaimed nation and state.[50]

The North, realizing the possibility of European recognition of the Confederacy, tried to undermine pro–Confederate sentiment by actively encouraging cotton production in other parts of the world, especially in Egypt. There was no little irony in the fact that the government of the world's greatest producer of cotton would encourage competitors to its most important export crop to emerge, but the military and political pressure was so overwhelming that it justified even extraordinary steps. Washington, wrote William H. Seward in April 1862, had "an obvious duty to examine the capacities of other countries for cotton culture and stimulate it as much as possible, and thus to counteract the destructive designs of the factious monopolists at home."[51]

As a counter to this move by the North, President Jefferson Davis tried different approaches, usually using cotton as an instrument of policy. At first he was so anxious to impress upon the world that a civilized and moderate administration held the reins of the Confederate government that he opposed an all-out war.[52] His original instructions to the agents he sent to Europe did not, therefore, include requests for substantial foreign aid or alliances. However, by 1862, when the effects of the blockade began to be felt more severely, the Confederate congress suggested that the president offer Britain, France, and Spain attractive commercial packages in return for their support. This policy reached its height in April of 1862 when Secretary Judah P. Benjamin was authorized to offer France not only generous trade privileges, but also 100,000 bales of cotton without cost, provided it would send ships to pick them up.[53] When France declined this baited offer, and Britain and Russia subsequently refused to join France in what they regarded as a futile mediation attempt, it became clear that the Confederate cotton policy could not coerce the European powers into recognition.

Britain, without whose cooperation no other European power would intervene in the American conflict, had many reasons to avoid choosing the southern side. Britain feared a Northern invasion of Canada if it abandoned its neutrality.[54] Also, whatever economic advantages the Confederacy could offer Britain, secretary of state William H. Seward's threat that any intervention in the Civil War would in the future justify United States intervention in European wars could not be taken lightly.[55] And it would have made little sense to risk losing Britain's best customer in exchange for one whose economic development and potential simply did not compare favorably with that of the United States.[56] British investments in United States railroads, banks, and mining and land companies, moreover, exceeded those in the English cotton industry.

Finally, while the British were opposed to slavery, their cotton merchants and manufacturers had for too long had their prosperity based on it. Profits derived from the trade in slave grown cotton had fueled the wealth of not only Britain but also France and Germany. Even for those who believed slavery to be an evil began to realize the economic problems if emancipation became a reality. The *Economist* was a case in point. Generally a strong opponent of slavery, its editors nonetheless feared that if abolition came to the American South "the catastrophe would be so terrible, its accomplishments so shocking, and its results everywhere and in every way so deplorable, that we most earnestly pray it may be averted.[57]

Conclusion

There was little indication at the time of the American Revolution that cotton would have the impact on the United States that it eventually would. This impact would be seen in every facet of American life, from its clothing through its economy. But it was the essence of America itself that allowed this impact to occur. If American ingenuity had not produced a means of separating the cotton from its seeds, none of what happened because of cotton's existence would have come to pass. Once the means of harvesting the cotton was solved, politicians procured the land to plant the crop by removing the indigenous population from some of the South's most productive farmland, making these Indians the first to feel the effects of the plant.

Since the success of a labor-intensive crop like cotton was directly tied to the ability of the landowner to procure workers who could survive and produce under the inhumane conditions in tending to the cotton crop of the Deep South, the promise of agricultural riches not only changed the history of the southern portion of the nation, but also caused the enslavement of hundreds of thousands of men and women, the effects of which have remained long after that bondage ended. Aside from the need for slaves to work the cotton crop, the connection of landowners to cotton denoted their worth. In 1805 there were just over one million slaves worth about $300 million; fifty-five years later there were four million slaves worth close to $3 billion. To put it another way, the value of capital invested in slaves roughly equaled the total value of all farmland and farm buildings in the South. Because of cotton, it is hardly surprising that southern slaveholders in 1860 were optimistic about the economic future of their region. They were, after all, in the midst of an unparalleled rise in the value of their human assets.

While an invention gave it the ability to process the cotton for use, a war, again with England, in 1812 caused the nation to begin its own manufacturing. Industrialists in New England, recognizing the potential for a domestic textile industry, began building cotton mills which benefited not only because of the invention of the cotton gin but also other machines invented both in the United States and abroad. This activity began the country's nascent foray into manufacturing, one that would eventually involve modern management practices and the amassing of great fortunes.

Employment also changed. Initially, under the British immigrant Samuel Slater, what was known as the "Rhode Island System" was established, which followed the customary patterns of family life in New England. Children aged 7 to 12 were among the first employees of the textile mill. Slater provided company-owned housing and stores, creating mill villages. Following his success, Francis Cabot Lowell built a new type of mill which was the first to produce cotton-to-cloth under one roof. Now, along with hiring workers from the local area who would return home after their day's work was done, Lowell recruited young New England farm girls to work the machines in his mill. The mill girls, as they came to be known, lived in boardinghouses provided by the company where they were kept under supervision and subject to a strict routine. The harsh conditions under which these women labored gave rise to the early labor movement, which initiated strikes in the mills in the 1820s and 1830s. These strikes would grow in strength after the Civil War when the mill workers were primarily immigrants.

Unskilled women and children could be employed in the textile industry because of the Armory System, which was developed in the 1820s and allowed cotton-factory workers to produce goods using a minimum of time and skill. Now manufacturing could be separated from assembly, allowing assembly to be carried out by sequentially adding parts to a product, a precursor to the modern assembly line, which became a prominent feature of production in the late 19th century. The Founding Fathers also became involved in cotton. Realizing its potential, Thomas Jefferson, a proponent of agriculture over manufacturing, facilitated the development of cotton-related machinery in his position as head of the patent office. Alexander Hamilton went even further, becoming involved in the procurement of foreign cotton manufacturing equipment and the opening of a mill.

American cotton had a profound effect internationally. By 1860 Great Britain, the birthplace of the industrial revolution and arguably the most powerful nation on earth, had become dependent on raw cotton furnished by its former colony. Nearly 4,000,000 British citizens out of a total population of 21,000,000 were affected by cotton textile manufacturing. Nearly 40 percent of Britain's total exports were cotton textiles and 75 percent of the cotton that supplied their mills came from the American South.

The effect of cotton on population was also profound. First, there was the forced migration of slaves from the older, northern part of the South to the newer cotton states in the lower southern states. As an example, in 1800 the slave population in Mississippi numbered 3,489; in 1860 the number climbed to 436,631. The new cotton lands besides Mississippi—Alabama, western Georgia, Louisiana, Arkansas, and Texas—were populated by another migration, that of whites looking to make a quick fortune. Again using Mississippi as an example, the white population in 1800 stood at 5,179; in 1860 it was 353,901. The economist Douglas C. North stated that cotton "was the most important proximate cause of expansion" in the 19th century American economy. The move into these new cotton lands was dictated by the price of cotton. Long swings in the prices were the result of periods of excess capacity, but once demand caught up to the level of supply, cotton prices would rise, resulting in the next move further west by planters and their slaves. These moves were financed by banks in the Northeast and England.

The cities also expanded. In the South, urban areas such as Mobile, Charleston, and Savannah increased their importance to the southern economy because of their use as cotton ports. New Orleans, because of its position on the Mississippi River as well as on the Gulf of Mexico, grew to the point where it was the only southern city among the first fifteen (by population) in the United States. Because the South needed to import agricultural and manufactured goods, other cities grew not because they shipped cotton, but because they supplied the South with necessary merchandise. Western farmers brought products into cities such as Cincinnati and Pittsburgh, which became river ports and centers of the early development of food processing for export to the New South.

Initially, transportation costs inhibited the supply of western foodstuffs, but once navigable waterways were created near the Mississippi, Ohio, and Illinois rivers and canals were built where necessary, there came about a substantial increase in supply. Now, with water transportation available, steamboats could made the upstream journeys that flatboat and keelboats could not, resulting in both lower shipping rates and a gain in travel time.

The boom in the South and the West was equaled by economic expansion in the Northeast. The financial, transport, and marketing services associated with cotton were prosperous, but more important was the demand for textiles that increased with the rising incomes in the new areas.

By 1860, New York city had literally become the capital of the South because of its dominant role in the cotton world. New York rose to its preeminent position as the commercial and financial center of America because of cotton. It has been estimated that New York received 40 percent of all cotton revenues, since the city supplied insurance, shipping, and financial services and additionally New York merchants sold goods to southern planters. Equally important was the fact that the raw cotton rarely traveled from the South to Europe or New England. The cotton boats sailed North to New York, and the cotton was offloaded and then reloaded onto ships bound for either New England or Europe. Those ships sailing to Europe were the first to sail on a schedule, ensuring that cargoes would reach their destination at specified times.

The antebellum United States witnessed an enormous increase in the production of short-staple cotton, and most of that cotton was exported to Great Britain and other European nations. By the mid–1830s, cotton shipments accounted for more than half the value of all exports from the United States. The income generated from the cotton exports was a major impetus for growth, not only in the South but in the rest of the economy as well. The low price of raw cotton produced by slave labor in the American South enabled textile manufacturers—both in the United States and in Britain—to expand production and provide benefits to consumers through a declining cost of textile products. As manufacturing of all kinds expanded at home and abroad, the need for food not only in southern cities but also in northern cities created a market for foodstuffs produced in the North. And the primary force at work was the economic stimulus from the export of southern cotton.

Cotton had a huge impact on the tariff policy of the United States, to the detriment of the South. After a number of tariffs were passed, usually befitting the North and the West, a compromise tariff was passed in 1857 which, even though characterized as "moderate," was considered an excessive level of protection by the South. In their eyes, it was an example of the willingness of the North and the West to make economic bargains at the expense of the South even though both sections enjoyed the benefits of southern cotton.

On the eve of the Civil War, cotton provided the economic underpinnings of the southern economy—both real and imagined: real because cotton dictated the South's huge role in a global economy that included Europe, New York City, New England and the American West; imagined because Confederate leaders believed an informal embargo on cotton would lead Great Britain into formal recognition of the Confederacy and to diplomatic intervention with other European countries on behalf of the South. This was the so-called King Cotton Diplomacy. Implementing it meant cutting off the supply of cotton to Britain's textile mills. While this "cotton famine" did eventually occur, when Britain's supply of raw cotton became exhausted it was not enough to draw England into the American Civil War. Cotton had benefited all of the sections of the nation that became involved in it, including the South, since without it they would not have had the wherewithal to commence the war. The Union's seizing and blockading southern ports showed that the failure of King Cotton diplomacy was merely a tactical blunder with no reflection on the power of cotton.

Chapter Notes

Introduction

1. George B. Tindall, *The Emergence of the New South, 1913–1946* (Baton Rouge: Louisiana State University, 1967), p. 124.
2. Joyce E. Chaplin, "Creating a Cotton South in Georgia and South Carolina, 1760–1815," *Journal of Southern History* 57 (1991), p. 199.
3. George S. Gibb, *Saco-Lowell Shops: Textile Machinery in New England, 1813–1949* (Cambridge: Harvard University Press, 1950), p. 10.
4. Ibid., p. 168.
5. William N. Parker, *Europe, America, and the Wider World* (Cambridge: Cambridge University Press, 1984), p. 45.
6. David L. Cohn, *The Life and Time of King Cotton* (New York: Oxford University Press, 1956), pp. 105–107.
7. V.S. Clark, *History of Manufacturers in the United States*, vol. 1 (New York: McGraw-Hill, 1929), p. 368.
8. Lance Davis, "Sources of Industrial Finance: The American Textile Industry, A Case Study," *Explorations in Entrepreneurial History* 9, no. 4 (April 1957), pp. 189–203.
9. Daniel Howe, *The Political Culture of American Whigs* (University of Chicago Press, 1979), pp. 104–106.

Chapter 1

1. F.W. Taussig, *Some Aspects of the Tariff Question* (Cambridge: Harvard University Press, 1915), p. 261.
2. Robert S. Woodbury, "The Legend of Eli Whitney and Interchangeable Parts," *Technology and Culture* 1 (Summer 1960), pp. 235–253.
3. John E. Sawyer, "The Social Basis of the American System of Manufacturing," *Journal of Economic History* 14 (1954), pp. 361–379.
4. Joseph Wentworth and George Wallis, *The Industry of the United States in Machinery Manufacturers, and Useful and Ornamental Arts* (London: G. Routledge, 1854), pp. iii-iv.
5. James Nasmyth, *Select Committee on Small-Arms*, Parliamentary Papers, 1854, XVIII, Q, p. 1367.
6. Joseph Wentworth and George Wallis, *The Industry of the United States in Machinery Manufacturers, and Useful and Ornamental Arts*, pp. iii-iv.
7. George Wallis, New York Industrial Exposition: Special Report of Mr. George Wallis, Parliamentary Papers, House of Commons, Command Paper, 1854, XXXVI, p. 5.
8. Eugene S. Ferguson, "On the Origin and Development of American Mechanical 'Know-how.'" *Midcontinent American Studies Journal* 3 (Fall 1962), pp. 2–15.
9. Zachariah Allen, *Science of Mechanics* (Providence, Rhode Island: Hutchens & Cory, 1829), p. 349
10. Frank W. Fox, "The Genesis of America Technology, 1790–1860: An Essay in Long-range Perspective, "*American Studies* 17, no. 2 (Fall 1976), pp. 39–40.
11. Alexis de Tocqueville, *Democracy In America*, ed. Phillips Bradley, vol. 1 (New York: A. Knopf, 1945), p. 46.
12. Wallis Report, p. 3.
13. Tocqueville, *Democracy in America*, p. 47.
14. Levi Frisbie, "Professor Frisbie's Inaugural Address," *North American Review* 6 (January 1818), p. 224–241.
15. Noah Webster, *A Grammatical Insti-*

tute of the English Language, part 1 (Albany: Charles R. & George Webster, 1796), p. 14.

16. Eugene S. Ferguson, "On the Origin and Development of American Mechanical 'Know-how,'" (Cambridge: MIT Press, 1992), p. 14.

17. Nathan Appleton: *Introduction of the Power Loom and Origin of Lowell* (Lowell: B.H. Penhallow, 1858), p. 12; Jonathan T. Lincoln, "Beginnings of the Machine Age in New England: Documents Relating to the Introduction of the Power Loom," *Bulletin of the Business Historical Society* 7, no. 5 (October 1933), pp. 10–12.

18. John S. Hekman, "The Product Cycle and New England Textiles," *Quarterly Journal of Economics* 94, no. 4 (June 1980), p. 701.

19. By 1831, when U.S. cotton textile production was slightly in excess of $40,000,000, factories accounted for $26,000,000 of the total value of output. By contrast, Albert Gallatin (secretary of the treasury under both Thomas Jefferson and James Madison), claimed that twenty years earlier roughly two-thirds of the clothing worn by the rural populace was the product of domestic family industry (T. Pitkin, *A Statistical View of the Commerce of the United States of America* (New Haven: Durrie and Peck, 1835), pp. 472, 482–484).

20. A. Gallatin, *Report on Manufactures: American State Papers, Finance,* vol. 2, report no. 325 (Washington D.C.: Government Printing Office, April 17, 1810), p. 430.

21. As an example, by 1823 there were streets in New York City which had front-lot values of $1,000 per foot and from that year onward the total assessed value of Manhattan real estate spiraled from $50,000,000 to over $76,000,000 in 1829, to slightly more than $104,000,000 in 1833, to $253,201,191 in 1836 (*Niles Weekly Register* 37 (November 7, 1829), p.164; vol. 38 (March 27, 1830), p. 85; vol. 44 (May 11, 1833), p.163; and vol. 51 (November 12, 1836), pp. 167, 176.

22. Allan Pred, "Manufacturing in the American Textile City: 1800–1840," *Annals of the Association of Geographers* 56, no. 2 (June 1966), p. 312.

23. V.S. Clark, *History of Manufacturers in the United States* (New York: McGraw-Hill, 1929), 4, pp. 244.

24. O. Handlin, *Boston's Immigrants, 1790–1880* (Cambridge: Harvard University Press, 1959), pp. 11, 74.

25. This notion that unskilled workers could not find employment was challenged by Samuel Colt, who explained to a British engineering group in 1851 that uneducated laborers made the best workers in his new mass production arms factory because they had so little to unlearn (Samuel Colt, "On the Application of Machinery to the Manufacture of Rotating Chambered-Breech Fire-Arms and the Peculiarities of Those Arms," *Minutes of the Proceedings of the Institute of Civil Engineers* 11 [London, 1851–1852], p. 63).

26. There were 34,102 spindles operating in the cotton mills of Baltimore County in 1839, but only 3,600 of these were within the city proper and they operated in the only steam-powered factory, which at this time employed 120 people. The situation was nearly identical in Philadelphia County, where only 3,120 of 40, 862 spindles fell within the city boundaries—and these were presumably steam-driven (*Aggregate Value and Produce, and Number of Persons Employed in Mines, Agriculture, Commerce, Manufactures, etc.*, Sixth Census of the United States, 1840 (Washington, D.C.: 1841), pp. 169–71, 217.

27. V.S. Clark, *History of Manufacturers in the United States,* p. 410.

28. Wesson was unusually well qualified to give an opinion on this subject. He was an enthusiastic advocate of a policy of industrialization for the South, and as such he was a student of southern industrial conditions. He was also the most successful textile manufacturer of the lower Mississippi Valley. His company was in such a strong position that its operations were unaffected by the Panic of 1857, which closed many mills of much larger size in both the North and South.

29. "The Textile Industry of the Old South as Described in a Letter by J M Wesson in 1858, *Journal of Economic History* 16, no. 2 (June 1956), pp. 201–204.

30. The seed-bearing capsule.

31. Arthur W. Page, "A Cotton Harvester at Last," *World's Work* 21, no. 13, pp. 748–760.

32. U.S. Commissioner of Patents, Report, 1850, Part 1, *Arts and Manufacturers* (Washington, 1850), pp. 233–234.

33. James H. Street, "Mechanizing the Cotton Harvest," *Agricultural History* 31, no. 1 (January 1957), pp. 12–13.

34. F.W. Loring and C.W. Atkinson, *Cotton Culture and the South Considered with Reference to Emigration* (Boston: A. Williams, 1869), Appendix H.

35. Joseph Gregoire de Roulhac Hamilton, ed., *The Papers of Thomas Ruffin,* vol. 1

(Raleigh: Edwards & Broughton, 1918–1920), p. 195.
36. Cornelius O. Cathey, "Agricultural Implements in North Carolina, 1763–1860," *Agricultural History* 25, no. 3 (July 1951), p. 135.
37. The weft is a thread or yarn of spun fiber.
38. Patent 931, 1769.
39. R.S. Fitton and A.P. Wadsworth, *The Strutts and the Arkwrights, 1758–1830: A Study of the Early Factory System* (Manchester, England: University of Manchester Press, 1973), p. 88.
40. Pollard, June 29, 1790, Patent Recs. Office, RG 241.
41. Between 1787 and 1789 New England entrepreneurs had been trying unsuccessfully to establish Arkwright's equipment. See William R. Bagnall, *The Textile Industries of the United States, Including Sketches and Notices of Cotton, Woolen, Silk and Linen Manufacturers in the Colonial Period*, vol. 1 (Cambridge and Boston: W.B. Clarke, 1893), pp. 83–84.
42. Including Alexander Hamilton.
43. John J. Fialka, "While America Sleeps," *Wilson Quarterly*, vol. 21, no. 1 (Winter 1997), pp. 48–51.
44. William Stevens, *A Journey of the Proceedings in Georgia, Beginning October 20, 1737*, vol. 2, London: S. Low, 1742), p. 325.
45. Jeannette Mirsky and Allan Nevins, *The World of Eli Whitney* (New York: Macmillan, 1952), pp. 303–304. This is why Whitney's gin is referred to as a "saw" gin.
46. Eli Whitney to his father, September 11, 1793, Eli Whitney Papers, Yale University, Sterling Memorial Library.
47. A major improvement on the Whitney principle came quickly. In 1796, Hodgen Homes was granted a patent for a gin in which saw-like teeth cut into iron disks replacing the spiked cylinder of the Whitney gin (Mirsky and Nevins, *"The World of Eli Whitney,"* p. 113–116).
48. "Manufactures of the United States in 1860, Compiled from the Original Returns of the Eighth Census" (Washington, 1865), p. ccxvi.
49. Aside from this problem, Whitney made some marketing mistakes: trying to rent rather than sell his machine and charging a ginning fee that made his technology more expensive than older methods.
50. Douglas C. North, *The Economic Growth of the United States*, (New York: Norton Library, 1961), pp. 52, 68.
51. "Extracts of a Letter from William McClure to Editor—Madrid, December 4, 1821: 'Progress of American Science,'" *American Journal of Science* 5 (New York, 1822), p. 197.
52. "Report on the Select Committee Appointed to Take into Consideration the State and Condition of the Patent Office," *Mechanics Magazine and Register of Inventions and Improvements* 7 (New York, May 1836), p. 330.
53. "Colt's Revolvers," from *Dover (England), Telegraph*, reprinted from *Appleton's Mechanics Magazine and Engineers' Journal* 2 (February 1852), p. 47.

Chapter 2

1. *Niles Register* 15, p. 135, quoting the *South Carolina Gazette*.
2. Thomas Cooper and D.J. McCord, *South Carolina Statutes at Large*, 10 vols. (Columbia: A.S. Johnson, 1836–1841), pp. 1837–1840.
3. A.S. Clayton, *Compilation of the Laws of Georgia, 1800–1810* (Augusta: Adams & Duyckinck, 1812), pp. 145–146.
4. H. Marbury and W.H. Crawford, *Compilation of the Laws of Georgia, 1755–1800* (Savannah: Seymour, Woolhopter & Stebbins, 1802), p. 371.
5. Reprinted in the *Athens (GA) Gazette*, April 18, 1816.
6. *Charleston Courier*, reprinted in the *American Railroad Journal* (December 13, 1834).
7. Flatboats were large oblong boxes which were floated downstream during high water. Typically they were broken up at the journey's end and sold for lumber. Keelboats were considerably more sophisticated, being built on a keel with plank-covered ribs and with a hull shaped somewhat like those of oceangoing vessels of the time. They operated with a large crew that sailed, rowed, poled, or pulled the vessel upstream.
8. James Mak and Gary M. Walton, "Steamboats and the Great Productivity Surge in River Transportation," *Journal of Economic History* 31 (September 1972), pp. 619–640.
9. U.S. Congress, House, Report on the Internal Commerce of the U.S., 1887, House Exec. Doc. 6, Part II, 50 Cong., I Sess. (1888), pp. 191 and 222.
10. Leland D. Baldwin, *The Keelboat Age on Western Waters* (University of Pittsburgh Press, 1941), pp. 180–182.
11. Ibid., p. 89.
12. *Western Monthly Magazine and Literary Journal* 4 (December 1835), p. 411.

13. *Tenth Census of the United States: Transportation* 4, pp. 662–666.
14. John James Audubon, *John James Audubon: Writing and Drawings* (New York: Library of America, 1999), p. 19.
15. Charles S. Davis, *The Cotton Kingdom in Alabama* (Philadelphia: Porcupine Press, 1974), p. 91.
16. Estwick Evans, *A Pedestrious Tour of Four Thousand Miles* (Cleveland: Arthur H. Clark, 1904), p. 325.
17. James Hall, *The West* (Cincinnati: H.W. Derby, 1848), p. 134
18. Louis C. Hunter, *Steamboats on the Western Rivers* (Cambridge: Harvard University Press, 1949), p. 366
19. John F. Stover, *American Railroads*, 2nd ed. (University of Chicago Press, 1997), pp. 10–20.
20. Aaron W. Marrs, *Railroads in the Old South, Pursuing Progress in a Slave Society* (Baltimore: Johns Hopkins University Press, 2009), p. 5.
21. *American Railroad Journal* 33 (1860), p. 670.
22. *1808 Report on Internal Improvements*, in Carter Goodrich et al., *Canals and American Economic Development* (New York: Columbia University Press, 1961), p. 246.
23. Inland Waterways Commission, *Preliminary Report*, 1908, pp. 205–209.
24. J. D. B. De Bow, ed., *The Industrial Resources of the Southern and Western States*, vol. 2 (New Orleans, Offices of De Bow's Review, 1852–1853), pp. 434, 450–454.
25. In 1850 nearly all of the 475,702 bales of cotton shipped to the eastern mills were transported by coasting vessels to eastern seaports. In 1855 there were 7,661 bales shipped to the North on the railroads. By 1859, the number was 106,678 of 786,521 (Joseph Nimmo, *Report on the Internal Commerce of the United States* (Washington: Government Printing Office, 1885), pp. 122, 128.
26. Stephen A. Caldwell, *A Banking History of Louisiana* (Baton Rouge: Louisiana State University Press, 1935), p. 42–55.
27. Robert G. Albion, *The Rise of the New York Port* (New York: Scribner's, 1939), p. 101.
28. Ibid., p. 120.
29. *De Bow's Review* 29, p. 484.
30. *Eighth Census of the United States, 1860, Agriculture*, p. clvii.
31. Herbert Wender, "Southern Commercial Conventions, 1837–1859," *Johns Hopkins University Studies in Historical and Political Science* 48, no. 4 [1930], chap. iii: "The Calhoun Convention."
32. E.P. Puckett, "The Attempt of New Orleans to Meet the Crisis in Her Trade with the West," *Proceedings of the Mississippi Valley Historical Association* 10 (1918–1919), pp. 481–495.
33. *De Bows Review* 29 (1860), "Southern Patronage to Southern Imports and Southern Industry," pp. 77–83.
34. *Seventh Annual Report of the Boston Board of Trade* (Boston, 1861), pp. 66–67.
35. Evelyn H. Knowlton, *Pepperell's Progress: History of a Cotton Textile Company, 1844–1945* (Cambridge, MA: Harvard University Press, 1948), p. 6.

Chapter 3

1. David J. Jeremy, "Damming the Flood: British Government Efforts to Check the Outflow of Technicians and Machinery, 1780–1843," *Business History Review* 51 (1977).
2. *Federal Gazette*, March 24, 1791. Parkinson initially argued that his was an "entirely new invention" that would be "of general utility to the United States."
3. Tench Coxe to Thomas Jefferson, March 14, 1791.
4. Only a few weeks earlier, Jefferson had submitted to Congress reports on the state of American fisheries and on Gouverneur Morris's mission to London in which Jefferson blasted English policy and proposed aggressive retaliatory economic diplomacy (Vernon G. Setser, *The Commercial Reciprocity Policy of the United States, 1774–1829* (New York: Da Capo, 1937), pp. 110–113.
5. Julian Boyd et al., eds., *The Papers of Thomas Jefferson* (Princeton: Princeton University Press, 1950), p. 340.
6. Joanne Loewe Neel, *Phineas Bond: A Study in Anglo-American Relations, 1786–1812* (Philadelphia: University of Pennsylvania Press, 1968), pp. 55–60.
7. Perry Walton, *The Story of Textiles* (Boston: J.S. Laurence, 1912), p. 144
8. Jefferson became secretary of state in 1790
9. Mitchell to Coxe, August 16, 1787; Coxe to Thomas Jefferson, September 15, October 4, 1787; Coxe to Mitchell, October 21, 1787; Mitchell to Coxe, May 4, June 4, 1788, Tench Coxe Collection, Historical Society of Pennsylvania.
10. Also Pennsylvania's delegate to the

Constitutional Convention and one of that state's first congressmen.

11. Coxe to George Clymer, January 17, 1790, Tench Coxe Collection. In May 1790, *American Museum* announced that Coxe possessed spinning machinery.

12. George Beckwith to William Wyndham Grenville, August 10, 1791, FO 4/12, 164–168, Public Records Office.

13. The secret war for the control of the British cotton machinery is described in David J. Jeremy, "British Textile Technology Transmission to the United States: The Philadelphia Region Experience, 1770–1820," *Business History Review* 47 (1973), pp. 24–52.

14. John E. Crowley, Jr., *The Privileges of Independence: Neomercantilism and the American Revolution* (Baltimore: Johns Hopkins University Press, 1993), pp. 77, 153.

15. John F. Kasson, *Civilizing the Machine: Technology and Republican Values in America, 1776–1900* (New York: Grossman, 1976), pp. 35–36.

16. George Cabot to Hamilton, September 6, 1791.

17. Moses Brown to John Dexter, July 22, 1791.

18. *Hamilton Papers* 9, p. 252.

19. Ibid. Hamilton borrowed this example from Coxe, who used it first in 1787 in a speech, *An Address to an Assembly of the Friends of American Manufactures*, pp. 13–14.

20. Ibid., p. 251.

21. Ibid., p. 262.

22. H.I. Dutton, *The Patent System and Inventive Activity during the Industrial Revolution, 1750–1852* (Great Britain: Manchester University Press, 1984), p. 21.

23. Christine MacLeod, "The Paradoxes of Patenting: Invention and Its Diffusion in 18th and 19th Century Britain, France, and North America," *Technology and Culture* 32 (1991), p. 898.

24. Christine MacLeod, *Inventing the Industrial Revolution: The English Patent System, 1660–1800* (Cambridge: Cambridge University Press, 2007), p. 108.

25. Hamilton, "Prospectus of the Society for Establishing Useful Manufacturers," August 1791, *Hamilton Papers*, vol. 9, p. 146.

26. Alexander Hamilton, *Report on Manufactures* (London: J. Debrett, 1793), p. 339.

27. John Morgan, "Whether it be most beneficial to the United States to promote agriculture, or to encourage the mechanic arts and manufacturers," *American Museum* 6 (July 1789), p. 73–74

28. *Hamilton Papers*, vol. 10, pp. 254, 271.

29. Hamilton, 3d draft of the ROM, p. 82.

30. Hamilton, ROM, p. 254. The opposition was not persuaded. James Logan charged that "under the *pretext* of serving the *agricultural interest*, Hamilton asked Congress to "grant exclusive privileges, bounties, and premiums, *to a few monied men*, to encourage them to extensive manufactures, and to enable them to import from Europe, necessary machines and workmen." *American Museum* 12 (October 1792), pp. 216–217

31. Washington to Congress, January 8, 1790 (Walter Lowrie and Mathew St. Clair Clarke, eds., *American State Papers, Documents, Legislative and Executive*, 38 vols., *Foreign Affairs*, vol. 1 [Washington, D.C.: Gales and Seaton, 1832–1861], p. 12).

32. Pamela O. Long, "Invention, Authorship, 'Intellectual Property,' and the Origin of Patents: Notes Toward a Conceptual History," *Technology and Culture* 32 (1991), p. 877.

33. Linda G. DePauw et al., eds., *Documentary History of the First Federal Congress of the United States of America*, vol. 1, *Senate Legislative Journal* (Baltimore: Johns Hopkins University Press, 1972), p. 271, p. 91n.

34. *Hamilton Papers*, 10, p. 296.

35. *Hamilton Papers*, vol. 10, p. 91. Benjamin Franklin commented in 1784 that "cheapness of land [in America was] inclining many to leave trades for agriculture" (*American Museum* 2 [September 1787], "Information for Those Who Would Wish to Remove to America," p. 214).

36. *Hamilton Papers*, X, p. 254, 270–271.

37. Hamilton rejected the prevailing economic view of the 18th century that assumed economic resources were limited and unlikely to grow significantly. Thus the U.S., which appeared in 1790 to be a conglomerate of sections and interests about to explode, survived all these crises, save slavery, with economic growth the glue (Peter F. Drucker, "On the 'Economic Basis' of American Politics," *Public Interest* 10 [1968], p. 35).

38. Hamilton, *ROM*, pp. 339–340.

39. Samuel Flagg Bemis, *Jay's Treaty: A Study in Commerce and Diplomacy* (New York: Macmillan, 1923), p. 49.

40. Hammond to Grenville, October 3, 1792.

41. Ibid., December 6, 1791.

42. *Hamilton Papers*, vol. 26, p. 828.

43. Paterson to Hamilton, February 10, 1791.

44. Neil Longley York, who examined the

numerous petitions for congressional assistance in the first two sessions, found many that asked for transportation subsidies. Congress turned them all down (York, *Mechanical Metamorphosis: Technological Change in Revolutionary America* (Westport, CT: Greenwood Press, 1985), p.174.

45. Paterson to Hamilton, February 10, 1791.

46. *Hamilton Papers,* vol. 10, p. 308.

47. I. Bernard Cohen, *Benjamin Franklin's Science* (Cambridge, MA: Harvard University Press, 1990), pp. 185, 199.

48. Franklin to William Shipley, November 10, 1755, in Leonard W. Labaree et al., eds., *The Papers of Benjamin Franklin*, vol. 6 (New Haven: Yale University Press, 1959), pp. 275-276.

49. James L. Huston, "The American Revolutionaries: The Political Economy of Aristocracy and the American Concept of the Distribution of Wealth, 1765–1900," *AHR* 98 (1993), p. 1081.

50. Peter Onuf and Nicholas Onuf, *Federal Union, Modern World: The Law of Nations in an Age of Revolutions, 1776–1814* (Madison, WI: Madison House, 1993), p. 203.

51. Ibid., p. 147.

52. Christine MacLeod, *Inventing the Industrial Revolution*, pp. 10–11.

53. Jacques Necker, *A Treatise on the Administration of the Finance of France*, trans. Thomas Mortimer, vol. 2 (London: Logographic Press, 1787), pp. 475–476.

54. Washington to Beverley Randolph, January 13, 1791.

55. Harry Ammon, *The Great Mission* (New York: Norton, 1973), p. 47

56. Doron Ben-Atar, "Alexander Hamilton's Alternative: Technology Piracy and the Report on Manufactures," *William and Mary Quarterly* 52, no. 3, Third Series (July 1995), pp. 389–414.

57. Alexander Hamilton and Henry Cabot Lodge, *The Works Of Alexander Hamilton*, Constitutional ed., vol. 4 (New York: G.P. Putnam's Sons, 1904), p. 70.

58. Andrew A. Lipscomb and Albert Ellery Bergh, eds., *The Writings of Thomas Jefferson*, vol. 2 (Washington, D.C.: Thomas Jefferson Memorial Association of the United States, 1903–1904), p. 229.

59. Thomas Jefferson, *Notes on Virginia* (Richmond: J.W. Randolph, 1853), Query 19.

60. Andrew A. Lipscomb and Albert Ellery Bergh, *The Writings of Thomas Jefferson*, vol. 12, p. 270.

61. Edwin Morris Betts, ed., *Thomas Jefferson's Farm Book: With Commentary and Relevant Extracts from Other Writings*, (Philadelphia: American Philosophical Society, 1944), p. 77.

62. Stephen B. Hodin, "The Mechanisms of Monticello: Saving Labor in Jefferson's America," *Journal of the Early Republic* 26, no. 3 (Fall 2006), p. 381.

63. Andrew A. Lipscomb and Albert Ellery Bergh, eds., *The Writings of Thomas Jefferson*, vol. 5 (Washington: Thomas Jefferson Memorial Association of the United States, 1903), pp. 58–59

64. Barbara McEwan, *Thomas Jefferson: Farmer* (Jefferson, NC: McFarland, 1991), p. 73.

65. Andrew A. Lipscomb and Albert Ellery Bergh, *Writings* 7, pp. 465–46.

66. Perry Walton, *The Story of Textiles*, p. 144.

67. James A. B. Scherer, *Cotton as a World Power: A Study in the Economic Interpretation of History* (New York: Frederick A. Stokes, 1916), p. 161.

68. Jefferson to Whitney, 1793.

69. Henry Clay gave this speech on March 30, 1824. He sought political measures to maintain and promote American industry and to limit foreign competition. Many American historians view the ideas espoused by Clay in this speech as formulating the basis for a political program that would come to be referred to as the "American system of manufacturers."

70. First American publisher to issue exclusively cartographic and geographic items.

71. Jefferson to John Melish, January 13, 1813.

72. One of Jefferson's strongest and most articulate political supporters and a fellow Virginia planter who also authored *Arator* and *An Enquiry into the Principles and Policy of the United States.*

73. Taylor to Monroe, October 26, 1810.

74. John Taylor, *Arator*, 6th ed. (Georgetown: J.M. Carter, 1814), p. 189.

75. James A.B. Scherer, *Cotton as a World Power: A Study in the Economic Interpretation of History*, p. 120.

76. Ibid., p. 76–77.

77. Stephen Yaffa, *Big Cotton* (New York: Viking, 2005), p. 72.

Chapter 4

1. David Eltis, *Economic Growth and the Ending of the Transatlantic Slave Trade*

(New York: Oxford University Press, 1987), p. 34.
2. Gene Dattel, *Cotton and Race in the Making of America* (Chicago: Ivan R. Dee, 2009), p. 8.
3. Catherine Drinker Bowen, *Miracle at Philadelphia: The Story of the Constitutional Convention, May to September 1787* (Boston: Little, Brown, 1966), p. 202–203.
4. Robert W. Fogel and Stanley L. Engerman, *Time on the Cross: The Economics of American Negro Slavery* (New York: W.W. Norton, 1974), pp. 86–89.
5. Harold G. Syrett, ed., *Papers of Alexander Hamilton*, vol. 19 (New York: Columbia University Press, 1976), pp. 443–444..
6. James A. B. Scherer, *Cotton as a World Power: A Study in the Economic Interpretation of History* (New York: Frederick A. Stokes, 1916), p. 199.
7. Ulrich B. Philips, *American Negro Slavery* (New York: D. Appleton, 1918), p. 190
8. James A. B. Scherer, *Cotton as a World Power: A Study in the Economic Interpretation of History*, p. 151.
9. Walter Johnson, *Soul by Soul: Life Inside the Antebellum Slave Market* (Cambridge, MA: Harvard University Press, 1999), p. 225.
10. Gene Dattel, *Cotton and Race in the Making of America*, p. 52
11. August Meier and Elliott Rudwick, *From Plantation to Ghetto* (New York: Hill and Wang, 1976), p. 57.
12. Robert William Fogel, *Without Consent or Contract: The Rise and Fall of American Slavery* (New York: Norton, 1989), pp. 44–45.
13. Lewis Cecil Gray, *History of Agriculture in the Southern United States to 1860*, vol. 1 (Gloucester, MA: Peter Smith, 1958), p. 666.
14. Robert Sobel, *The Money Manias: Tales of Entrepreneurs and Investors During the Eras of Great Speculation in America, 1770–1970* (New York: Weybright and Talley, 1973), p. 90.
15. Charles S. Syndor, *Slavery in Mississippi* (Gloucester, MA: P. Smith, 1965), pp. 240, 242.
16. Robert Russell, *North America, Its Agriculture and Climate* (Edinburgh: Black, 1857).
17. Frederick Law Olmsted, *A Journey to the Back Country* (New York: Schocken Books, 1970), pp. 351–352.
18. An embankment designed to prevent the flooding of a river.
19. Robert W. Harrison, "Levee Districts and Levee Building in Mississippi: A Study in State and Local Efforts to Control Mississippi River Floods," published by Delta Council, Mississippi Levee Commissioners, Board of Levee Commissioners for the Yazoo-Mississippi Delta and Mississippi Agricultural Experiment Station (October 1951), pp. 7–8.
20. James A. Scherer, *Cotton as a World Power: A Study in the Economic Interpretation of History*, pp. 218–222.
21. This company was a major supplier of armaments to the Confederacy during the Civil War.
22. Cassius Marcellus Clay, "Slavery: The Evil—The Remedy," republished by Horace Greeley in the *New York Tribune*, 1848.
23. Robert W. Fogel and Stanley Engerman, *Time on the Cross: The Economics of American Negro Slavery*, pp. 171–172.
24. Ibid., pp. 172–173.
25. J.E. Cairnes, *The Slave Power: Its Character, Career, and Probable Designs; Being an Attempt to Explain the Real Issues Involved in the American Contest* (reprint, New York: Kelles, 1968), p. 147.
26. *The Southern States: Embracing a Series of Papers Condensed from the Earlier Volumes of De "Bow's Review,"* p. 61.
27. Ibid., p. 122.
28. Douglass C. North, *The Economic Growth of the United States, 1790–1860* (New York: Norton Library, 1966), p. 122.
29. A.H. Conrad and John R. Myers, "The Economics of Slavery in the Ante-Bellum South," *Journal of Political Economy* 6, no. 2 (April 1958), p. 95.
30. Robert W. Fogel and Stanley L. Engerman, *Time on the Cross: The Economics of American Negro Slavery*, p. 204.
31. Ibid., pp. 212, 86–94.
32. Elizabeth Fox-Genovese and Eugene D. Genovese, *Fruits of Merchant Capital* (New York: Oxford University Press, 1983), p. 37.

Chapter 5

1. John A. James, "The Optimal Tariff in the Antebellum United States," *American Economic Review* 71, no. 4 (September 1981), p. 726.
2. Hamilton to James Duane, September 3, 1780.
3. John C. Miller, *Alexander Hamilton: Portrait in Paradox* (New York: Harper, 1959), pp. 134, 388.
4. U.S. Congress, *New American State Papers: Manufactures*, vol. 1, p. 37.
5. John C. Miller, *Alexander Hamilton: Portrait in Paradox*, pp. 222–225.

6. "Continentalist No. V," April 18, 1782, Papers of Alexander Hamilton, vol. 3, pp. 78–79.
7. U.S. Congress, *American State Papers, Finance*, vol. 1, pp. 158–161.
8. Ibid., p. 161.
9. Annals of Congress, vol. 3, (January 1791), p. 349, and (April 1792), p. 569.
10. Gerald Clarfield, "Protecting the Frontiers: Defense Policy and the Tariff Question in the First Washington Administration," *William and Mary Quarterly* 32 (July 1975), p. 459.
11. John C. Miller, *Alexander Hamilton: Portrait in Paradox*, pp. 393–400.
12. Hamilton to Thomas Pinckney, June 25, 1794, *Papers of Alexander Hamilton*, vol. 16, p. 527.
13. Hamilton to Benjamin Lincoln, June 28, 1794, and *Report on the Subject of Manufacturers*, Third Draft, *Papers of Alexander Hamilton*, vol. 10, p. 104.
14. John C. Miller, *Alexander Hamilton: Portrait in Paradox*, p. 546.
15. Robert B. Zevin, "The Growth of Cotton Textile Production After 1815," In *The Reinterpretation of America's Past*, ed. Robert Fogel and Stanley Engerman (New York: Harper & Row, 1971), pp. 122–147.
16. Caroline F. Ware, *The Early New England Cotton Manufacture* (New York: Russell & Russell, 1966), p. 66.
17. Willard L. Thorp, *Business Annals* (New York: National Bureau of Economic Research, 1926), pp. 117–118.
18. *Annals of Congress*, p. 966.
19. Edward Stanwood, *American Tariff Controversies in the Nineteenth Century*, 2 vols. (New York: Houghton Mifflin, 1903), pp. 131–132.
20. Mark Bils, "Tariff Protection and Production in the Early U.S. Cotton Textile Industry," *Journal of Economic History* 44 (December 1984), pp. 1033–1045.
21. Caroline Ware, *The Early New England Cotton Manufacture*, p. 72.
22. Duty on an item based on its value rather than any other factor such as, e.g., quantity, size or weight.
23. Henry Louis Stettler III, "Growth and Fluctuations in the Ante-Bellum Textile Industry" (PhD diss., Department of Economics, Perdue University, 1970), p. 212.
24. Robert B. Zevin, *The Growth of Cotton Textile Production After 1815*, p. 123.
25. Annals of Congress, 14 Cong., 1st Sess., p. 1330.
26. James R. McKissick, *Notes on the Early History of Cotton and Cotton Manufactures in South Carolina* (Spartanburg, SC: Band & White, 1927), p. 18–19.
27. Ibid., p. 19.
28. Victor S. Clark, *History of Manufactures in the United States*, 3 vols. (New York: McGraw-Hill, 1929), 1, opp. p. 536 (cotton mills), opp. p. 562 (woolen mills).
29. Annals of Congress, 14 Cong., 1st Sess., pp. 1634–1635.
30. Ibid., p. 1261.
31. Ibid., p. 1351.
32. *Niles' Weekly Register* 11 (December 1816), p. 284.
33. Annals of Congress, 14 Cong., 1 Sess., pp. 1329–1332.
34. Annals of Congress, 15 Cong., 1 Sess., pt. 2, & p. 1732.
35. See speech of Representative Nathaniel Silsbee of Massachusetts, *Annals of Congress*, 16 Cong., 1, Sess., pt. 2, 1989.
36. Frank W. Taussig, *Tariff History of the United States* (London: G.P. Putnam's Sons, 1931), pp. 30–31.
37. Annals of Congress, 16 Cong., 1 Sess., pt. 2, p. 2071.
38. Norris W. Preyer, "Southern Support of the Tariff of 1816: A Reappraisal," *Journal of Southern History* 25, no.3 (August 1959), pp. 306–322.
39. Charles Francis Adams, ed., *Memoirs of John Quincy Adams*, vol. 4 (Philadelphia: J.B. Lippencott, 1874–1877), p. 497.
40. Clyde N. Wilson, "Calhoun's Economic Platform," in *Slavery, Secession, and Southern History*, Robert Louis Paquette & Louis A. Ferleger, eds. (Charlottesville: University of Virginia Press, 2000), pp. 87–88.
41. *Memorial of a Convention of the Friends of National Industry ... Delegates from Maryland, Rhode Island, Connecticut, New York, New Jersey, Pennsylvania, Massachusetts, Delaware, and Ohio*, 16 Cong., 1st sess., 31, H.R. Doc. 9 (December 20, 1819), p. 3.
42. *Remonstrance of the Virginia Agricultural Society of Fredericksburg*, 16th Cong., 1st sess. H.R. Doc. 24 (February 2, 1821), p. 4.
43. United Agricultural Society of Virginia, 16th Cong., 1st sess., Finance 570 (January 17, 1820), p. 460.
44. *Annals*, 18th Cong., 1st sess., p. 1979.
45. Charles H. Evans, comp., *Exports, Domestic and Foreign*, 48th Cong., 1st sess., H.R. Misc. Doc. 492 (1884), p. 68.
46. Frank W. Taussig, *The Tariff History of the United States*, pp. 88–89.

47. Ibid., pp. 135–136.
48. True economic profit after taking into account the profit that could be made by investing elsewhere.
49. Mark Bils, "Tariff Protection and Production in the Early United States Cotton Textile Industry," *Journal of Economic History* 44 (December 1984), pp. 1033–1045.
50. Harley C. Knick, "International Competitiveness of the Antebellum American Textile Industry," *Journal of Economic History* 52 (September 1992), pp. 559–584.
51. Robert B. Zevin, "The Growth of Cotton Textile Production After 1815," in Robert Fogel and Stanley Engerman, eds., *The Reinterpretation of America's Past* (New York: Harper & Row, 1974), pp. 126–127.
52. Annals of Congress, House of Representatives, 16th Cong., 1st sess., p. 2078.

Chapter 6

1. Nicholas Biddle to Jim McKim, 1827, quoted in Ralph C. Catterall, *Second Bank of the United States* (Chicago: University of Chicago Press, 1960), p. 100.
2. Register of Debates, Senate, 23rd Cong. 1st sess. (May 26, 1834), p. 1808.
3. John M. Dobson, *History of American Enterprise*, (Upper Saddle River, NJ: Prentice Hall), p. 91.
4. Congressional Globe, Senate, 35th Cong., 1st sess. (March 4, 1858), p. 961.
5. David L. Cohn, *The Life and Times of King Cotton* (New York: Oxford University Press, 1956), p. 112.
6. Ibid., p. 113.
7. Ibid., p. 116.
8. To discount is to sell for cash, with a sum deducted from the face value of the note.
9. Report on U.S. Bank, 1841, p. 18.
10. *Financial Register*, 1838, Vol. 2, p. 140, Liverpool report of July 10, 1838.
11. Richardson Wright, *Hawkers and Walkers in Early America* (Philadelphia: J.B. Lippencott, 1927), pp. 37–38.
12. Ibid., p. 65.
13. Robert Sutcliff, *Travels in Some Parts of North America, in the Years 1804, 1805, and 1806* (Philadelphia: B & T Kite, 1812), pp. 90–91.
14. Fred Mitchell Jones, *Middlemen in the Domestic Trade of the United States, 1800–1860* (Urbana: University of Illinois, 1937), p. 62.
15. William Bostwick Papers, Beinecke Rare Book and Manuscript Library, Yale University.
16. Ibid.
17. Fenner's *Southern Medical Reports*.
18. Stuart Bruchey, *Cotton and the American Economy, 1790–1860*, (New York: Harcourt, Brace & World, 1967), p. 110.
19. Guy S. Callender, ed., *Selections from the Economic History of the United States, 1765–1860* (Boston: Ginn, 1909), pp. 283–284.
20. Ibid., pp. 290–294
21. Stuart Bruchey, *Cotton and the Growth of the American Economy, 1790–1860*, p. 157.
22. Hinton B. Helper, *Compendium of the Impending Crisis of the South* (New York: A.B. Burdick, 1860), pp. 144, 288–289.
23. Robert William Fogel and Stanley L. Engerman, *Time on the Cross: The Economics of American Negro Slavery* (New York: W.W. Norton, 1974), pp. 90–94.
24. Ibid., p. 250.
25. Robert G. Albion, *The Rise of New York Port, 1815–1860* (New York, Scribner's), p. 116.
26. Avery Luvere Carlson, *A Monetary and Banking History of Texas* (Fort Worth: Fort Worth National Bank, 1930), pp. 1–18.
27. McKinney to Williams, January 27, 1839, Williams Papers.
28. Williams to Anson Jones, in Anson Jones, *Republic of Texas* (reprint: Chicago: Rio Grande Press, 1966), p. 146.
29. Arthur Ikin, *Texas* (Waco: Texian Press, 1964), p. 68.
30. *Telegraph and Texas Register*, June 24, 1840.
31. Abigail Curlee Holbrook, "Cotton Marketing in Antebellum Texas," *Southwestern Historical Quarterly* 73, no. 4 (April 1970), pp. 431–455.
32. Hines Holt to Farish Carter, March 28, 1841 (first quotation); Richard Long to Carter, May 7, 1842, Farish Carter Papers, Southern Historical Collection, University of North Carolina, Chapel Hill.
33. Lynn Willoughby Ware, "Cotton Money: Antebellum Currency Conditions in the Apalachicola/Chattahoochee River Valley," *Georgia Historical Quarterly* 74, no. 2 (Summer 1990), pp. 220–221, 233.

Chapter 7

1. Albert Gallatin, "Manufactures," *American State Papers, Finance*, vol. 2, p. 427.
2. *Twelfth Census of the United States: 1900*, "Manufactures," vol. 3, p. 54.

3. Clive Day, "Early Development of the American Cotton Manufacturing, *Quarterly Journal of Economics* 39 (December 1924), p. 452.

4. Victor S. Clark, *History of Manufactures in the United States*, 2nd ed., vol. 1 (New York: McGraw-Hill, 1929), p. 398.

5. Massachusetts General Court, *House Document*, 1842, #4, p. 2.

6. *General Statutes of Massachusetts*, Chapter 53, Section 3, Laws of 1860.

7. Firms that marked the cotton mills' output.

8. R.G. Albion, *Rise of the Port of New York, 1815–1860* (New York: Scribner's, 1939), p. 63.

9. *Dry Goods Economist*, Jubilee Issue (1896), pp. 103–104.

10. Quoted in the *Boston Commercial Bulletin*, August 17, 1872.

11. *Fall River Monitor*, July 7, 1827.

12. A mill girl who wrote about her experiences at Lowell.

13. Hannah Josephson, *The Golden Threads: New England's Mill Girls and Magnates* (New York: Duell, Sloan and Pearce, 1949), p. 95.

14. Nathan Appleton to the Middlesex Mechanics Association, December 30, 1846. Ironically, at the time this letter was written wages were being reduced and the work day lengthened. He was one of the original mill owners, a Boston Associate.

15. Lawrence was one of the mill owners in Lowell. By 1854, he had become an ardent abolitionist. Speaking of his conversion, he said, "[W]e went to bed one night old fashioned, conservative, Compromise Union Whigs & waked up stark mad Abolitionists" (James M. McPherson, *Battle Cry of Freedom: The Civil War Era* [New York: Oxford University Press, 1988], p. 120).

16. Arthur L. Eno, *Cotton Was King: A History of Lowell, Massachusetts* (Somersworth, NH: New Hampshire Publishing, 1976), p. 128.

17. David Crockett, *The Life of David Crockett*, (New York: Scribner's, 1923), p. 246.

18. William T. Thompson, *Major Jones' Sketches of Travels* (Charlottesville: University of Virginia Press, 2000).

19. Stephen Yafa, *Big Cotton* (New York: Viking, 2005), p. 96.

20. *Voice of Industry*, September 25, 1846.

21. *Factory Girls' Album and Operatives' Advocate*, Exeter (New Hampshire), February 4, 1846. This magazine was an open advocate of the rights of female operatives..

22. Lucy Larcom, "Among Lowell Mill Girls," *Atlantic Monthly* (November 1881).

23. Samuel Adams Drake, *History of Middlesex County, Massachusetts*, vol. 2 (Boston: Estes and Lauriat, 1880), p. 102.

24. Hannah Josephson, *Golden Threads: New England Mill Girls and Magnates*, p. 71.

25. Bagley's Letter, *Voice of Industry*, September 8, 1846.

26. *Voice of Industry*, June 12, 1846.

27. Strike.

28. *Zion's Herald*, October 5, 12, 1836.

29. Edith Abbot, *Women in Industry: A Study in American Economic History* (New York: Source Book Press, 1970), p. 131n.

30. Linda K. Kerber, *Women of the Republic: Intellect and Ideology in Revolutionary America* (Chapel Hill: University of North Carolina Press, 1980).

31. *Voice of Industry*, June 12, 1846.

32. *Factory Girls' Album*, February 14, 1846.

33. *Voice of Industry*, February 19, 1847.

34. Jama Lazerow, "Religion and the New England Mill Girl: A New Perspective on an Old Theme," *New England Quarterly* 60, no. 3, (September 1987): p. 452.

35. Nathan Appleton, *Labor: Its Relations in Europe and the United States Compared* (Boston: Eastburn's Press, 1844), pp. 12–14.

36. John Aiken, *Labor and Wages at Home and Abroad* (Lowell: D. Bixby, 1849), p. 16.

37. John G. Nicolay and John Hay, eds., *Abraham Lincoln: Complete Works*, vol. 1 (New York: F.D. Tandy, 1894), p. 625.

38. American antebellum workers' and suffrage organizer.

39. Seth Luther, *An Address to the Working Men of New England on the State of Education and on the Condition of the Producing Classes in Europe and America*, 2nd ed. (New York: The Author, 1832), p. 6.

40. *Factory Girl's Album and Operative's Advocate*, "Beauties of Factory Life" (November 1846).

41. Harriet Robinson, *Loom and Spindle; or, Life Among the Early Mill Girls* (Kailua, HI: Press Pacifica, 1976), pp. 194–195.

42. Caroline F. Ware, *Early New England Cotton Manufacture* (New York: Russell and Russell, 1966), pp. 251–252.

43. Ray Ginger, "Labor in a Massachusetts Cotton Mill, 1853–60," *Business History Review* 28, no. 1 (March 1954), p. 72.

44. Helen L. Sumner, *History of Women in Industry in the United States* (New York: Arno Press, 1974), p. 34.

45. Edgar W. Martin, *The Standard of Living in 1860: American Consumption Levels on the Eve of the Civil War* (University of Chicago Press, 1942), pp. 398–401.
46. From the savings accounts of the Lyman Mills in Holyoke, Massachusetts.
47. Constance McLaughlin Green, *Holyoke, Massachusetts* (New Haven: Yale University Press, 1939), p. 59.
48. Ibid., pp. 41–44.
49. Mary Morrison to Stephen Holman, May 28, 1856, Lyman Mills Papers.
50. Evelyn H. Knowlton, *Pepperell's Progress: History of a Cotton Textile Company, 1844–1945* (Cambridge: Harvard University Press, 1948), p. 59.
51. Lyman Mills Papers.
52. Jane Wallace to Stephen Holman, December 8, 1858, Lyman Mills Papers.
53. Ibid., October 9, 1858.
54. Elisha Bartlett, *A Vindication of the Character and Condition of the Females Employed in the Lowell Mills ...* (Lowell: L. Huntress, 1841), p. 14.
55. Samuel Batchelder, *Introduction and Early Progress of the Cotton Manufacture in the United States* (Boston: Little, Brown, 1863), p. 89.
56. H.C. Carey, *Essay on the Rate of Wages...* (New York: Kelley, 1965), pp. 78–79
57. Nathan Appleton, *Introduction of the Power Loom, and Origin of Lowell* (Lowell: B.H. Penhallow, 1858), p. 32.
58. Carew Manufacturing Co. Papers, Time Book, 1850–1866. A situation similar to Holyoke's obtained in Chicopee where "foreign girls have been employed in such numbers that what American girls are employed there, experience considerable difficulty in finding society among their workmates congenial to their tastes and feelings," *Hampden, Freeman*, March 13, 1852.
59. Holyoke, Town Records, 1853, p. 8.
60. *History of the H.F. Co.*, pp. 11–13; Lyman Mill Papers, Davis to Mills, March 5, 1857.
61. *Holyoke Freeman*, May 28, June 25, 1853.

Chapter 8

1. Fred Bateman and Thomas Weiss, *A Deplorable Scarcity: The Failure of Industrialization in the Slave Economy* (Chapel Hill: University of North Carolina Press, 1981), p. 26.
2. *American Farmer*, September 28, 1827, "Cotton Bagging."
3. Ibid., January 18, 1828, "A Report on the Establishment of Cotton and Woolen Manufacturers and on the Growing of Wool; Made to the House of Commons of North Carolina by Mr. Fisher, from Rowan, on Tuesday, January 1, 1828."
4. *Athenian*, January 4, 1828.
5. Ibid., January 27, 1828.
6. *Tuscumbia North Alabamian*, March 13, 1841.
7. *Montgomery Independent*, copied in *Niles Weekly Register* 69 (1845), p. 188.
8. *Mobile Daily Register*, February 15, 1850.
9. Collier's speech is quoted in its entirety in Richard W. Griffin, "North Carolina: The Origins and Rise of the Cotton Textile Industry" (PhD diss., Ohio State University, 1954), pp. 310–314.
10. Ibid., p. 67.
11. *Gales and Seaton's Register of Debates in Congress*, 22nd Congress, 1st sess., vol. 8, pt. 3: 1832, p. 3555.
12. *Athenian*, March 31, 1829.
13. Deed Book "Q," p. 58–60.
14. *Southern Banner*, February 22, 1834, "Died."
15. *Gales and Seaton's Register of Debates in Congress*, 22nd congress, 1st sess., vol. 18, pt. 3: 1832, p. 3549–3550.
16. *New York Journal of Commerce*, as quoted in the *Athenian*, May 5, 1829.
17. *Athenian*, July 26, 1831.
18. Broadus Mitchell, *The Industrial Revolution in the South* (New York: New American Library 1930), pp. 240–241.
19. *Montgomery Tri-Weekly Flag & Advertiser*, January 13, 1849.
20. *Montgomery Alabama Journal*, October 24, 1850.
21. *Montgomery Tri-Weekly Flag & Advertiser*, September 23, 1848.
22. *Mobile Herald & Tribune*, May 18, 1847.
23. "Southern Convention," *Southern Quarterly Review* 18 (1850), p. 198
24. See, for example, Mary Howard Schoolcraft, *The Black Gauntlet* (Freeport, NY: Books for Libraries, 1971).
25. Shadrach Mims, *History of Prattville* (Prattville, AL: A.R.B.C., 1976), in Susan F.H. Tarrant, *Hon. Daniel Pratt: A Biography, with Eulogies on His Life and Character* (Richmond: Whittet & Shepperson, 1904), p. 23.
26. *Prattville Southern Statesman*, May 26, 1855.

27. *Montgomery Tri-Weekly Flag & Advertiser*, June 24, 1847.
28. Pratt Public Letter, March 12, 1849, published in the *Montgomery Tri-Weekly Flag & Advertiser*, March 31, 1849.
29. *De Bow's Review* 4 (1847), p. 136, and vol. 10 (1851), p. 226.
30. Shadrach Mims, *History of Autauga County* (Prattville, AL: A.R.B.C., 1976), pp. 262, 266–267
31. August Kohn, *The Cotton Mills of South Carolina* (Spartanburg: Reprint Co., 1975), p. 21.
32. *Edgefield Advertiser*, November 21, 1850, August 31, 1854, September 28, 1854; Martin, "Advent of Gregg and Graniteville," p. 414.
33. Reprinted by the *Raleigh (NC) News and Observer*, October 5, 1924.
34. *Montgomery Tri-Weekly Flag & Advertiser*, May 6, 1848.
35. Randall Martin Miller, *The Cotton Mill Movement in Antebellum Alabama* (NY: Arno, 1978), p. 70.
36. *The Plough, the Loom, & the Anvil* 1 (May 1849), p. 714.
37. Congressman and planter from Virginia who advocated a commercial agrarian society.
38. Speaker of the House of Representatives and a planter from South Carolina who favored southern secession.
39. J.L. Watkins, *King Cotton* (New York: Negro Universities Press, 1969), p. 101.
40. Fred Bateman, "The Participation of Planters in Manufacturing in the Antebellum South," *Agricultural History* 48, no. 2 (April 1974), p. 289fn.
41. George D. Green, *Finance and Economic Development in the Old South: Louisiana Banking, 1804–1861* (Stamford: Stamford University Press, 1972), p. 360fn.
42. Minutes of the Demosthenian Debating Society, June 17, 1842.
43. Laurence Shore, *Southern Capitalists: The Ideological Leadership of an Elite, 1832–1885* (Chapel Hill: University of North Carolina Press, 1986), pp. 31–40.

Chapter 9

1. This letter, dated July 7, 1749, is quoted in R.H. Loughbridge, *Cotton Production in Georgia* (Washington, D.C.: Government Printing Office, 1884), pp. 53–54.
2. Thomas Ellison, "A Centennial Sketch of the Cotton Trade of the United States," published in Latham, Alexander & Co.'s *Annual Report on Cotton Movement and Fluctuations*, 1892, p. 27.
3. *DeFoe's Weekly Review*, January 31, 1708.
4. Albert S. Bolles, *Industrial History of the United States* (Norwich: H. Bill, 1879), p. 7.
5. Ibid., p. 92.
6. T.A. Pitkin, *A Statistical View of the Commerce of the United States* (New York: Augustus M. Kelley, 1967), p. 109.
7. Thomas Ellison, *The Cotton Trade of Great Britain* (New York: A.M. Kelley, 1968), pp. 83–84.
8. J.B. McMasrer, *History of the People of the United States*, vol. 2 (New York: Farrar, Straus), p. 34.
9. Thomas Jefferson, *Notes on Virginia*, pp. 278, 281.
10. George White, *Statistics of Georgia* (Savannah: W. Thorne Williams, 1849), p. 38.
11. Denison Olmsted, "Memoir of Eli Whitney, Esq.," *American Journal of Science* (1832).
12. Thomas Ellison, *The History of Great Britain* (London: E. Wilson, 1886), p. 34.
13. David Ramsey, *History of South Carolina*, vol. 2 (Newberry: W.J. Duffie, 1858), p. 218.
14. Ibid., p. 214.
15. Thomas Ellison, *The History of Great Britain*, p. 56.
16. Ibid., p. 78.
17. Slavery had been outlawed in England in 1833.
18. First promulgated in 1689 limiting imports of wheat and corn to encourage British exports.
19. Thomas P. Martin, "Some International Aspects of the Anti-Slavery Movement, 1818–1823," *Journal of Economic and Business History* 1 (1928–1929), pp. 141–143.
20. William Huskisson Papers, British Museum.
21. Huskisson to Backhouse, June 15, 1829, *American Historical Review* 7 (1901–1902), pp. 517–518.
22. The *Baltimore Gazette*, quoted in *Niles Register*, September 6, 1828.
23. *Charleston (SC) City Gazette*, September 15, 1829.
24. C.S. Boucher, "In Re that Aggressive Slavocracy," *Mississippi Valley Historical Review* 8 (1921–1922), pp. 13–79.
25. Thomas P. Martin, "The Upper Missis-

sippi Valley in Anglo-American, Anti-Slavery and Free Trade Relations, 1837–1842," *Mississippi Valley Historical Review* 15 (1928–1929), pp. 204–220.
26. A member of the British parliament who was also an antislavery orator and activist.
27. *London Economist,* October 10, 1846.
28. British radical, orator, and member of Parliament.
29. Hansard, *Parliamentary Debates,* Ser. 3, XCII, pp. 476ff.
30. Great Britain, *Parliamentary Papers, 1847–1848,* VIII, Pt. III, 238.
31. *Hunt's Merchant's Magazine* 9, p. 523.
32. D.A. Farnie, *The English Cotton Industry and the World Market, 1815–1896* (Oxford: Claredon Press, 1979), p. 180.
33. Douglass C. North, *The Economic Growth of the United States, 1790–1860* (Englewood Cliffs, NJ: Norton Library, 1966), p. 112.
34. *The Economist,* February 2, 1861, p. 117.
35. Ibid., January 19, 1861, p. 58.
36. J.T. Danson, "On the Existing Connection Between American Slavery and the British Cotton Manufacture," *Journal of the Statistical Society of London* 20, no. 1, (March 1857), pp. 1–21.
37. Ruth K. Nuermberger, *The Free Produce Movement: A Quaker Protest Against Slavery* (Durham, NC: Duke University Press, 1942), p. 66.
38. Thomas Ellison, *The Cotton Trade of Great Britain,* p. 86.
39. Arthur W. Silver, *Manchester Men and Indian Cotton, 1847–1872* (Great Britain: Manchester University Press, 1966), p. 78.
40. Henry Richard, *Memoirs of Joseph Sturge* (London: S.W. Partridge, 1864), p. 386.
41. E.J. Donnell, *History of Cotton* (Wilmington, DE: Scholarly Resources, 1973), pp. 454 and 466
42. R.A. Arnold, *History of the Cotton Famine* (London: Saunders, Otley, 1865), pp. 36–37.

43. Ibid., p. 37
44. John Watts, *The Facts of the Cotton Famine* (London: Cass, 1968), p. 90.
45. Laura A. White, *Robert Barnwell Rhett: Father of Secession* (Gloucester: P. Smith, 1931), p. 196.
46. Frank Moore, ed., *The Rebellion Record: A Diary of American Events,* vol. 1 (New York: G.P. Putnam, 1861–1863), "Diary of Events," p. 16.
47. Dunbar Rowland, ed., *Jefferson Davis, Constitutionalist: His Letters, Papers and Speeches* vol. 5 (Jackson, MS: Torgerson Press, 1923), pp. 62–63.
48. Henry Blumenthal, *A Reappraisal of Franco-American Relations, 1830–1871* (Chapel Hill: University of North Carolina Press, 1959), p. 123.
49. Mary Boykin Chesnut, *A Diary from Dixie,* ed. Ben Ames Williams (Boston: Houghton Mifflin, 1949), p. 92.
50. Frank L. Owsley, *King Cotton Diplomacy* (University of Chicago Press, 1959), p. 20.
51. Seward quoted in Thayer to Seward, March 5, 1863.
52. Jefferson Davis, *The Rise and Fall of the Confederate Government,* vol. 1 (New York: T. Yoseloff, 1958), p. 469.
53. *Journal of the Congress of the Confederate States of America, 1861–1865,* vol. 2 (Washington, D.C.: Government Printing Office, 1904–1905), pp. 192–193.
54. Robin W. Winks, *Canada and the United States: The Civil War Years* (Baltimore: Johns Hopkins University Press, 1960), p. 378.
55. Henry Blumenthal, *A Reappraisal of Franco-American Relations, 1830–1871,* p. 124.
56. Robert Huhn Jones, "Anglo-American Relations, 1861–1865, Reconsidered," *Mid-America* 45 (January 1963), pp. 39–40.
57. *The Economist,* January 19, 1861, p. 58.

Bibliography

American Farmer, September 28, 1827. "Cotton Bagging."
American Farmer, January 1, 1828. "A Report on the Establishment of Cotton and Wollen Manufacturers and on the Growing of Wool: Made to the House of Commons of North Carolina by Mr. Fisher."
American Railroad Journal 33 (1860), p. 670.
Annals of Congress, 14 Cong., 1st. sess., pp. 1329–1332, 1634–1635.
_____, 15 Cong., 1st sess. pp. 2, 1732.
_____, 16 Cong., 1st sess., pt. 2, pp. 1989, 2071.
_____, House of Representatives, 16 Cong., 1st. sess., p. 2078.
_____, 18 Cong., 1st. sess., p. 1979.
_____, vol. 3, (January 1791), p. 349, and (April 1792), p. 569.
Appleton, Nathan. Letter to Middlesex Mechanics Association, December 30, 1846.
"Bagley." Letter. *Voice of Industry*, September 8, 1846.
Bateman, Fred. "The Participation of Planters in Manufacturing in the Antebellum South. *Agricultural History* 2 (April 1974), p. 289 fn.
Beckwith, George. Letter to William Wyndham, Greenville, August 10, 1791, FO 4/12, p. 164–168, Public Records Office.
Ben-Atar, Doron. "Alexander Hamilton's Alternative Technology Piracy and the Report on Manufacturers." *William and Mary Quarterly* 52, no. 3. Third Series (July 1995), pp. 389–414.
Bils, Mark. "Tariff Protection and Production in the Early U.S. Cotton Industry." *Journal of Economic History* 44, (December 1984), pp. 1033–1045.
Bostwick, William. Papers. Beinecke Rare Book and Manuscript Library, Yale University.
Boucher, C.S. "In Re That Aggressive Slavocracy." *Mississippi Valley Historical Review* 9 (1921–1922), pp. 13–79.
Brown, Moses. Letter to John Dexter, July 22, 1791.
Cabot, George. Letter to Alexander Hamilton, September 6, 1791.
Carew Manufacturing Company Papers. Time Book, 1850–1866 (a situation similar to Holyoke's, obtained in Chicopee where "foreign girls have been employed in such numbers that what American girls are employed there, experience considerable difficulty in finding society among their workmates congenial to their tastes and feelings" (*Hampden Freeman*, March 13, 1852).
Cathey, Cornelius O. "Agricultural Implements in North Carolina, 1763–1860." *Agricultural History* 25, no. 3 (July 1951), p. 135.
Chaplin, Joyce E. "Creating a Cotton South in Georgia and South Carolina, 1760–1815." *Journal of Southern History* 57 (1991), p. 199.
Clarfield, Gerald. "Protecting the Frontiers: Defense Policy and the Tariff Question in the First Washington Administration." *William and Mary Quarterly*, 32 (July 1975), p. 459.

Clay, Cassius Marcellus. "Slavery: The Evil—The Remedy." Republished by Horace Greeley in the *New York Tribune*, 1848.

"Colt's Revolvers," reprinted from *Dover (England) Telegraph. Appleton's Mechanics Magazine and Engineers' Journal* 2 (February 1853), p. 47.

Congressional Globe. Senate, 35th Cong., 1st sess., March 4, 1858, p. 961.

Conrad, A.H., and John Myers. "The Economics of Slavery in the Ante-bellum South." *Journal of Political Economy* 66, no. 2 (April 1958), p. 95.

"Continentalist No. V." April 18, 1782, Papers of Alexander Hamilton, vol. 3, p. 78–79.

Coxe, Tench. Correspondence: Mitchell to Coxe, August 18, 1787, May 4, 1788, June 4, 1788; Coxe to Mitchell, October 21, 1787; Coxe to Thomas Jefferson, September 15, October 4, 1787; Letter to George Clymer, Jan. 17, 1790; Letter to Thomas Jefferson, March 14, 1791. Tench Coxe Collection, Historical Society of Pennsylvania.

Danson, J.T. "On the Existing Connection Between America Slavery and the British Cotton Manufacture." *Journal of the Statistical Society of London* 30, no. 1 (March 1857), pp. 1–21.

Day, Clive. "Early Development of the American Cotton Manufacturing." *Quarterly Journal of Economics* 39 (December 1924), p. 452.

De Bow's Review 4 (1847), pp. 136, vol. 10 (1851), p. 226, vol. 29 (1860), p. 484.

De Bow's Review 29 (1860). "Southern Patronage to Southern Imports and Southern Industry," pp. 77–83.

Drucker, Peter F. "On the Economic Basis of American Politics." *The Public Interest* 10 (1968), p. 35.

Eighth Census of the United States, 1860, Agriculture, p. clvii.

Ellison, Thomas. "A Centennial Sketch of the Cotton Trade of the United States." Published in Latham, Alexander & Company's *Annual Report on Cotton Movement and Fluctuations*, 1892, p. 27.

Evans, Charles H., comp. "Exports, Domestic and Foreign." 48th Cong., 1st sess., H.R., Misc. Doc. 492 (1884), p. 68.

Factory Girls' Album and Operatives' Advocate (November 1846). "Beauties of Factory Life."

Fenner's Southern Medical Reports.

Ferguson, Eugene, S. "On the Origin and Development of American Mechanical 'Know-how'—Mid-continent." *American Studies Journal* 3 (Fall 1962), pp. 2–15.

Fialka, John, J. "While America Sleeps." *Wilson Quarterly* 1 (1976), vol. 21, no. 1 (Winter 1997), p. 48–51.

Financial Register 2 (1838). "Liverpool Report."

Fox, Frank W. "The Genesis of American Technology, 1790–1860: An Essay in Long-Range Perspective." *American Studies* 17, no. 2 (Fall 1976), pp. 39–40.

Frisbie, Levi. "Professor Frisbie's Inaugural Address." *North American Review* 4 (January 1818), pp. 224–241.

Gales and Seaton's Register of Debates in Congress, 22nd Congress, 1st sess., vol. 8, pt. 3; 1832, p. 3555, and vol. 18, pt. 3; 1832, pp. 3549–3550.

Gallatin, Albert. "Manufacturers." *America State Papers, Finance* 2, p. 247.

General Statutes of Massachusetts, chapter 53.

Ginger, Ray. "Labor in the Massachusetts Cotton Mill, 1853–1860." *Business History Review* 28, no. 1 (March 1954), p. 72.

Great Britain. Parliamentary Papers, 1847–1848, VIII, pt. III, p. 238.

Griffen, Richard W. "North Carolina: The Origins and Rise of the Cotton Textile Industry." Ph.D. diss., Ohio State University, 1954, pp. 310–314.

Hamilton, Alexander. *The Papers of Alexander Hamilton*. Vols. 1–27. Edited by Harold C. Syrett. New York: Columbia University Press, 1961–1987. Selected letters.

Hammond to Grenville, October 3, 1792 and December 6, 1791.

Hansard. Parliamentary Debates, Ser. 3, XCII, p. 476ff.

Harrison, Robert W. "Levee Districts and Levee Building in Mississippi: A Study in State and Local Effort to Control Mississippi River Floods." Published by Delta Council, Mississippi Levee Commissioners, Board of Commissioners for the

Yazoo-Mississippi Delta and Mississippi Agricultural Experiment Station (October 1951), pp. 7–8.

Hekman, John S. "The Product Cycle and New England Textiles." *Quarterly Journal of Economics* 94, no. 4 (June 1980), p. 701.

History of the H.F. Company. Lyman Mills Papers. Davis to Mills, March 8, 1857.

Hodin, Stephen B. "The Mechanisms of Monticello: Saving Labor in Jefferson's America." *Journal of the Early Republic* 26, no. 3 (Fall 2006), p. 381.

Holbrook, Abigail Curlee. "Cotton Marketing in Antebellum Texas." *Southwestern Historical Quarterly* 73, no. 4 (April 1970), pp. 431–455.

Holt, Hines. Letter to Farish Carter, March 28, 1841. Farish Carter Papers, Southern Historical Collection, University of North Carolina, Chapel Hill.

Holyoke, Massachusetts, Town Records, 1853, p. 8.

Huskisson, William. Letter to Backhouse, June 15, 1829. *American Historical Review* 7 (1901–1902), pp. 517–518.

———. Papers, British Museum.

Huston, James L. "The American Revolutionaries: The Political Economy of Aristocracy and the American Concept of the Distribution of Wealth, 1795–1900. *American Historical Review* 98 (1993), p. 1081.

Inland Waterways Commission. Preliminary Report, 1908, pp. 205–209.

James, John A. "The Optimal Tariff in the Antebellum United States." *American Economic Review* 71, no. 4 (September 1981), p. 726.

Jefferson, Thomas. Letter to John Melish, January 13, 1813.

———. Letters to Eli Whitney, 1793.

Jeremy, David J. "British Technology Transmission to the United States: The Philadelphia Region Experience, 1770–1820." *Business History Review* 47 (1973), pp. 24–52.

———. "Damming the Flood: British Government Efforts to Check the Outflow of Technicians and Machinery, 1780–1843." *Business History Review* 1 (1977), pp. 19–21.

Jones, Robert Huhn. "Anglo-American Relations, 1861–1865, Reconsidered." *Mid-America* 45 (January 1963), pp. 39–40.

Journal of the Congress of the Confederate States of America, 1861–1865. Vol. 2. Washington: Government Printing Office (1904–1905), pp. 192–193.

Knick, Harley C. "International Competitiveness of the Antebellum American Textile Industry." *Journal of Economic History* 52 (September 1992), pp. 559–584.

Lance, David. "Sources of Industrial Finance: The American Textile Industry; A Case Study." *Explorations in Entrepreneurial History* 9, no. 4 (April 1957), pp. 189–203.

Larcom, Lucy. "Among Lowell Mill Girls." *Atlantic Monthly*, November 1881.

Lazerow, Jana. "Religion and the New England Mill Girl: A New Perspective on an Old Theme." *New England Quarterly* 60, no. 3 (September 1987), p. 452.

Lincoln, Jonathan T. "Beginnings of the Machine Age in New England: Documents Relating to the Introduction of the Power Loom." *Bulletin of the Business Historical Society* 7, no. 5 (October 1933), pp. 10–12.

Long, Pamela O. "Invention, Authorship, 'Intellectual Property' and the Origin of Patents: Notes Toward a Conceptual History." *Technology and Culture* 32 (1991), p. 877.

Long, Richard. Letter to Farish Carter, May 7, 1842. Farish Carter Papers, Southern Historical Collection, University of North Carolina, Chapel Hill.

MacLeod, Christine. "The Paradoxes of Patenting: Invention and its Diffusion in 18th and 19th Century Britain, France, and North America." *Technology and Culture* 32 (1991), p. 898.

Mak, James, and Gary M. Walton. "Steamboats and the Great Productivity Surge in River Transportation." *Journal of Economic History* 31 (September 1972), pp. 619–640.

"Manufacturers of the United States in 1860, Compiled from the Original Returns of the Eighth Census." Washington, D.C.: Government Printing Office, 1865), p. ccxvi.

Martin, Thomas P. "The Advent of William

Gregg and the Graniteville Company." *Journal of Southern History* vol. 11 no. 3 (August 1945).

———. "Some International Aspects of the Anti-Slavery Movement, 1818–1823." *Journal of Economic and Business History* 1 (1928–1929).

———. "The Upper Mississippi Valley in Anglo-American Anti-Slavery and Free Trade Relations, 1837–1842." *Mississippi Valley Historical Review* 15 (1928–1929), pp. 204–220.

Massachusetts General Court. House Document, 1842, #4, p. 2.

McClure, William. "Extracts of a Letter from William McClure to Editor—Madrid, Dec. 4, 1821: Progress of American Science." *American Journal of Science* 5 (New York, 1822), p.197.

Memorial of a Convention of the Friends of National Industry.... Delegates from Maryland, Rhode Island, Connecticut, New York, Pennsylvania, Massachusetts, Delaware, and Ohio. 16th Cong., 1st sess., 31, H.R. Doc. 9, December 20, 1819, p. 3.

Minutes of the Demosthenian Debating Society, June 17, 1842.

Morgan, John. "Whether It Be Most Beneficial to the United States to Promote Agriculture, or to Encourage the Mechanical Arts and Manufacturers." *American Museum* 6 (July 1789), pp. 73–74.

Morrison, Mary. Letter to Stephen Holman, May 28, 1856. Lyman Mills Papers

Nasmyth, James. Select Committee on Small Arms. Parliamentary Papers, 1854, XVIII, Q, p. 1367.

Olmsted, Denison. "Memoir of Eli Whitney Esq." *American Journal of Science* (1832)

Page, Arthur W. "A Cotton Harvest at Last." *World's Work* 21, no. 13, pp. 748–760

The Plough, the Loom, and the Anvil 1 (May 1849), p. 714.

Pollard, June 29, 1790, Patent Recs. Office, RG 241.

Pratt. Public Letter, March 12, 1849. *Montgomery Tri-Weekly Flag & Advertiser*, March, 31, 1849.

Pred, Allan. "Manufacturing in the American Textile City: 1810–1840." *Annals of the Association of Geographers* 56, no. 2, (June 1966), p. 312.

Preyer, Norris W. "Southern Support of the Tariff of 1816: A Reappraisal." *Journal of Southern History* 25, no. 3 (August 1959), pp. 306–322.

Puckett, E.P. "The Attempt of New Orleans to Meet the Crisis in Her Trade with the West." *Proceedings of the Mississippi Valley Historical Association* 10 (1918–1919), pp. 481–495.

Register of Debates. Senate, 23rd Cong., 1st sess. March 4, 1858, p. 961, and May 26, 1834, p. 1808.

Remonstrance of the Virginia Agricultural Society of Fredericksburg. 16th Cong., 1st sess., H.R. Doc. 24, February 2, 1821), p. 4.

"Report on the Select Committee Appointed to Take into Consideration the State and Condition of the Patent Office." *Mechanics Magazine and Register of Inventions and Improvements* (May 1863), p. 330.

Report on the U.S. Bank, 1841. Washington, D.C., p. 18.

Sawyer, John E. "The Social Basis of the American System of Manufacturing." *Journal of Economic History* 14 (1954), pp. 361–379.

Seventh Annual Report of the Boston Board of Trade. Boston, 1861, pp. 66–67.

Sixth Census of the United States, 1840. Washington, D.C.: Government Printing Office, 1841, pp. 169–171, 217.

"Southern Convention." *Southern Quarterly Review* 18 (1850), p. 198.

"The Southern States Embracing a Series of Papers Condensed from the Earlier Volumes of *DeBow's Review*." Washington, D.C.: 1856.

Stettler, Henry Louis, III. "Growth and Fluctuations in the Anti-Bellum Textile Industry." Ph.D. Thesis, Department of Economics, Purdue University, 1970, p. 212.

Street, James H. "Mechanizing the Cotton Harvest." *Agricultural History* 31, no. 1 (January 1957), pp. 12–13.

Tenth Census of the United States: Transportation. Vol. 4. Washington, D.C.: Government Printing Office, 1888, pp. 662–666.

Twelfth Census of the United States: Man-

ufacturers. Vol. 3. Washington, D.C.: Government Printing Office, 1900, p. 54.
United Agricultural Society of Virginia. 16th Cong., 1st. sess., Finance 570 (January 17, 1820), p. 460.
U.S. Commissioner of Patents Report, 1850. Part 1. *Art and Manufacturers*. Washington, D.C.: Government Printing Office, 1850, pp. 233–234.
U.S. Congress. House, Report on the Internal Commerce of the U.S., 1887. House Exec., Doc. 6, Part II, 50 Cong., 1st sess. (1888), pp. 191, 222.
_____. New American State Papers: Manufacturers. Vol. 1, p. 37
Wallace, Jane. Letter to Stephen Holman, December 8, 1858. Lyman Mills Papers.
Wallis, George. New York Industrial Exposition: Special Report of Mr. George Wallis. Parliamentary Papers, House of Commons, 1854, XXXVI, p. 3, 5.
Ware, Lynn Wiloughby. "Cotton Money: Antebellum Currency Conditions in the Apalachicola/Chattahoochee River Valley." *Georgia Historical Quarterly* 74, no. 2 (Summer 1990), pp. 220–221, 223.
Washington, George. Letter to Beverley Randolph, January 13, 1791.
Wesson, J.M. "The Textile Industry of the Old South as Described in a Letter by J.M. Wesson in 1858." *Journal of Economic History* 16, no. 2 (June 1956), pp. 201–204.
Whitney, Eli. Letter to his father, September 11, 1793. Eli Whitney Papers, Yale University, Sterling Memorial Library.
Woodbury, Robert S. "The Legend of Eli Whitney and Interchangeable Parts." *Technology and Culture* 1 (Summer 1960), pp. 235–253.

Books

Abbot, Edith. *Women in Industry: A Study in American Economic History*. New York: Source Book Press, 1970.
Adams, Charles Francis. *Memoirs of John Quincy Adams*. 12 vols. Philadelphia: J.B. Lippencott, 1874.
Aiken, John. *Labor and Wages at Home and Abroad*. Lowell: D. Bixby, 1849.

Albion, Robert G. *The Rise of the New York Port*. New York: Scribner's, 1939.
Allen, Zachariah. *Science of Mechanics*. Providence: Hutchens & Cory, 1829.
Ammon, Harry. *The Great Mission*. New York: Norton, 1973.
Appleton, Nathan. *Introduction of the Power Loom and Origin of Lowell*. Lowell: B.H. Penhallow, 1858.
_____. *Labor: Its Relations in Europe and in the United States Compared*. Boston: Eastburn's Press, 1844.
Arnold, R.A. *History of the Cotton Famine*. London: Saunders, Otley, 1865.
Audubon, John James. *John James Audubon: Writings and Drawings*. New York: Library of America, 1999.
Bagnall, William R. *The Textile Industry of the United States, Including Sketches and Notes of Cotton, Wollen, Silk, and Linen Manufacturers in the Colonial Period*. Boston: W.B. Clarke, 1893.
Baldwin, Leland, D. *The Keelboat Age on Western Waters*. Pittsburgh: University of Pittsburgh Press, 1941.
Bartlett, Elisha. *A Vindication of the Character and Condition of the Females Employed in the Lowell Mills*. Lowell: L. Huntress, 1841.
Batchelder, Samuel. *Introduction and Early Progress of Cotton Manufacture in the United States*. Boston: Little, Brown, 1863.
Bateman, Fred, and Thomas Weiss. *A Deplorable Society: The Failure of Industrialization in the Slave Economy*. Chapel Hill: University of North Carolina Press, 1981.
Bemis, Samuel Flagg. *Jay's Treaty: A Study in Commerce and Diplomacy*. New York: Macmillan, 1923.
Betts, Edwin Morris, ed. *Thomas Jefferson's Farm Book: With Commentary and Relevant Extracts from Other Writings*. Philadelphia: American Philosophical Society, 1944.
Blumenthal, Henry. *A Reappraisal of Franco-American Relations, 1830–1871*. Chapel Hill: University of North Carolina Press, 1959.
Bolles, Albert. *Industrial History of the United States*. Norwich: H. Bell, 1879.

Bowen, Catherine Drinker. *Miracle at Philadelphia: The Story of the Constitutional Convention, May to September 1787.* Boston: Little, Brown, 1966.

Boyd, Julian P., ed. *The Papers of Thomas Jefferson.* Princeton: Princeton University Press, 1950.

Bruchey, Stuart. *Cotton and the American Economy: 1790–1860.* New York: Harcourt Brace & World, 1967.

Cairnes, J.E. *The Slave Power: Its Character, Career, and Probable Design; Being an Attempt to Explain the Real Issues Involved in the American Contest.* New York: Kelles, 1968 [1862].

Caldwell, Stephen A. *A Banking History of Louisiana.* Baton Rouge: Louisiana State University Press, 1935.

Callender, Guy S., ed. *Selections from the Economic History of the United States, 1765–1860.* Boston: Ginn, 1909.

Carey, H.C. *Essay on the Rate of Wages.* New York: Kelley, 1965.

Carlson, Avery Luvere. *A Monetary and Banking History of Texas.* Fort Worth: Fort Worth National Bank, 1930.

Catterall, Ralph C. *Second Bank of the United States.* Chicago: University of Chicago Press, 1960.

Chesnut, Mary Boykin. *A Diary from Dixie.* Edited by Ben Ames Williams. Boston: Houghton Mifflin, 1949.

Clark, Victor S. *History of Manufactures in the United States.* 2nd ed. Vol. 1. New York: McGraw-Hill, 1929.

Clayton, A.S. *Compilation of the Laws of Georgia.* Augusta: Adams & Duyckinck, 1812.

Cohen, I. Bernard. *Benjamin Franklin's Science.* Cambridge: Harvard University Press, 1990.

Cohn, David L. *The Life and Times of King Cotton.* New York: Oxford University Press, 1956.

Cooper, Thomas, and D.J. McCord. *South Carolina Statutes at Large.* Columbia: A.S. Johnson, 1836–1841.

Crockett, David. *The Life of David Crockett.* New York: Scribner's, 1923.

Crowley, John E. *The Privileges of Independence, Neomercantilism and the American Revolution.* Baltimore: Johns Hopkins University Press, 1993.

Dattel, Gene. *Cotton and Race in the Making of America.* Chicago: Ivan R. Dee, 2009.

Davis, Charles, S. *The Cotton Kingdom in Alabama.* Philadelphia: Porcupine Press, 1974.

Davis, Jefferson. *The Rise and Fall of the Confederate Government.* 2 vols. New York: T. Yoseloff, 1958 [1881].

DeBow, J.D.B. *The Industrial Resources of the Southern and Western States.* Vol. 2. New Orleans: Offices of De Bow's Review, 1852–1853.

De Pauw, Linda G., et al. *Documentary History of the First Federal Congress of the United States of America.* Vol. 1, *Senate Legislative Journal.* Baltimore: Johns Hopkins University Press, 1972.

Dobson, John M. *History of America Enterprise.* Upper Saddle River, N.J.: Prentice Hall, 1988.

Donnell, E.J. *History of Cotton.* Wilmington, DE: Scholarly Resources, 1973.

Drake, Samuel Adams. *History of Middlesex County Massachusetts.* 2 vols. Boston: Estes and Laureat, 1880.

Dunbar, Rowland, ed. *Jefferson Davis, Constitutionalist: His Letters, Papers, and Speeches.* 10 vols. Jackson: Torgerson Press, 1923.

Dutton, H.I. *The Patent System and Inventive Activity During the Industrial Revolution.* Manchester, UK: University of Manchester Press, 1984.

Ellison, Thomas. *The Cotton Trade of Great Britain.* New York: A.M. Kelley, 1968.

_____. *The History of Great Britain.* London: E. Wilson, 1886.

Eltis, David. *Economic Growth and the Ending of the Transatlantic Slave Trade.* New York: Oxford University Press, 1987.

Eno, Arthur L. *Cotton Was King: A History of Lowell, Massachusetts.* Somersthworth, N.H.: New Hampshire Publishing, 1976.

Evans, Estwick. *A Pedestrious Tour of Four Thousand Miles.* Cleveland: Arthur H. Clark, 1904.

Farnie, D.A. *The English Cotton Industry and the World Market, 1815–1896.* Oxford: Clarendon Press, 1979.

Ferguson, Eugene S. *On the Origin and Development of American Mechanical Knowhow.* Cambridge: MIT Press, 1992.

Fitton, R.S., and A.P. Wadsworth. *The Strutts and the Arkwrights, 1758–1830: A Study of the Early Factory System*. Manchester: University of Manchester Press, 1973.

Fogel, Robert William. *Without Consent or Contract: The Rise and Fall of American Slavery*. New York: Norton, 1989.

Fogel, Robert William, and Stanley L. Engerman. *Time on the Cross: The Economics of American Negro Slavery*. New York: W.W. Norton, 1974.

Fox-Genovese, Elizabeth, and Eugene D. Genovese. *Fruits of Merchant Capital*. New York: Oxford University Press, 1983.

Gibb, George S. *Saco-Lowell Shops: Textile Machinery in New England*. Cambridge: Harvard University Press, 1950.

Goodrich, Carter, et al. *Canals and American Economic Development*. New York: Columbia University Press, 1961.

Gray, Lewis Cecil. *History of Agriculture in the Southern United States to 1860*. Vol. 1. Gloucester, MA: Peter Smith, 1958.

Green, Constance McLoughlin. *Holyoke, Massachusetts*. New Haven: Yale University Press, 1939.

Green, George D. *Finance and Economic Development in the Old South: Louisiana Banking, 1804–1861*. Stamford, CT: Stamford University Press, 1972.

Hall, James. *The West*. Cincinnati: H.W. Derby, 1848.

Hamilton, Alexander. *Report on Manufacturers*. London: J. Debrett, 1793.

Hamilton, Alexander, and Henry Cabot Lodge. *The Works of Alexander Hamilton*. New York: G.P. Putnam, 1904

Hamilton, Joseph Gregoire de Roulhac, ed. *The Papers of Thomas Ruffin*. Raleigh: Edwards & Broughton, 1918–1920.

Helper, Hinton B. *Compendium of the Impending Crisis of the South*. New York: A.B. Burdick, 1860.

Howe, Daniel. *The Political Culture of American Whigs*. Chicago: University of Chicago, 1979.

Hunter, Louis C. *Steamboats on the Western Rivers*. Cambridge: Harvard University Press, 1949.

Iken, Arthur. *Texas*. Waco: Texian Press, 1964.

Jefferson, Thomas. *Notes on Virginia*. Richmond: J.W. Randolph, 1853.

Jones, Fred Mitchell. *Middlemen in the Domestic Trade of the United States*. Urbana: University of Illinois Press, 1937.

Josephson, Hannah. *The Golden Threads: New England Mill Girls and Magnates*. New York: Duell, Sloan, and Pearce, 1949.

Kasson, John F. *Civilizing the Machine: Technology and Republican Values in America, 1776–1900*. New York: Grossman, 1976.

Kerber, Linda K. *Women of the Republic: Intellect and Ideology in Revolutionary America*. Chapel Hill: University of North Carolina Press, 1980.

Knowlton, Evelyn H. *Pepperell's Progress: History of a Cotton Textile Company, 1844–1945*. Cambridge: Harvard University Press, 1948.

Kohn, August. *The Cotton Mills of South Carolina*. Spartanburg: Reprint, 1975.

Labree, Leonard W. *The Papers of Benjamin Franklin*. Vol. 6. New Haven: Yale University Press, 1959.

Lipscomb, Andrew A., and Albert Ellery Bergh, eds. *The Writings of Thomas Jefferson*. Washington, D.C.: Thomas Jefferson Memorial Association of the United States, 1903–1904.

Loring, F.W., and C.W. Atkinson. *Cotton Culture and the South Considered with Reference to Emigration*. Boston: A. Williams, 1869.

Loughbridge, R.H. *Cotton Production in Georgia*. Washington, D.C.: Government Printing Office, 1884.

Lowrie, Walter, and M. St. Clair Clarke. *American State Papers: Documents, Legislative and Executive*. Washington, D.C: Gales and Seaton, 1832.

Luther, Seth. *An Address to the Working Men of New England on the State of Education and on the Condition of Producing Classes in Europe and America*. 2nd ed. Boston: The Author, 1832.

MacLeod, Christine. *Inventing the Industrial Revolution: The English Patent System, 1660–1800*. Cambridge: Cambridge University Press, 2007.

Marbury, H., and W.H. Crawford. *Compilation of the Laws of Georgia*. Savannah: Seymour, Woolhopter, & Stebbins, 1802.

Marrs, Aaron W. *Railroads in the Old South, Pursuing Progress in a Slave Society.* Baltimore: Johns Hopkins University Press, 2009.

Martin, Edger W. *The Standard of Living in 1860: American Consumption Levels on the Eve of the Civil War.* Chicago: University of Chicago Press, 1942.

McEwan, Barbara. *Thomas Jefferson: Farmer.* Jefferson, NC: McFarland, 1991.

McKissick, James R. *Notes on the Early History of Cotton and Cotton Manufacturers in South Carolina.* Spartanburg: Band & White, 1927.

McMaster, J.B. *History of the People of the United States.* New York: Farrar, Straus, 1964.

McPherson, James M. *Battle Cry of Freedom: The Civil War Era.* New York: Oxford University Press, 1988.

Meier, August, and Elliot Rudwick. *From Plantation to Ghetto.* New York: Hill and Wang, 1976.

Miller, John C. *Alexander Hamilton: Portrait in Paradox.* New York: Harper, 1959.

Miller, Randall Martin. *The Cotton Mill Movement in Antebellum Alabama.* New York: Arno Press, 1971.

Mims, Shadrach. *History of Autauga County.* Prattville, AL: A.R.B.C., 1976.

_____. *History of Prattville.* Prattville, AL: A.R.B.C., 1976

Mirsky, Jeannette, and Allan Nevins. *The World of Eli Whitney.* New York: Macmillan, 1952.

Mitchell, Broadus. *The Industrial Revolution in the South.* New York: New American Library, 1930.

Moore, Frank, ed. *The Rebellion Record: A Diary of American Events.* New York: G.P. Putnam, 1861–1863.

Necker, Jacques. *A Treatise on the Administration of Finance.* London: Logographic Press, 1787.

Neel, Joanne Loewe. *Phineas Bond: A Study in Anglo-American Relations.* Philadelphia: University of Pennsylvania Press, 1968.

Nemmo, Joseph. *Report on the Internal Commerce of the United States.* Washington: Government Printing Office, 1885.

Nicolay, John G., and John Hay, eds. *Abraham Lincoln: Complete Works.* 2 vols. New York: F.D. Tandy, 1905.

Nuermberger, Ruth K. *The Free Produce Movement: A Quaker Protest Against Slavery.* Durham: Duke University Press, 1942.

Olmsted, Frederick Law. *A Journey to the Back Country.* New York: Schocken, 1970

Onuf, Peter, and Nicholas Onuf. *Federal Union, Modern World: The Law of Nations in an Age of Revolution.* Madison: Madison House, 1993.

Ousley, Frank L. *King Cotton Diplomacy.* Chicago: University of Chicago Press, 1959

Parker, William N. *Europe, America, and the Wider World.* Cambridge: Cambridge University Press, 1984.

Phelps, Ulrich B. *American Negro Slavery.* New York: D. Appleton, 1918.

Pitkin, T.A. *A Statistical View of the Commerce of the United States.* New York: Augustus M. Kelly, 1967.

Ramsey, David. *History of South Carolina.* Newberry: W.J. Duffie, 1858.

Richard, Henry. *Memoirs of Joseph Sturge.* London: S.W. Partridge, 1864.

Robinson, Harriet. *Loom and Spindle; or, Life Among the Early Mill Girls.* Kailua, HI: Press Pacifica, 1976.

Russell, Robert. *North America: Its Agriculture and Climate.* Edinburgh: Black, 1857.

Scherer, James A.B. *Cotton as a World Power: A Study in the Economic Interpretation of History.* New York: Frederick A. Stokes, 1916.

Schoolcraft, Mary Howard. *The Black Gauntlet.* Freeport, NY: Books for Librarians Press, 1971.

Setser, Vernon. *The Commercial Reciprocity Policy of the United States, 1774–1829.* New York: Da Capo, 1937.

Shore, Laurence. *Southern Capitalists: The Ideological Leadership of an Elite, 1832–1855.* Chapel Hill: University of North Carolina, 1986.

Silver, Arthur W. *Manchester Men and Indian Cotton.* England: University of Manchester Press, 1966.

Sobel, Robert. *The Money Manias: Tales of Entrepreneurs and Investors During the*

Eras of Great Speculation in America, 1770–1970. New York: Weybright and Talley, 1973

Stanwood, Edward. *American Tariff Controversies in the Nineteenth Century*. 2 vols. New York: Houghton Mifflin, 1903.

Stevens, William. *A Journal of the Proceedings in Georgia, Beginning October 20, 1737*. 3 vols. Atlanta: Franklin Printing, 1906 [1742].

Stover, John F. *American Railroads*. Chicago: University of Chicago Press, 1961.

Sumner, Helen. *History of Women in Industry in the United States*. New York: Arno Press, 1974.

Sutcliff, Robert. *Travels in Some Parts of North America in the Years 1804, 1805, and 1806*. Philadelphia: B&T Kite, 1812.

Syndor, Charles S. *Slavery in Mississippi*. Glouster, MA: P. Smith, 1965.

Syrett, Harold G., ed. *Papers of Alexander Hamilton*. New York: Columbia University Press, 1961–87.

Tarrant, Susan F.H. *Hon. Daniel Pratt: A Biography with Eulogies on His Life and Character*. Richmond: Whittet & Shepperson, 1904.

Taussig, Frank W. *Some Aspects of the Tariff Question*. Cambridge: Harvard University Press, 1915.

_____. *Tariff History of the United States*. London: G.P. Putnam, 1931.

Taylor, John. *Arator*. 6th ed. Georgetown: J.M. Carter, 1814.

Thompson, William T. *Major Jones' Sketches of Travels*. Charlottesville: University of Virginia, 2000.

Thorp, Willard L. *Business Annals*. New York: National Bureau of Economic Research, 1926.

Tindall, George B. *The Emergence of the New South, 1913–1946*. Baton Rouge: Louisiana State University, 1967.

Tocqueville, Alexis de. *Democracy in America*. New York: A.A. Knopf, 1945.

Walton, Perry. *The Story of Textiles*. Boston: J.S. Laurence, 1912.

Ware, Caroline. *Early New England Cotton Manufacture*. New York: Russell & Russell, 1966.

Watkins, J.L. *King Cotton*. New York: Negro University Press, 1969.

Watts, John. *The Facts of the Cotton Famine*. London: Cass, 1968.

Webster, Noah. *A Grammatical Institute of the English Language*. Part I. Albany: Charles R. & George Webster, 1796.

Wentworth, Joseph, and George Wallis. *The Industry of the United States in Machinery Manufacturers and Useful and Ornamental Arts*. London: G. Routledge, 1854.

White, George. *Statistics of Georgia*. Savannah: W. Thorne Williams, 1849.

White, Laura A. *Robert Barnwell Rhett: Father of Secession*. Glouster: P. Smith, 1931.

Wilson, Clyde N. "Calhoun's Economic Platform." In *Slavery, Secession, and Southern History*. Edited by Robert Louis Paquette and Louis A. Ferleger. Charlottesville: University of Virginia Press, 2000.

Winks, Robin W. *Canada and the United States: The Civil War Years*. Baltimore: Johns Hopkins University Press, 1960.

Wright, Richardson. *Hawkers and Walkers in Early America*. Philadelphia: J.B. Lippincott, 1927.

Yafa, Stephen. *Big Cotton*. New York: Viking, 2005.

York, Neil Longley. *Mechanical Metamorphosis: Technological Change in Revolutionary America*. Westport, CT: Greenwood Press, 1985.

Zevin, Robert B. "The Growth of Cotton Production after 1815." In *The Reinterpretation of America's Past*. Edited by Robert Fogel and Stanley Engermann. New York: Harper & Row, 1974.

Newspapers and Periodicals

Athens (GA) Athenian, 1828, 1829, 1831
Athens (GA) Gazette, 1816
Charleston (SC) City Gazette, 1829
Charleston (SC) Courier, 1834
De Foe's Weekly Review, 1708
Dry Goods Economist, Jubilee Issue, 1872
The Economist, 1861
Edgefield Advertiser, 1850, 1854
Factory Girls' Album and Operatives' Advocate, 1846
Fall River (MA) Monitor, 1827
Federal Gazette, 1791
Holyoke (MA) Freeman, 1853

Hunt's Merchant Magazine
London Economist, 1846
Mobile (AL) Daily Register, 1850
Mobile (AL) Herald Tribune, 1847
Montgomery (AL) Journal, 1850
Montgomery (AL) Tri-Weekly Flag & Advertiser, 1847, 1848, 1849
Niles Weekly Register, 1816, 1829, 1830, 1833, 1836, 1845
Prattville (AL) Southern Statesman, 1855
Raleigh (NC) News and Observer, 1924
Telegraph and Texas Register, 1840
Tuscumbia (AL) North Alabamian, 1841
Voice of Industry, 1846, 1847
Western Monthly Magazine and Literary Journal 4, 1835
Zion's Herald, 1836

Index

antislavery (British) 165–166
Appleton, Nathan 16, 84–85, 124
Arkwright, Richard 3, 22–25; cotton spinning machine 47–49
Armory System 172
Audubon, John James 36

Bagley, Sarah 128–129
balance of payments 9
bank (of the United States) 95–96
banks (plantation or property) 100
banks (state) 99–100
Biddle, Nicholas 96, 101, 160–161
Blake, Eli Whitney 12–13
Boston Associates 121
Bostwick, William 103–105

Cairnes, John Elliot 72
Calhoun, John C. 44–45, 85–87, 89–91
canals 39
Cartwright, Edmund 3, 23, 25
Civil War (effect on Europe) 167
Claiborne, Col. John, F.H. 19–20
Clay, Cassius Marcellus 70
Clay, Henry 7
Clayton, Augustus 140–141
Collier, Henry W. 139–140
Colt, Samuel 12
cotton: export 159; increase in demand 108; mechanization of manufacturing 20–22; mercantile houses 119–120; mills and water power 18; movement to new fields 105–107; speculation 102–103, 112; stocks in 1860 167
"Cotton Is King" 169
"cotton triangle": inland 43; ocean 41–42
Coxe Trench 46–47, 53
Crockett, David 125

Danson, J.T. 164–165
De Bow, J.D.B. 44, 73
Demosthenian Debating Society 150–151

Engerman, Stanley 5, 74–77

factors (factorage) 5–6, 97–99, 101
Fall River, Massachusetts 120–122
Fisher Report 137–138
flatboats 35
Fogel, Robert William 74–77
Franklin, Benjamin 55
Frederick Olmsted Law 71–72

Gallatin, Albert 17, 38, 117
Georgia (transportation) 31–33
Gregg, William (Graniteville) 146–148

Hamilton, Alexander 49–57, 63–64, 79–82
Hammond, Senator James Henry 96–97
Hayne, Col. Robert Y. 34
Helper, Hinton Rowan 70–71
Holyoke, Massachusetts 135
Huskisson, William 159–160

India 161–163
Indian (American) 6
Irish 123

James, Henry 15
Jefferson, Thomas 46, 57–61, 156

"King Cotton" 97

Larcon Lucy 123
Lowell (city) 122
Lowell, Francis Cabot 4, 16, 25–26
Lowndes, William 85–87

201

M'Cay, Professor 163
migrations 173
"Mill Girls" 122–123, 126–131, 134
mills: workers 131–134; working conditions 126, 135
Mims, Shadrach 146

Necker, Jacques 56
New England 6–7, 16, 90
"new form" cotton mill 118
New Orleans 108–110
New York City 5, 40–44, 103–104, 112–113, 120, 145, 173–174
North, C. Douglas 73–74
Notes on Virginia 57–58

packet system of shipping 40–43
Parkinson, George 46–47
peddlers 102
Pollard William 24–25
Pratt, Daniel (Prattville) 143–146

railroads 37–40
"Report on Manufacturers" 50

Sawyer, John 12
Seven Houses 95
Slater, Samuel 4, 14, 26

slaves: labor in cotton mills 142; leased 69; migration 65; value 6, 66, 70, 171
Smith, Adam 7
South (antebellum) 111
South Carolina (transportation) 33–34
Southern mill labor 142–143
steamboats (riverboats) 35–37

Tariff of 1789 80
Tariff of 1816 84
Tariff of 1824 88–90
Tariff of 1828 90–92
Tariff of 1832 92
Tariff of 1846 (Walker Tariff) 92
Tariff of 1857 174
Tausseg, F.W. 92
Texas 113–115
Thompson, George 124–125
"turn out" 128
turnpikes 38

unions 122, 136

Ware, Caroline 83
Washington, George 61, 79
Webster, Daniel 69–69
Whitney, Eli 4, 11, 26–28, 59, 157
Woodbury, Robert 11

www.ingramcontent.com/pod-product-compliance
Ingram Content Group UK Ltd.
Pitfield, Milton Keynes, MK11 3LW, UK
UKHW042006140426
5217IPUK00015B/1011